FAMILIES: CANADA

Rachel Schlesinger

FAMILIES: CANADA

Benjamin Schlesinger
Faculty of Social Work
University of Toronto

McGraw-Hill Ryerson Limited

Montreal	Toronto	New York	St. Louis	San Francisco
Beirut	Auckland	Bogotá	Düsseldorf	Johannesburg
London	Lisbon	Lucerne	Madrid	Mexico
Panama	New Delhi	Paris	San Juan	São Paulo
Sydney	Singapore	Tokyo		

Families: Canada

Printed and bound in Canada

Design and cover: Sharon Black

5 6 7 8 9 0   D   8 7 6 5 4 3 2

Canadian Cataloguing in Publication Data

Schlesinger, Benjamin, date
 Families, Canada

First ed. published in 1972 under title: Families, a Canadian perspective.
Includes bibliographical references.

ISBN 0-07-082897-0 pa.

1. Family—Canada. I. Title

HQ560.S34 1979 301.42'0971 C79-094045-0

THE AUTHOR

Dr. Benjamin Schlesinger, a Professor on the Faculty of Social Work, University of Toronto, is a leading expert on the Canadian Family. His academic background includes a Master of Social Work and a Ph.D in Child Development and Family Relationships. Dr. Schlesinger has written 8 books, numerous monographs and more than 200 papers published in Canadian and foreign journals on various aspects of family life. He has given workshops for students, teachers, nurses and social workers across Canada; appeared on radio and television to discuss the Canadian family; and taught, as visiting professor, at universities in Australia, New Zealand, Jamaica and Puerto Rico as well as across Canada. Among the subjects on which Dr. Schlesinger has done extensive research are: One-Parent Families in Canada; Remarriage; The Aged; Fatherhood; Grandparenthood; Attitudes towards Family Planning; Multi-Problem Families; and the Effects of Divorce on Children.

ACKNOWLEDGEMENTS

A number of the author's articles, some with different titles and in slightly different form, were originally published in journals: "The Unmarried Mother Who Keeps her Child" in *Social Worker* (December 1976); "The Widowed" in *Social Sciences;* "Children in Reconstituted Families" in *Stepparent's Forum* (September-October 1976, November-December 1976); "The Family and Decision Making" in *Child and Family;* "The ABC's of Adolescent Sexuality" in *The Canadian Nurse* (October 1977).

The following authors or co-authors have contributed articles to *Families: Canada—*

R. Margaret Cook, former Director, Youth Counselling Service, Addiction Research Foundation of Ontario. *Alcoholism and the Family.*

Katherine Tasios Dominic, M.S.W., Social Worker. *Weekend Fathers.*

Ellen T. Libman, Graduate Student, Faculty of Social Work, University of Toronto. *Adoption Disclosure.*

Gregory P. Lubimiv, M.S.W., Social Worker. *Adoption Disclosure.*

Diana Marshall, M.A. Family Counsellor. *Communal Family Living.*

Rubin Todres, Ph.D. Assistant Professor, Faculty of Social Work, University of Toronto. *Motherless Families and Singlehood.*

Marriage Contract in Appendix by Philip Spencer, a Toronto lawyer.

Questions, activities and projects at the end of each article by:
Evelyn Shapka
Family Studies Program Leader
North York Board of Education
North York, Ontario

Joan Stewart
Family Studies teacher
George Vanier Secondary School
North York, Ontario

CONTENTS

PREFACE

In 1972 my book *Families: A Canadian Perspective* was published by McGraw-Hill Ryerson. At that time it was the first Canadian effort to present various family patterns to the reader.

The present book is a completely revised volume in which I have kept (and updated) five articles from the 1972 book. The present volume is not a textbook in the traditional sense. It is an attempt to present to the reader the up-to-date topical issues dealing with family life in the late 1970s in Canada. Thus we have included the following selected topics, among others, for discussion: one-parent families; reconstituted families; communal family life; child abuse; wife abuse; adolescent sexuality; singleness; working women; "occupation homemaker"; grandparenthood; the male role in family life; child-care services in Canada; and satisfactions in family life today.

Some of the articles have been jointly written by some of my graduate students and myself, and some have been written partly or in full by others. Several articles have appeared in journals.

I have been interested in examining family life in Canada since 1960. My teaching at the Faculty of Social Work, University of Toronto, my research projects, and seminars from coast to coast have focused constantly on the wide boundaries of the family.

For each topic included in this book, I have included questions for discussion, as well as activities and projects, several of which will take the student out into the community. The questions, activities and projects lend themselves to individual, group or class work. Preview this section for questions which should be answered before reading the article. For further reading a list of selected books, films and audiotapes has been included after each topic, most of them with a Canadian focus where at all possible. A list of appropriate Canadian films and audiotapes is also included.

The appendix includes 16 tables of statistics dealing with the

Canadian family. It also contains an explanation of the 1978 Ontario Family Law Reform Act, an article on the Vanier Institute of the Family, a sample marriage contract and a list of sources of information and material related to Canadian family life.

I would like to thank my editor, Penny Fine, who has been very helpful in producing this book from early beginnings to final publication. A special thank you to my own family, my wife Rachel, and children Avi, Leo, Esther, and Michael for allowing me to live in a warm and intimate family in Canada.

Introduction—Families: Canada

Choosing to have a family used to be uninteresting. It is, today, an act of intelligence and courage. To love family life, to see in family life the most potent moral, intellectual and political cell in the body politic is to be marked today as a heretic.
(Michael Novak, "The Family Out of Favor," *Harper's*, April 1976, p. 37)

No other social institution in Canada holds such a sense of immediacy to our very selves. The family is the cradle of existence, the source of biological inheritance, the transmitter of culture. The family bestows on us our history and enables us to locate ourselves in time. It is the substance of the past, the wellspring of the present, and the foundation of the future.

The family is the central social institution of society and the anchor of a viable community. It is no wonder that in different historical periods other institutions have sought to take the family over, influence and destroy it. But it persists—although often battered and bruised. Whatever the form, its existence has served to satisfy the human need that generated its creation and development. The family has been around for a long time, which is testimony to its profound importance in social history. Similar to many things that are around a long time, the family is taken for granted, especially when it does the job. Even when it lumbers along tattered by time, worn by use, and often the object of a nostalgic outpouring for an earlier time, the family remains a major, if not *the* major institution in our lives.

CANADIAN FAMILY TRENDS

In 1976 there were 5 727 895 families* living in Canada. For Canadian census purposes, the "definition of a family" is a group of persons consisting of:
    . . . a husband and wife (with or without children who have never been married, regardless of age) or a parent with one or more children never married, living in the same dwelling. A family may consist, also, of a man or woman living with a guardianship child or ward under 21 years of age for whom no pay was received.
    I have highlighted eleven selected trends in the Canadian family today to give a picture of present changes. I have included the implications for the educational system in Canada, since these trends will affect our schools and students.

1. Size of Family

Canadians are having fewer children. The lowest birthrate is in Quebec, the highest in Newfoundland. The average family size in 1976 was 3.5, two adults and nearly two children. "Non-parenthood" is on the increase. In 1975 32% of families had no children.

* See the Appendix for detailed statistical tables on the Canadian family.

Implications

The lower birthrate has resulted in empty classrooms in our public schools, and the release of "surplus" teachers. It is estimated that in 1981, at least 20% of those women 30-34 years of age who have ever been married will be childless, approximately double the current rate. Thus we cannot foresee a sudden "baby boom" to fill our classrooms. "Non-parenthood" or "childless marriages" will become a more viable option for Canadians than in the past.

2. One-Parent Families

Nearly every tenth family in Canada is headed by a single parent. Of these 80% are headed by women and 20% by men. Divorce, separation and the single mother and her child as a family unit are on the increase. Women today are being widowed when they are older.

Implications

A larger percentage of students in our classrooms are from single parent households. They may have special needs, including needs for more attention and for male models. Some may feel uncomfortable when we discuss family life in the class. More teenagers are becoming pregnant, and more are keeping their babies.

3. Marriage

Marriage rates have not declined drastically. Canadians are still "rushing" to the altar. Of all the brides in 1976 25.5% were under the age of 20 years and 7.2% of the grooms were under the age of 20. The average age of marriage in Canada was 27.9 years for men and 25.3 for women. The average age has gone up slightly in recent years.

Implications

Will our classrooms include more married students at the high school level? How can we help our student not to rush into marriage? With a life expectancy of 69 years for men and 76 years for women, the decision to marry should not be made hastily. We also know statistically that a teen-age marriage has five times as much chance of breaking up as a later union.

4. Remarriage—Reconstituted Families

Nearly 13% of all the annual marriages in Canada in 1976 involved at least one partner who had been married previously. Of all the people involved in second unions 71% were divorced and 29% were widowed. The average age of a second marriage for a divorced male was 38.3 years, for a divorced female 34.9 years, for a widower 58.6 years and for a widow 52.7 years. The remarriage rate is rising annually.

Implications

Canadians are forming reconstituted families at an increasing rate. More of our children live in these families.

5. Aging

About 8% of our population are senior citizens. In 1976 we had 1 973 185 pensioners (over the age of 65). By 1980, every tenth Canadian will be a senior citizen.

Implications

Can we use any of our senior citizens in our schools? They can come as volunteers or paid helpers to work with many of the children who would benefit from their guidance, patience, warmth and experience. We have in our growing aged population a tremendous untapped resource for our schools. We may also fill our empty classrooms with senior citizens involved in taking courses or in leisure activities.

6. Working Women

Nearly 40% of our labour force in Canada in 1976 were women. Of these 60% were married. These working mothers had 275 000 children under the age of 3; 345 000 children aged 3-5; and 1 994 000 children aged 6-16 years. Only 4.3% of Canadian children in the under 3 age group were in day care, and 18.4% of the 3-5 age group were in day care in 1976.

Most Canadian women have to work either because they are the sole-support parent or the high cost of living and inflation has forced them to.

Implications

We are finding more families in which both parents work full-time. The need for more and better day-care services is pressing. Many students are "latchkey" children, who come home to an empty house after school.

7. Poverty and Family Life

In our country the "rich become richer" and the "poor families poorer." In 1975, the average family income was $16 263 before deductions. However, 40% of our population earned less than $9 666 per annum. When we examine the distribution of family income in our country we find that in 1951 the bottom fifth (economically speaking) of our families made up 6.1% of Canadian families, in 1973 they also made up 6.1%. There has been no change in 21 years.

Implications

Unless society will deal with some of the basic issues related to poverty, we will not be able to do very much for our poor children in our schools.

8. Human Sexuality

In 1976 nearly one third of our 50 000 abortions annually were performed on women under the age of 20. Every eleventh baby was born to a single mother, of whom 46% were under the age of 19 years. About 80% kept their babies. The venereal disease rate among teenagers is rising.

Implications

The results of the trend in teenage sexuality suggest that we can not stand back and wait, but have to help our students realize that "sex is not a game."

9. Unemployment

There are at least 2 million people under the age of 25 in the "youth market." About 50% are unemployed. It's estimated that in the 1980s, 3 million young people will be looking for work.

Implications

What training will be helpful in the 1980s? Which educational stream can help the student prepare for the world of work?

10. Child Abuse

Family violence, including child abuse, has been reported increasing in Canada. In 1973 approximately 1 100 cases of child abuse were reported by the provincial child welfare authorities. It is estimated that at least three times as many cases are not reported.

Implications

We should not stand by and allow this to go on. Reporting to the proper authorities should be mandatory.

11. Mobility, the High Cost of Housing and Family Life

Every year nearly one quarter of our families move at least once within each province. The high cost of housing in many areas of Canada has forced families to move into inadequate housing. The average cost in 1976 of a house in Calgary was \$54 000, in Vancouver it was \$60 000, in Toronto \$65 000. Apartment rents are also rising.

Implications

Our school population is quite mobile. It's difficult for many of our school children to establish roots. Moving can bring with it many problems, including adjusting to new friends, new teachers and, at times, new values. The school counsellor should find out the "moving history" of a youngster who develops problems in school.

THROUGH THE "LOOKING GLASS"

What is needed in Canadian society is a change in our patterns of living that will bring adults and children back into each other's lives. To effect such a change will require profound modifications in our social and economic institutions. Among the most needed reforms in Canada are: increased opportunity and status for part-time jobs; flexible work schedules so that one parent can be at home when children return from school; enhancement of the status and power of women in all walks of life—both on the job and at home; the breaking down of the wall between school and community so that children become acquainted with the world of work, and parents and other adults besides teachers can take an active part in activities at school; the inclusion, as an integral part of the high school curriclum, of supervised experience in the care of younger children; and above all, the provision of adequate health and child-care services, housing and income maintenance to the Canadian families whose resources are insufficient to ensure normal development for a growing child.

I hope that in the future we will redesign our Canadian cities and suburbs so that there will be a real outdoors for all children's play. Children should be able to experience the unpredictability and endless fascination of growing things and be rescued from much of the current boredom with only-too-predictable toys and school tasks.

In my examination of Canadian family life I can heartily agree with the summary presented by Professor Jean Veevers in the report on the 1971 Census of Canada "Family Profile,"* when she pointed out that by and large, the Canadian family is demonstrated to be a viable and dominant social institution, and to have remained so over the past decade. The changes that have occurred are not so much replacing the Canadian family with an alternative form as they are modifying certain aspects of the existing structure. In considering the family in terms of its future or lack of it, the gradual trends involved do not lend support to the hypothesis of its imminent demise. Declining fertility reflects not so much a rejection of parenthood roles as a preference for intensive involvement with fewer children. Even the most drastic symptom of family change, the increasing divorce rate, reflects not a disillusionment with marriage in general, but a disillusionment with marriage to a particular spouse. The increased acceptance of serial monogamy suggests that marital disruption is less a sign of family *disorganization* than of family *reorganization*, resulting from the fact that most adults prefer to spend most of their lives in a family context.

* Jean E. Veevers, *The Family in Canada.* (Ottawa: Statistics Canada, November 1977) Vol. 5, Part 3.

READINGS

Elkin, Frederick. *The Family in Canada*. Ottawa: Vanier Institute of the Family, 1964.
An account of knowledge related to the Canadian family in the 1960s.

Ishwaran, K., ed. *The Canadian Family*. 2nd edition. Toronto: Holt, Rinehart and Winston, 1976.
Thirty-six selections related to family life in Canada.

Larson, Lyle. *The Canadian Family in Comparative Perspective*. Toronto: Prentice-Hall, 1975.
An introduction to the basic perspectives, concepts and issues in the study of marriage and the family. Includes 21 selections from the writings of other authors.

Schlesinger, Benjamin, ed. *The Chatelaine Guide to Marriage*. Toronto: Macmillan, 1975.
A selection of 18 articles from *Chatelaine* dealing with marriage and divorce. The editor introduces these topics.

Vanier Institute of the Family. *Canadian Resources on the Family*. Ottawa: 1972 and 1974.
This catalogue contains both printed material and audio-visual material dealing with the Canadian scene.

Veevers, Jean. *The Family in Canada*. Ottawa: Statistics Canada, Profile Studies, Vol. 5, Part 3, 1977.
An examination of the 1971 Census Data related to Canadian families.

Wakil, Parvez S. *Marriage and Family in Canada*. Calgary: Journal of Comparative Family Studies, 1976. A monograph.

Wakil, Parvez S., ed. *Marriage, Family and Society: Canadian Perspectives*. Toronto: Butterworths, 1975.
Thirty selections which deal with selected aspects of Canadian family life.

I
THE VARIETY OF FAMILY FORMS

Introduction

In examining a textbook on the family, written in 1934, by Dr. Nimkoff I found the following definition of the family:

The family may be defined most simply as a relationship of indeterminate duration existing between parent(s) and offspring. This definition emphasizes the fact that, to be a family, both parent(s) and progeny must remain together for an indefinite period after the birth of the young.

Today as we examine the various family patterns, we may have to change this outlook. The following table lists the six various family patterns in Canada.

TYPES OF FAMILIES IN CANADA

1. *Nuclear Family:* husband, wife, children

2. *Childless Couples:* husband and wife

3. *One Parent Families:* widows, widowers, divorcées, divorced men, separated and deserted men and women, non-married mothers. (These families can be mother-headed or father-headed only, except in the case of non-married motherhood)

4. *Adopted Families:* husband and wife and adopted children

5. *Reconstituted Families:* second marriages, or "blended families"

   Theoretically there are eight different "types" of remarriages:

   a. a divorced man married to a single woman
   b. a divorced man married to a widowed woman
   c. a divorced man married to a divorced woman
   d. a single man married to a widowed woman
   e. a single man married to a divorced woman
   f. a widowed man married to a single woman
   g. a widowed man married to a widowed woman
   h. a widowed man married to a divorced woman

   In unions that involve children several different combinations of family units are possible: the father and his children can acquire a new wife and mother; the mother and her children can acquire a new husband and father; the father and his children can join the mother and her children. Further variations of these combinations are possible if the spouses have children after their second marriage.

6. *Communal Families:* A group of families, or a group of families with children and some single adults.

As you can see the variations have expanded from our traditional view of a family, namely "mother, father, and children." The contributions in this section examine these patterns in detail. I have also included some material on satisfactions and dissatisfactions in family life today.

1
Childless Couples: A new voluntary family option

The following Canadian couple has opted for childlessness. The wife works for an advertising agency. Her husband is in a managerial position with a retail store. They own an $80 000 townhouse. In the beginning, the couple had a tough time financially and so delayed having children for economic reasons. Then they found that they grew to like life without children.

"At first we wavered. We thought, wouldn't it be nice not to be lonely when we're 50," said the wife, who helped look after a brother and sister as a child and felt she'd never had a childhood.

He explained: "There are parents and then there are people who should never be parents. I am one who should never be a parent. Children are very nice so long as they are someone else's." He is an only child.

He said he realized early in his marriage that children weren't for him. "I believe if you father a child you have to be prepared to spend time with the child, to give of yourself. I tend to be a private person. When I come home at night I don't want to give of myself for a time—not to anyone— not even to my wife. I don't think children would understand."

He was also concerned about the high cost of children. "Raising a child is very expensive. I didn't feel I wanted to spend all that money on a child."

It wasn't career ambitions that kept his wife from motherhood. "I'm not a women's libber," she said.

She describes herself as "very demanding of myself. I set high standards for myself." She didn't think she would be a good mother. "I think I would expect too much of a child," she said.

She believes that a mother should be a full-time mother, not a career woman too. "I'm a firm believer that you can't do more than one thing at a time exceptionally well," she said.

She also felt that if she spent her days childrearing, she wouldn't be "the kind of wife my husband would like me to be at the end of the day."

He said he always wanted his wife to be "anything but the classic housewife." Women who have nothing to talk about but the kids and the laundry are not for him. "I want a loving, concerned wife, but I also want her to be a woman with interests outside the home."

Criticism from others has been a problem. "When you decide not to have children people think you hate children," he said.

"People are always asking if we have a pet instead," she added. "I resent the inference that our cat is a substitute for a child."

The couple think accusations that they are selfish people are justified. "We have what I consider a nice home. We drive a nice car. We've just begun to travel. I wouldn't want to give that up. I guess I have turned into a selfish person," she said.

In our society childless couples are accused at times of being: stupid, selfish, neurotic, childish, hedonistic, short-sighted, unthinking, un-natural, shameful, deceitful, missing out on life, immature and self-serving.

WHY BECOME PARENTS?

Amazingly little research has been done on the motivation for parenthood. No one really understands why people want to become parents. Some people may describe children as being a liability rather than an asset. Rearing children places enormous demands on parents in terms of emotional and financial costs. Yet, when a choice exists, the vast majority of people choose to be parents.

For years high fertility has been attributed to the maternal instinct myth. Essentially this notion holds that women, as a consequence of their biology, want and must have children. Not only have they had little or no choice in the matter, but once they have a child it is assumed that they "instinctively" love and know how to care for the child. Characteristically, this simplistic view overlooks the following exceptions: (1) the intense desire of many women to terminate pregnancy; (2) the increasing reports of child abuse, which suggest that some mothers do not instinctively love their children; and (3) the many women who do choose to remain childless who apparently suffer no psychic or physical distress.

In the past children were considered, especially by women, to be their raison d'être. The highest accomplishment was to rear happy, healthy, productive children. Whether the demise of the urgent necessity to perpetuate the species has served to change attitudes, or the increased oppor-

tunities to find fulfillment via other outlets have changed attitudes is unclear. Regardless, bearing and rearing children have lost supremacy in the hierarchy of life accomplishments for many people. Potential parents no longer feel an obligation or a commitment to have children. They can and often prefer to find their fulfillment elsewhere.

Unlike most relationships, parenthood is irreversible. It is impossible to divorce your children! Though they may be given up for adoption or foster care, beyond infancy these solutions are not often socially acceptable. Perhaps conceiving and bearing a child is the biggest gamble of a lifetime. It is impossible to judge what the characteristics of the prospective child may be. Assuming one is fortunate in bearing a physically and mentally healthy child, there is still the possibility of personality clashes. How can you know if you will like each other? Additionally, some potential parents question their skills and aptitudes for parenting. Far from being selfish, they may decide to spare an unsuspecting child from the trauma of being reared by psychologically, emotionally or financially inadequate parents.

The cost of a child

It has been estimated that it costs $54 000 to raise your first child up to the age of 18 years.

The value of children

As children are economic liabilities in Canada, parents usually want children for non-economic reasons, such as emotional and psychological fulfillment. Eight categories of non-economic values of children follow. These were developed by Dr. Thomas J. Espenshade of the East-West Center in Honolulu, Hawaii.
1. *Adult Status and Social Identity.* Having children is tangible evidence that one

has reached adulthood, perhaps more so than completing school, taking a first job, or even getting married.

2. *Expansion of the Self, Tie to a Larger Entity, "Immortality."* As a rule children outlive their parents, and this may furnish parents with a sense of immortality, the realization that their characteristics, as reflected in their progeny, will survive after them.

3. *Morality.* This dimension refers to the subordination of self-interest to a higher goal. Children afford parents the opportunity to sacrifice for the good of someone else.

4. *Primary Group Ties, Affiliation.* The family has historically been a stable and permanent institution, and affiliation with it may offer a sense of emotional security.

5. *Stimulation, Novelty, and Fun.* A birth creates the sense that something new and different is happening, and in so doing may help to relieve the tedium of everyday life.

6. *Creativity, Accomplishment, Competence.* The challenges involved in raising children may fulfill these needs.

7. *Power, Influence, Effectiveness.* Having children enables parents to influence the course of others' lives.

8. *Social Comparison, Competition.* Where offspring are a sign of prestige or wealth, large numbers of children may elevate the parents' position in the community. They may also attest to the parents' sexuality. These motives are perhaps most commonly found in non-industrialized societies."

STUDIES OF CHILDLESS COUPLES

One of the pioneers in research related to voluntary childlessness in North America is Professor Jean E. Veevers, a sociologist

at the University of Western Ontario, in London. In summarizing the findings of her numerous studies she points out that voluntarily childless wives are acutely aware of the fact that almost all people strongly disagree with their views on the value of motherhood, and strongly disapprove of them for endorsing an antinatalist (anti-birth) position. In addition, voluntarily childless wives feel subjected to a variety of direct and indirect social sanctions apparently intended to punish them for their immoral attitudes and/or to induce them to conform to the dominant fertility norms. In spite of this many childless wives are relatively unperturbed. For those wives who are in stable marriages and who have the support of their husbands, it is quite possible to develop and to maintain a comfortable and integrated world view justifying the preference for a child-free existence. The voluntarily childless are able to redefine the conventional meanings of parenthood by cynically and skeptically questioning romantic beliefs which are generally thought to be unquestionable. They often look negatively on the attributes of the kinds of persons who choose to become parents; they seriously question the motives involved both in having children oneself and in recommending that others do likewise; and they disparage the consequences of having children.

In examining studies of childless couples in North America various trends appear regularly. These couples are more egalitarian in the distribution of power to make decisions and in the delegation of responsibility for household tasks. They tend to cross over the traditional sex role boundaries of husband and wife. Even when the wife is not employed, there is a greater sharing of these tasks, decisions and leisure time.

Several subjective qualities of the marriage also distinguish the voluntarily childless couples from the others. They stress companionship as both an organizing principle of their marriages and as a valued attribute. The area of most discontent is a desire for more togetherness in the marriage.

The childless indicate that they see having children as a threat to the *egalitarianism* of their relationship when they stress the interference children would have with the wife's career goals. More importantly, they speak of a fear that the traditional sex segregation of tasks brought on by parenthood would diminish their equal footing in the household. For example, one husband states, "Having children would be an obligation I don't want and I question how much responsibility I would accept." Many wives say they simply do not view themselves as mothers and do not trust their husbands to share the child-care duties.

The *freedom and spontaneity* with which the childless pursue their activities together is also threatened by having children, in their eyes. Both husbands and wives say things like, "If we had children, we wouldn't be able to drop everything and go to parties . . ." or "we would not have as much freedom to travel, taking off on the spur of the moment."

The *personal growth,* which is fostered within the marriage relationship, would be curtailed, "Children would limit the freedom of expansion we now have . . ." "I feel it's an enormous responsibility which would complicate my life. I'm more concerned with fulfilling my own goals."

Through such answers we can begin to understand two of the ways in which the childless marriage functions to influence or maintain the decision to remain childless. 1. The distinguishing characteristics of the marriage are themselves felt to be incompatible with having children. 2. The personal goals which are fostered by the marriage relationship are also thwarted by the assumption of parenthood.

A QUESTIONNAIRE FOR PROSPECTIVE PARENTS

The National Organization for Non-Parents, with its headquarters in Baltimore, U.S.A., has developed some questions for couples who are thinking about childlessness or having children. Here are a few for you to consider and discuss.

1. What do I want out of life for myself? What do I think is important?
2. Could I handle a child and a job at the same time? Would I have time and energy for both?
3. Would I be ready to give up the freedom to do what I want to do, when I want to do it?
4. Would I be willing to cut back my social life and spend more time at home? Would I miss my free time and privacy?
5. Can I afford to support a child? Do I know how much it takes to raise a child?
6. Do I want to raise a child in the neighbourhood where I live now? Would I be willing and able to move?
7. How would a child interfere with *my* growth and development?
8. Would a child change my educational plans? Do I have the energy to go to school and raise a child at the same time?
9. Am I willing to give a great part of my life—at least 18 years—to being responsible for a child? and spend a large portion of my life being concerned about my child's well being?
10. Have my partner and I really talked about becoming parents?
    a) Does my partner want to have a child? Have we talked about our reasons?
    b) Could we give a child a good home? Is our relationship a happy and strong one?

c) Are we both ready to give our time and energy to raising a child?

d) Could we share our love with a child without jealousy?

e) What would happen if we separated after having a child, or if one of us should die?

f) Do my partner and I understand each other's feelings about religion, work, family, child raising, future goals? Do we feel pretty much the same way? Will children fit into these feelings, hopes and plans?

g) Suppose one of us wants a child and the other doesn't? Who decides?

Although childless couples are clearly not free from conflict, it is too early to state with any assurance what the future may hold for these couples in Canada. It is clear that for the present, the couples are saying that "two's company . . . three's a crowd."

Also we should remember that you can like children but dislike parenting. More and more Canadian couples will be opting for the new voluntary option of childless couples who will form a sizeable proportion of Canadian families. However, it is interesting to note that more than 360 000 babies were born in Canada in 1977.

READINGS

Barrett, Michael and Taylor, Chris. *Population and Canada*. Toronto: Faculty of Education, Guidance Centre, 1977.
A booklet examining population trends in Canada. Has excellent bibliography.

Bouma, Gary D., and Bouma, Wilma J. *Fertility Control: Canada's Lively Social Problem*. Toronto: Longman, 1975.
A discussion of fertility control in Canada.

Marsden, Lorna R. *Population Probe: Canada*. Toronto: Copp-Clark, 1972.
An examination of population research in Canada.

Peck, Ellen and Senderowitz, Judith eds. *Pronatalism: The Myth of Mom and Apple Pie*. New York: Thomas Y. Crowell, 1974.
Twenty-three authorities examine the question: Do you really want a baby?

Peck, Ellen. *The Baby Trap*. New York: Pinnade Press, 1972.
"Are children important?" the author asks.

Silverman, Anna and Silverman, Arnold. *The Case Against Having Children*. New York: David McKay, 1971.
A discussion of childlessness as a viable option.

QUESTIONS, ACTIVITIES AND PROJECTS

1. Respond to the Questionnaire for Prospective Parents at the end of this chapter. From your responses do you see yourself as being ready to have a child now? In the foreseeable future?
   List the factors which you would have to consider before making the decision of whether or not to have a child.

2. Prepare a chart from Dr. Espenshade's list of categories of non-economic values of children on page 10. Survey parents to see how they compare their reasons for having children with those listed under Dr. Espenshade's categories.

2
Communal Family Living

Benjamin Schlesinger
Diane Marshall

INTRODUCTION

Communalism is one of the alternative lifestyles within Western culture. It exists in both rural and urban settings, and a number of working models attest to its viability. The basis of this communal lifestyle is the sharing of work, housing and social duties by the members, who are bound by religious, political, cultural, economic and emotional ties. The parental responsibilities and the expectations of the members in their relationships with the children vary from commune to commune. For example, in the Hutterite colonies the parents of the Hutterite youth are responsible first and foremost to the colony as a whole. Children are subject to the rules and rhythm of colony life, and all Hutterite adults have a duty to discipline all children. Child-care responsibilities fall onto those members of the colony to whom that particular task has been assigned, and the needs of all members, especially the children (who have to learn self-discipline), are secondary to the needs of the colony as a whole. The socialization of the Hutterite child is the responsibility of each member and produces community-oriented adults who repress their individuality, accept all other colony members and adjust to the routine of colony life. What is peculiar to communal life and parent-child relationships within a self-defined commu-

nity like the Israeli kibbutz or the Hutterite colony is their common basis in the concepts of equality and shared labour, seeking to organize around a cooperative, rather than competitive, mode.

Essentially, the communes of the sixties and seventies throughout North America have been experiments in social solidarity, based primarily on friendship. These communes seek to combat the depersonalization of modern technological, bureaucratic society. They reject much of the middle class culture which is taken for granted by most North Americans.

The North American communal movement has been both colourful and romantic. It has affirmed the "now," the natural and the expressive. It has sought full equality, a fair division of labour and a non-sexist view of roles.

We will look at the implications of this form of alternative family for parenting.

AN URBAN ALTERNATIVE COMMUNITY

The Toronto group consists of eight couples, five of whom have children (a total of seven preschoolers) and several single people, all of whom live in the same building in the city's east end. The core group of this community shared a cooperative farm for several years, prior to moving to an urban location. The families share economic goods—such as cars, washing machine, vacuum cleaners, etc.; they also care for one another's children and the men work together in a work collective. Perhaps the best description of the community is found in the words of two of the group's members:

I see myself as part of a caring, sharing, cooperative support group—which may, but does not have to include any or all of the aspects of life that are political, economic, religious, work, child-care, friendship. I do not see any particular 'vision,' solidified structure or overall expectation of one another, but rather a growing, organic, constantly changing unit very much susceptible to human weakness; however, open to questioning . . .

and

Our alternate lifestyle community is characterized by no clear intention but is united by:

a) work: collectivized labour which is self-controlled, stable, and involved in basic service at subsistent wages . . . People are paid according to their marital status, number of children, and need.

b) political: identity ranges within a sphere called perhaps Christian radicalism—with a shared skepticism of secular political structures. It ranges from the extremes of resistance and anarchy to involvement in local government.

Certainly, the community shares a broad scope of interests and activities in the general area of politics. They see themselves as something of a "resistance" community. They follow a "small is beautiful" work pattern. They seek to take a stand against corporate powers. They seek alternate parenting and child-care methods in that the women operate a co-op daycare and

share babysitting. The group consciously develops internal friendships—the members are warm and caring friends, helping one another emotionally and practically through times of need. The communal members seek to be non-sexist in their relationships and the women meet weekly for study and discussion around issues of feminism.

THE STUDY

The five couples with seven preschool children were interviewed and asked to complete a questionnaire. It was divided into four major sections: Community, Marital Relations, Work and Parenting. The Parenting section was the most comprehensive. It asked questions about pre-pregnancy, pregnancy, birth, post-partun experiences, philosophy of child rearing, attitudes toward discipline, sex-roles, nutrition, recreation, toys, and, finally, child-care arrangements. The results of the findings will be presented under three headings: Similarities, Dissimilarities, and Problem Areas.

Similarities

Strikingly, all the men and women interviewed were what can best be described as "intentional parents." They all expressed a deep desire to have a child, and saw their child(ren) as an expression of their love and commitment to one another and to their view of life. While in certain couples there was a dominant partner in the actual decision to have a child, by the time of the baby's birth there was complete agreement, anticipation and joy. All the parents (men and women) expressed a sense of wonder and a "peak experience" in the actual birth of their babies. The fathers each helped in the labour and deliveries, and in the aftercare of their new-born infants.

Nutrition is very important in the whole community's lifestyle. The women all breast-feed—some up to age 2—and many members are vegetarian. There is a natural, back-to-the-earth awareness of food and the place of diet in one's life.

All of the parents expressed similar views in response to the question "Do you have a particular philosophy of parenting?" Each parent viewed the children as persons: unique, not to be labelled or stereotyped. Some said they were disturbed by the proliferation of books on parenting—they felt that perhaps an intuitive approach to parenting would be better than one based on the ideas in books. The major unresolved question in the area of philosophy of child-rearing seemed to relate to the amount of "freedom" that the children should have. Most of the parents approved of a nonviolent approach to discipline: either removing the child from the object (or vice versa) or sending the child to a room, but without physical punishment.

The desire to combat sex-role stereotyping became clear in the parents' attitudes towards the children's toys. The parents refuse to give dolls to the girls and trucks to the boys, but make a variety of creative playthings available to all the children. While people are at different stages in this process, it would be fair to say that the community does not have a view of "masculinity" or "femininity." Rather they seek a liberation from roleplaying which affirms people's distinctive gifts as persons. This process appears to be a difficult one, as the women must be often at home because of the ages of the children and the men are at work in the collective.

However, it is a major goal of all the families to have the men and the women work in an outside job on a part-time basis, so that both can share the task of parenting and of bringing in income. At the present time, the men see their involvement in the work collective as a positive and creative experience. The income is distributed according to need, and an alternative to the depersonalization of corporate powers is being formed. Interest-free loans are made to one another when in need.

Everyone viewed friendships as vital components of the community. All the women attend the "women's meeting," which includes singles and non-parents. They see this meeting as an important ingredient in their growth and maturation as persons. Certain problems, such as feeling over-exposed, appear to have been overcome by trust and sharing.

Child care is increasingly becoming a communal responsibility. Regular cooperative day care exists, and people care for one another's children when someone is sick or has a short-term job. The single people and non-parents in the community also participate in baby sitting. Thus, a stable environment for the children is provided, allowing them to develop trust in several adults in the community.

Dissimilarities

There are various areas in which families operate differently. One is in the area of relationships with grandparents and one's own family of origin. For some of the couples there is very little contact, nor is more desired; for others, grandparents, aunts, uncles and other extended kin, play an important role in the children's lives. There appears to be some ambivalence about relating to natural families—one couple, for example, who are not legally married, have felt that their own parents have cut them out of their lives since the birth of their daughter.

Religious commitments and involvements vary. The question of the place and role of the institutional Church is very much a matter of dispute. Few members have a consistent relationship to the structured Church, though several have studied theology at one time.

The question of schedules varies from family to family. Some couples have fairly regular eating, bedtime and toilet training routines; others are flexible and, for some, schedules are non-existent. This difference has been one reason for the decision that families would live separately and somewhat self-contained, even though in the same building.

A major controversy has centred around the question of whether or not the men's work collective (which includes several single men) actually respects family needs. The collective does carpentry and general house repairs. The long hours of work, which are necessary in order to survive at lower wages, are seen as essential in order to provide an economic alternative for poor people. However, frequently the results include delayed dinner hours and less time spent with the children or in recreational pursuits. This seemed to be an area where the men and the women disagreed; the former felt the collective was a positive and creative experience, the latter felt victimized occasionally by the long hours of work and the burden of child care.

Problem Areas

Privacy was seen as being an area of future concern. The term "privacy" appeared to be one of those scare terms that no one quite knew how to define, nor how to organize their own needs around. Certainly the view of economics and of friendship which exists within the community acts against extremes of privacy and isolation; however, the dilemma of feeling over-exposed is also a potential threat.

Recreation was an area largely ignored by the community. Certainly, a level of voluntary poverty does not allow lavish recreational pursuits; but the members all recognized that, as their children get older, this will be an area requiring a great deal of thought and creativity. In the interim, a sense of *meaning* in work and community seems to give impetus to the members and serves as a kind of recreation. However, leisure as such is a scarcity in the structure of this community.

In the area of child-rearing, there were some differences of opinion. Some people indicated that differences in priority regarding child care have caused a slowing down in the development of other areas of community. But, by and large, the presence of so many children, all at similar stages of development, is seen as presenting a challenge in terms of becoming a very real "alternative" community. The whole question of the development of a unique sense of "self" versus a collective identity amongst the children was raised. Some of the parents were aware that the literature on kibbutzim indicated a breakdown in certain later stages of psychosocial development if the growth into self-consciousness and hence later intimacy is prevented by too heavy a group-consciousness. However, the fact that the members discuss this possibility openly is a positive sign for the development of the community.

Finally, male-female relationships are seen as problem areas in the practical application of the beliefs of the commune. For example, both men and women wish to work part-time, and so all share child-care responsibilities. Yet, in practice, the men are more highly skilled than the women, and so can earn more money in the job market. Further, the women's strong views about breastfeeding restrict their hours. Most women are now working at least one day per week but, by and large, it is the other women who share the child care on those days, not the men. However, this area is in an early stage of evolution and it is important that the women share the care of each others' children in a mutual and cooperative way in order to free one another for outside pursuits. In this respect, the women have worked through the foundations of true cooperation much in the same way as the men have done in the work collective.

Conclusions

In conclusion, we can say that this urban Toronto community is characterized by several features typical of alternative lifestyle situations. The members share goods and material income; they are basically non-consumers; they believe strongly in conservation; they are seeking a just division of labour; they are attempting to eliminate or at least moderate sexism; and they are seeking creative new forms of child care. In their search for intimacy, they are essentially attempting to find integration and wholeness through a kind of institutionalization of friendship. They are strongly motivated to be parents, and to create a *human* environment where children can be accepted by all. Although organized as an extended family, with couples and their children remaining monogamous in their own private quarters, they fulfill the criteria of mutual sharing and a common economic base which characterize them as an alternative "community."

We have discovered in our investigation that "good" parenting is to be found among members of this alternative lifestyle community. The ingredients of love, trust, affection and physical care are all component parts of this approach to family life. It is too early to judge how children will develop in the future of this Toronto commune, but it would be of great interest to follow up their progress. One must give credit to the families who have chosen this way of life as a demonstration of their freedom and option in the contemporary nuclear society.

READINGS

Carter, Novia. *Something of Promise: The Canadian Communes.* Ottawa: Canadian Council on Social Development, 1974.
   A four months study of communal living in Canada.
Kanter, Rosabeth Moss. *Committment and Community: Communes and Utopias in Sociological Perspective.* Cambridge, Mass.: Harvard University Press, 1972.
Kanter, Rosabeth Moss, ed. *Communes: Creating and Managing the Collective Life.* New York: Harper and Row, 1973.
Vanier Institute of the Family. *Varieties of Family Lifestyle: A Selected Annotated Bibliography.* Ottawa: 1977.
   This bibliography covers varied lifestyles which include common-law unions, communal living, intentional childlessness, etc.
Vanier Institute of the Family. *The New Life.* Ottawa: 1977.
   A report on an inquiry workshop dealing with contemporary familial lifestyles in Canada.

QUESTIONS, ACTIVITIES AND PROJECTS

1. *Compare the values of children raised in a commune with those of children raised in the traditional North American nuclear family. Include areas such as independence, the work ethic, sex roles, privacy, sharing and love.*
2. *In an article in* Saturday Night, *August 1974, Philip Marchand commented that "the trouble with communes is that they don't work." Develop a class list of social conditions and personal commitment needed to make the communal philosophy work.*

3
Adoption Disclosure

Benjamin Schlesinger
Ellen T. Libman
Gregory P. Lubimiv

Every person has a basic right to privacy as a general principle.

The common good or community welfare takes precedence over the individual's right to privacy.
—(Ontario Association of Children's Aid Societies, "Policy Statement on Confidentiality and Release of Information", April 1977)

Our concern for the rights of one party has always been tempered by our equal concern for safeguarding the rights of the other parties involved.
—(Report: "Committee on Record Disclosure to Adoptees," Government of Ontario, June 22, 1976)

Over the past decade there has been increasing interest in the adoptive family, and adoption as a process. As more interest was shown it became evident that not enough information was available, especially in the form of statistics. We do not know how many Canadians are adopted; we do not know whether interracial, older-child, or, in fact, any particular type of adoption generally turns out well or badly.

The uneasiness concerning adoption was not only coming from the outside, but more importantly began to grow from within. Over the past several years more and more adoptees have been searching for their "roots." In their quest they have found themselves fenced in by policies and regulations which seek to maintain confidentiality and anonymity and result in extinguishing, or attempting to extinguish, any physical bonds or attachment between the adoptee and the birth family.

The prime issue which evolved in Canada from this is disclosure versus non-disclosure. This controversy touches the lives of many people. It includes the adoptee, the birth parents, the adoptive parents and the agency personnel who deal with adoption (social workers, judges, etc.). Each of these parties have interests at stake and although there is no definite division of opinions, each group tends to have general characteristics and views which differentiate them from one another.

THE ADOPTEES

There is a growing number of adopted persons in Canada who have become adults and who question their adoption process. To the law which denies many of these persons access to information about their birth and birth parents they are perpetually seen as non-adults. The adoptees are, in many cases, considered adopted children and never obtain a true adult status in the eyes of society.

Although the number of adoptees who are emerging into public view or who are searching for their birth parents, are increasing, it is not a new phenomenon. It is felt that most adoptees, as children and as adults, have questioned their origin and wondered who or where their "real" parents are—but, few would act upon their search. It was thought, and still is by many, that a searcher was a "disturbed" person who could not come to grips with reality. The fear of having this label applied was a barrier to the adoptee who wished to search for his/her parents.

A greater fear was that of hurting the adoptive parent, who may not understand why their son or daughter must find, or find out about, their birth parent. Today this is still prevalent with searchers and non-searchers alike. Many of the adoptees who are involved in looking for their birth parents conceal this from their adoptive parents.

In the past, as well, there were few, if any, support systems available to an adoptee looking for information. The growth of numerous organizations in the U.S.A. and in Canada, such as "Parent Finders" and "Concerned United Birth Parents," has improved the situation. However, this does not eliminate the anger and frustration some adoptees direct against social agencies, social workers and the system for not helping them in their venture.

The adoptees who search for their birth parents believe they have a right to the information and, although there is anxiety about what they will find, they follow every clue and leave no stone unturned. They do not, however, imply that they search because they have turned against their adoptive parents. Instead of trying to replace their adoptive families with their birth families they are merely attempting to put together all the pieces of their life. Most

adoptees undertaking a quest for their origins do so as a sincere effort to gain a better understanding of themselves and their situation.

It is noted that some adoptees begin a search after marriage and after having or deciding to have children of their own, in order to gain as much information as possible about their birth parents' health and medical history.

Some adoptees never end their search, a few find hunting becomes a part of their lives and some find their birth mother and/or birth father and wish they had never begun the search. There have been and will continue to be tragedies, but this does not daunt them. These adoptees feel the possible damages are tiny in comparison to the upset and turmoil of not knowing their roots.

When one considers the probable number of adoptees presently in Canada this issue is transformed from a minor phenomenon to a major concern. As more and more adoptees acknowledge their turmoil and become involved in the issue of disclosure, there is mounting pressure on governments to re-assess their policies and open the files to them.

THE ADOPTIVE PARENTS

When an adoption is finalized, the child becomes a legal member of an adoptive family, and that family raises the child as their own. It would certainly be the ideal situation for these parents if the past could be washed away and life would go on as though there were no birth mother or birth father other than themselves. In the past, a few adoptive parents attempted to erase or change the past by not telling the adoptive child that he/she was adopted. This practice may still occur today and seems related to the fact that some parents do not feel comfortable in having to tell their child about adoption and in having to answer all the questions related to this fact.

The adoption procedure from application to finalization is also a factor to consider when looking at the adoptive parents' profile. In this process a couple is "put to the test" by an agency and called upon to "prove" they will make adequate parents. As a result many feel the need to magnify their strengths, minimize their weaknesses and in general compete with other applicants. This is especially true today because of the undersupply of available children. As a result, adoptive parents often tend to take on the role of "super-parents"—a role which, more often than not, remains with them. This, too, can influence a parent to become over-protective of the child and overly sensitive to criticism from outside the immediate family.

There is also the reality that the child has birth parents who the adoptee will be curious about. This can be very threatening to the close family who is not willing to contemplate sharing the adoptee with an unknown outsider, or to the adoptee not seeing them as the "real" parents.

It may very well be that the most vulnerable person in this debate is the adoptive parent who has everything to lose and nothing to gain.

The British Columbia government looked at the question of adoption disclosure in 1975. The Commission on Family Law, chaired by Mr. Justice Thomas Berger, recommended the establishment of an adoption registry which would help adoptees and birth parents reunite. The suggestion provoked a worried reaction from couples who had adopted children. An Organization to Save the Adopted Family was founded and the uproar it caused was enough to deter the British Columbia government from following up on the proposal with this legislation.

Not all adoptive parents are unable to understand why their adopted child must ask questions and wonder about their birth parent. However it is difficult for many adoptive parents to deal with the anxiety surrounding the fear of losing the child in whom they invested their love, or in the fear of losing their role as primary parents. As one adoptive parent stated, "I'm not bothered by the fact that they "want" to search—that seems entirely natural—but, by the fact that they 'give in' to this impulse."

When the adoptee "gives in" and begins to search how does the adoptive parent react? How do they view the reason for the search? The questions are endless and vary according to the individual circumstances. What does not vary greatly is the worry this situation creates. Many adoptive parents fear that the search implies that their child may not be satisfied with their love.

Another factor to consider is the premise under which the adoption took place. The adopted child was "given" to the adoptive parents legally and all other rights of any birth parent were absolutely abolished. Thus, a move to change the present system of confidentiality represents a betrayal of the "as if born" concept which had been presented to the adoptive parents at the time of adoption. It may also be interpreted as a destructive move which would continually undermine the parent's position with their adopted child.

There is the natural urge of a parent to protect their child, whether over 18 years or under, from danger, especially when their son or daughter "doesn't realize" the threat. Many parents see in disclosure and reunion a source of sorrow and stress, not only for themselves, but for their children. For this reason they will fight to keep this from happening, even if it means going against their child who "doesn't know any better."

Perhaps, in general, one of the greatest difficulties is that the purpose of adoption is to provide a home and a set of parents for a child. It also includes giving tremendous amounts of love, and experiencing heartaches and sacrifices as they raise the child. When the adoptee shows interest in finding more about his/her roots or in contacting the birth parents, the parents' fear of losing or having to share their child with a virtual "stranger" becomes more real.

With these factors in mind, it is not hard to understand the adoptive parents' position, both in relation to their worries and fears, and in relation to their hopes and desires.

THE BIRTH PARENTS

The birth parent is in a complicated position and is the most "hidden" member of the triad. Traditionally, the birth parent has been the "stained" person whom society shuns, even today, although there has been a slow shift in social norms.

Many of the adoptees today were the children of a young single woman who experienced pressure on her to give up the baby. In the past, the unwed parents had great pressure put on them by ministers, social workers and their own parents. If they really cared about the future of their child, they were told, they would relinquish him/her, because a child born out of wedlock was doomed to a life of misery.

During this era (1950s-1960s), it seems to have been generally accepted that upon giving a child up for adoption these women could then make fresh starts, pretend there was never any pregnancy and forget any infant was ever born to them. This myth was and is prevalent belief, but is one which is changing after more birth parents come to public view and express themselves openly. They tell their story as only they can. They speak of shame, guilt and love. They talk about wishing things were different and being thankful someone could give their child what they felt they could not offer to him/her.

However, by signing away their rights on a piece of paper, most found they could not sign away their hearts. Natural parents may terminate all their legal rights and responsibilities, but their emotional involvement does not come to an end. For adoptive parents, this has always been a sensitive and threatening area. It has now become an open and highly charged issue.

It must not be forgotten that many children who were adopted were taken forcefully from their parent(s) because of abuse, neglect, desertion, etc. However, for many of these birth mothers, and birth fathers, the turmoil, anger and sorrow that their child is lost to them remains, even though they may have been to blame.

For the birth parents the question of disclosure and possible reunions could be a threatening one. Many, after giving up a child, have rebuilt their lives, married and had other children whom they have kept. Often, these same parents would like to have their files updated so that some day their child will see that they were able to make it. However, occasionally, the birth mother has not been able to tell her husband and/or family of her past and so may suffer in fear of a telephone call or a knock on the door which will bring the past into the present.

It is interesting to note that it is generally believed that birth parents are much more open to disclosure than adoptive parents and have aligned themselves much closer to the adoptee organizations which exist.

At the same time, though, it would also seem likely that most birth parents have not yet emerged from their secret worlds in order to become a part of the movement for changing existing policies. Thus, it is also not known, as yet, if these "hidden" people would wish any revision of policy, although there are indications that there is acceptance of being more involved at some point in time. In the study conducted by Baran, Pannor and Sorosky of 38 birth parents in the United States (36 females and 2 male) it was found that the majority wanted to have contact with the children they gave up.

In the same research they found the natural parents were grateful towards the adoptive families for giving their children what they couldn't. This is contrary to the belief of many adoptive parents and agency personnel that the birth parent is hostile and resentful towards their replacement, and is a strong argument towards disclosure and more easily accessible reunion.

The most elusive individuals in the adoption issue are the birth fathers. As such, they are also probably the most misunderstood group. Prior to the 1960s the birth mother rarely gave the name or identity of the putative (supposed) father and this has resulted in few adoptees searching for birth fathers.

Although there is not very much information available on this group it appears the father is not a reckless, irresponsible Don Juan, as many believe, but, rather was concerned about his children, but hindered by immaturity and family pressures.

At present, more and more birth fathers are coming into the picture, which makes the situation even more stressful not only for the adoptee and the adoptive parents, but especially the birth mother who most often lost contact with the father and has negative feelings towards him.

Together, the birth mother and birth father comprise an important part of an adoptee's life and vice versa. These things cannot be changed and must be accepted. The question which remains is what to do about this and how do the birth parents best fit in?

SOCIAL AGENCIES

In the forefront of the adoption issue stand the social workers, judges and bu-

reaucrats. They become the symbols of the "system" which people attack or praise and it seems they are often seen as mechanical systems rather than the human systems they are.

In the issue of disclosure, it is widely felt that agency personnel are supportive of the rules and policies they carry out, but this is not necessarily the case. Social workers caught at the core of the controversy feel torn about it themselves.

In speaking with individuals dealing with adoption practice, there are as wide and diverse opinions as with any of the other groups (i.e. adoptive parents) and many feel as threatened or afraid or as cautious.

Many social workers today go against the adoption policy of confidentiality by "leaking" out information to an adoptee who is desperately seeking a birth parent. Many more wish they could be allowed to do the same but cannot overstep their accountability to an agency.

On the other hand, a great number of social workers, lawyers, ministers and laymen believe disclosure must not come about so easily if the individual's rights will be harmed by disclosure.

With so many opinions existing it becomes easier to understand why there have been no great changes in this area up to date. There is no general agreement as to what changes should occur. At present, though, indications are that policies should be reviewed and some alterations made.

CONCLUSIONS

The growing number of those who are seeking either information or reunion with biological parents affect thousands of adoptees, natural parents, parents who have already adopted and those who are considering adoption. This situation also affects social agencies and the allied professions of law and medicine.

Because society had delegated to social

agencies responsibility for protecting the interests and well-being of all three parties involved in adoption, social agencies have an obligation to hear the messages that adult adoptees are sending. Adult adoptees are a primary source of knowledge about adoption as an institution. Their perceptions are unique, for adult adoptees are actually the only persons who can tell us what it is like to live adoption in a society in which most people are not adopted. Their views should be sought because they can add an important new dimension to what is known about a large group of people in our society.

There is a more important reason why people in social agencies should respond to the adoptees' pleas. This is a humanitarian reason: adult adoptees who are "seeking" are individuals who are asking for help—help in obtaining information or in dealing with distress and pain. This fact alone is cause enough for social agencies to be non-judgmental, to respond with an open mind, respect, empathy, and the caring that is social work's reason for being. Such receptivity will inevitably mean a re-examination of agency policy and practice; it may well cause a change in both policy and practice.

The issue of adoption disclosure in Canada will not go away. The question is "how much of what we know will we tell?"

READINGS

Anderson, C. Wilson. "Adoption: People Seeking Identity," *Social Service Review*, 51 (March 1977), 141-154.

Baran, A., Pannor, Ruben and Sorosky, Arthur D. "Adoptive Parents and The Sealed Record Controversy," *Social Casework*, 55 (Nov. 1974), 534-535.

Baran, Annette, Pannor, Reuben and Sorosky, Arthur D. "The Lingering Pain of Surrendering a Child," *Pyschology Today*, 11 (June 1977), 58-60; 88.

———. "Open Adoption," *Social Work*, 21 (March 1976), 91-100.

Colon, Fernando. "In Search of One's Past: An Identity Trip," *Family Process*, 12 (Dec. 1973), 429-438.

Cominos, Helen. "Minimizing the Risks of Adoption through Knowledge," *Social Work*, 16 (Jan. 1971), 73-79.

Dalsheimer, B. "Adoptive Runs in My Family, *Ms. Magazine*, August, 1973, 82-83; 112-113.

Dukette, Rita. "Perspectives for Agency Response to the Adoption Record Controversy," *Child Welfare*, 54 (Sept./Oct. 1975), 545-555.

Family Involvement Magazine. "Special Issue: Adoption and Roots," 9 (November 2, 1977).

———. "Special Issue: Birthparents Tell Their Story," 9 (November 5, 1977).

Fisher, Florence L. *The Search for Anna Fisher*. New York: Arthur Field, 1973.

Freedman, Joel. "An Adoptee in Search of Identity, *Social Casework*, 22 (May, 1977), 531-536.

Howard, Mary. "I Take After Somebody, I Have Relatives, I Possess a Real Home," *Psychology Today*, 9 (December 1975), 33.

Jaffee, Benson. "Adoption Outcome: A Two-Generation View," *Child Welfare*, 53 (April 1974), 211-224.

Jaffee, Benson and Fanshel, D. *How They Fared in Adoption: A Follow-up Study*. New York: Columbia University Press, 1970.

Kirk, H. *Shared Fate*, New York: Free Press, 1964.

Lifton, Betty Jean. *Twice Born: Memoirs of an Adopted Daughter*. New York: McGraw-Hill, 1975.

Parttridge, Penny. "An Adoptee Talks to Groups of Adoptive Parents About the Search for Origin," *Child Welfare*, 56 (December 1977), 683-686.

Paton, Jean M. *Orphan Voyage*, New York: Vintage, 1968.

———. "The Reunion of Adoptees and Birth Relatives," *Journal of Youth and Adolescence*. 3 (1974), 195-206.

Sorosky, Arthur D., Banan, Annette and Pannor, Reuben. "Adoptive Parents and the Sealed Record Controversy," *Social Casework*, 55 (Nov. 1974), 531-536.

Sorosky, Arthur D., Baran, Annette and Pannor, Reuben. "Opening the Sealed Record in Adoption: The Human Need for Continuity," *Journal of Jewish Communal Service*, 51 (Winter 1974), 188-196.

Sorosky, A. D., Baran, Annette and Pannor, Reuben. "Effects of Sealed Record Adoption," *American Journal of Psychiatry*, 123 (August 1976), 900-904.

Sorosky, A. D., Baran, Annette and Pannor, Reuben. "Identity Conflicts in Adoptees," *American Journal of Orthopsychiatry*, 45 (January 1975), 18-27 (A good review of literature)

"The Review of Adoptees and Birth Relatives," *Journal of Youth and Adolescence*, 3 (1974), 195-206.

Trieseliotis, John ed. *In Search of Origins: The Experiences of Adopted People.* London: Routledge and Kegan Paul, 1973.

FILMS:

Joey, N.F.B., 28 min., black/white, 1964.
  A study of placing an older child for adoption.
A Further Glimpse of Joey, N.F.B., 28 min., black/white, 1966.
  Joey has found a home. The film shows his adjustment problems.

AUDIOTAPES:

Available from C.B.C. Learning Systems, Box 500, Station A, Toronto, Ontario, M5W 1E6.

Adoption

A visit with the family broadcasters Barbara and Lyal Brown, who have one daughter of their own and three adopted children of mixed race (part-Negro, part-Chinese, and part-Indian). Cat. No. 135L: one hour

QUESTIONS, ACTIVITIES AND PROJECTS

1. *Write a short skit about an adopted teenager who demands from his/her parents the right to search out his/her birth parents. Select a cast to portray mother, father and teenager. Have the skit acted out for the class. (a) As an observer, list the emotions that are displayed by the parents and by the teenager. (b) During the skit, which party did you identify with most? Give your rationale for supporting that person.*

2. *Invite a worker from the Children's Aid Society to present the agency's views about disclosing information on adoption procedures. Prepare a list of questions to which you wish the speaker to respond.*

4A

SINGLE PARENT FAMILIES:

The Unmarried Mother Who Keeps Her Child

INTRODUCTION

In 1973, 31 005 children were born to single mothers in Canada. This constituted 9% of all live births that year. It is estimated that at least 80% of the single mothers opted to keep their children, thus forming an alternate one-parent family group, that of the "single mother and her child." An examination of the three largest age groups of the single mothers found that 46% were under the age of 19; 31% in the 20-24 year category; and 13% in the 25-29 year age group.

HISTORICAL BACKGROUND

Legal rights and services for unmarried parents and their children are a relatively modern phenomena, with the first piece of effective legislation being enacted in 1921. Originally, the unwed mother had no rights or services, and consequently concealed or even destroyed her offspring. In 1826 the first piece of legislation on this subject was passed in Upper Canada, an Act "to prevent the destroying and murdering of bastard children." The law was a punitive one, making provision to try a mother for the murder of her child, or in the case of concealment, for a lesser offense. The following year the Guardian-ship Act took the child into account, specifying that an illegitimate child could be placed with a guardian. However, exploitation and cruelty towards these children were rampant and the Act was generally ineffective. The Illegitimate Children's Act in 1914 attempted to make the father liable for the child's maintenance. The Act enabled the mother to present an Affidavit of Paternity to the court. However, as there was no provision in the legislation to make the father legally responsible, action could rarely be taken. Finally, in 1921, through the efforts of both the medical and social work professions, "The Children of Unmarried Parents Act" was passed marking a new approach to children born out of wedlock. The Act, no longer referring to such children as illegitimate, focused on aiding the unmarried mother to provide for her child. Affiliation orders made between the Province of Ontario and the putative (supposed) fathers were now legally binding, requiring the father to contribute to the cost of his child's maintenance. In practice the mother was also financially responsible; however, the new Act provided her with the right to appeal for statutory guardianship with a provincial child welfare officer. If she were still unable to care for the child, or in the case of abandonment or neglect, the Children's Aid Society was given a mandate to assume guardianship. In turn, it could transfer the guardianship role to adoptive parents.

In the following years sociologists sought explanations of illicit pregnancy. A shift from an emphasis on moral deficiency and bad companions to one taking into account the role of environmental or cultural factors took place. Earlier, moral judgments were reflected in the external applications of labels and in the absence of social supportive services. However, a recognition of poverty, broken homes and their influences brought about a change in public attitude. In the 1950s Sigmund Freud's explanations of all behaviour as purposive became popular, contributing to the development of a psychological interpretation of illegitimacy. Thus, the out-of-wedlock pregnancy was accepted as symptomatic and purposeful, an attempt by the personality to ease an unresolved conflict. Attention also became focused on societal attitudes, for while illicit pregnancy continued to be censored, a "fun morality" which includes premarital sex is implicitly condoned if not encouraged by much of our mass media. Nevertheless, although our society continues to see the unmarried mother as a "role violator," in theory at least, neither our legislation nor our services reflect any moral judgement. Rather, they recognize the social, emotional and financial problems which are likely to beset the unmarried parent.

The most important decision to be made by the unmarried mother is what to do with her child. In some cases the unwed mother, because she lacks the capacity to plan realistically or to foresee the consequences of her action, will require assistance in planning for the future care of her child. She is faced with a number of alternatives. If she chooses to keep the baby she may return to her parents' home or

marry the putative father (or another man) or set herself up independently. On the other hand, she may decide to place the child for adoption.

THE UNMARRIED MOTHER

For any individual, entry into a new role may be experienced as a crucial event. For the unmarried girl who becomes pregnant the problem is two-fold: not only is she faced with the transition to a changed status, but in addition her new role of mother is an unexpected and may be an unwanted one. The role of the unmarried mother is also an ambiguous one. While the married, widowed, separated or divorced woman finds both a socially recognized status and role behaviour anchored in the social system, the unmarried mother is socially recognized only as a role "violator," for the role of mother in our society prescribes the counter-role of father, and both are within wedlock. Should the unmarried mother be an adolescent, she may also experience role conflict, for the pregnant teenager must, at the same time, get used to two roles which would ordinarily occur in sequence. As a result, the way she sees and reacts to events and people can switch, depending on the role which is governing her behaviour at the time.

The girl's relationship with her family can be another area of concern. The literature on illegitimacy indicates that many unmarried mothers did not have warm, close relationships with their families in their early years. Often, as a result of her experiences, the girl also has extremely negative feelings towards men. When seeking help from a social agency, the unwed mother is often assigned to a male case worker. Although they may be at a disadvantage in some ways, male workers are in a unique position of being able to demonstrate positive male attributes. The unwed mother is then able to test out her attitudes toward men. In addition to her personal feelings and adjustments towards her family the unmarried mother must make several practical decisions. Since her confinement and future plans as well as the disposition of her child may involve her family, she must evaluate the emotional and practical support which they can offer.

THE SCHOOL AND THE UNMARRIED MOTHER

During this period full of uncertainty and change, schooling could provide some continuity; yet most schools require unwed mothers to drop out of classes as soon as their pregnancy becomes known. The reasons given may be the impact on the girl and her inability to function in a school situation or her detrimental influence on the morals of the school. Whether school officials in fact fear that pregnancy is "catching" or if these rationales are cover-ups for moral biases is not the significant issue. The important point is that education, an important prerequisite for taking care of oneself in our rapidly changing technological society, becomes interrupted for these girls and often leaves them with little motivation to return to school after the birth of the baby. Thus, not only are they deprived of the stabilizing experience of involvement in a study program but also of the social contact which school ordinarily provides and stimulates. While most maternity homes offer educational programs, for those who stay in the community there are few alternatives. However, currently an emphasis on helping the school-age unwed mother to complete her education has been put into practice in some areas in Canada. A bold program, unique at the time to Canadian education, was reported in the February 1971 issue of *Chatelaine:*

Some 100 girls averaging sixteen and a half years, have taken advantage of the opportunity of continuing their education at a school operated by the adult education department of the Calgary School Board, which supplies a building, services and bus tickets. Students pay a tuition fee of $5 per month. There's a full-time teaching staff and many community agencies which cooperate to help the students. In addition to regular academic subjects covering grades seven to twelve, there are also classes in business education, home economics and sewing.

This type of program offers the girls an opportunity to continue their education and focus on their potential for achievement. Those programs which relate to the student's imminent life style—as do, for example, courses in home economics, sewing and business education—and an environment which is task-oriented, non-threatening, informal and highly supportive have been found to be most conducive to learning.

The unwed mother who works may not find her routine as disrupted as that of the student. Interestingly, it is rarely suggested that pregnancy will interfere with her individual functioning. Employers also seem to be more tolerant of unmarried pregnant women, allowing them to continue working for longer periods before delivery. This attitude has become more widespread with the Women's Equal Employment Opportunity Act (December 1970) prohibiting dismissal because of pregnancy.

CANADIAN STUDIES

London, Ontario

The Family and Children's Services of the City of London and County of Middlesex carried out a Longitudinal Study to find out more about how the unmarried mother and her child fared in the community and to learn also of the kind of problems she is likely to encounter.[1]

The study concerned itself specifically with the interpersonal relationships, the emotional and economic adjustments of the unmarried mother and how the first-born child of an unmarried mother, retained by her, fared in the community. Fifty-nine unmarried mothers, mostly white, and ranging between the ages of 17 and 19 years old, were chosen for the study. They represented a cross section of the general population of the area served by the agency. Personal follow-up interviews were conducted at six, twelve, and eighteen months after the baby's birth.

Information gathered from the study indicated that most of the mothers had relatively long-term and probably meaningful relationships with the fathers of their children. The data also found only about one out of five of the fathers assumed any financial responsibility toward the mother or for the care of the child. The study showed that towards the end of the last interview, more than two-thirds of the mothers were self-supporting and one in four had married. This could indicate that having a child out of wedlock is not necessarily associated with inability to become self-supporting, nor is it a hindrance to the opportunity for future marriage.

The data collected indicated a process of adjustment for the unmarried mother which was critical at twelve months, but by the end of the eighteenth month things had become fairly stable. The data revealed also anxieties and problems in such areas as caring for the child.

The study found that most of the unmarried mothers and their babies lived in adequate accommodations. A large number of them lived in publicly subsidized low-rental housing. Less than 10% of the unmarried mothers lived in a common-law union at the time of conception; this figure decreased to 6% by the time the baby was eighteen months old.

The mothers who lived alone with their children experienced a very lonely existence, while those who had a good relationship with their parents were able to create a happy emotional atmosphere for the grandparents, themselves and the child. Most of the mothers had the major responsibility of caring for their children. The mothers complained that the lack of day-care facilities was a problem for them. They also complained that the amount of financial assistance that they received was very inadequate. Only a few mothers felt that they had received adequate personal help in the form of guidance or advice, psychological or emotional support or opportunities for satisfying social contacts.

The study indicated that at the twelve month period, the mothers experienced a critical time. It was at this time that outside help, including the help received from the family, diminished. It was at this time too that the roles they were in became apparent to them. Only a few of the mothers had regrets regarding their marital status at the time of the baby's birth. Many stated that they experienced an unsatisfactory social life, as most of their time was spent in caring for the child.

In this study, the author found that marriage was offered to some of the mothers by men other than the putative father. Many of the mothers indicated that they saw marriage as their ultimate goal, closely followed by happiness and financial security. Much optimism was expressed in regard to obtaining these goals. Some even stated their willingness to return to school so as to complete their educational program. They did not see that as a major problem.

The author of the study stated that in her opinion there was a significant hard core minority, perhaps 25%, where the potential for adequate child care was lower than for the group as a whole, and where the danger of future child neglect was prominent. The most outstanding needs of the mothers that were clearly identified in the study were those of financial and emotional assistance.

The community from which the Longitudinal Study was drawn does carry a comprehensive range of services for the unmarried mother and her child through the Family and Children's Services Department. Services provided include counselling follow-up if the mother keeps her child, and adoption for the child if indicated. Those other services, such as maternity home care, prenatal care, financial assistance, and income maintenance, although provided under other auspices (private and public), are clearly coordinated for the recipient by the Family and Children's Services social worker.

Toronto, Ontario

The Children's Aid Society of Metropolitan Toronto (CAS) has carried out surveys on the unwed mother who keeps her child and who functions as solo-parent in the community.[2] In one of the studies, mothers from the CAS and CCAS (Catholic Children's Aid Society), with a control group, were participants. The study revealed that over 70% of the CCAS and CAS groups and 60% of the control group were no more than twenty years or younger when interviewed. It also indicated that 80% of these young mothers were the primary full-time caring person of the child or children, and that 37% of them were living on their own with their children.

From the study, it was revealed that income or lack of it, tended to be a problem to the mothers. About 80% of these young mothers were living on an income of $4 000 or less. Naturally, this inadequate amount did not allow them the pleasure of securing baby-sitters; neither did it allow them the opportunity of indulging in any kind of recreational expenditures. The average educational level of most of these mothers was that of Grade 10.

Other information obtained from the study, revealed that a large percentage of the mothers retained only a few, in some cases none, of their old friends. Many of the mothers were raising their children in a very isolated environment.

The study revealed also that a large percentage of the young mothers felt that their role as a mother inhibited their social life to some extent. About 30% felt that their mothering role minimally inhibited their social life. About 80% felt strongly that it was essential that they get at least occasional relief from their child caring role. About 70% of the mothers stated their desire to see on-going groups for single parents as part of an agency program.

Vancouver, BC

In a study in Vancouver of ninety single mothers, Susan Poulos[3] ranked the most frequent problems faced by them:

> Rank order of problems faced by single mothers in a Vancouver study
> 1. Day care
> 2. Income management
> 3. Personal adjustment
> 4. Living arrangements
> 5. Child rearing and care
> 6. Getting along in the community
> 7. Employment
> 8. Sex education
> 9. Job training
> 10. Family court action
> 11. Health

Finding suitable day-care facilities for their children was felt as a problem by 80% of the mothers interviewed. The older mothers (over 25 years of age) considered this more of a problem than the younger mothers (72% as opposed to 53%). Age of the child did not seem to influence the experienced severity of this problem. Those mothers who were self-supporting found day care to be a far greater problem than those who were not self-supporting (83% as opposed to 45%). The simplest explanation for this would seem to be a greater number of the former group are probably employed. An alternate explanation may be the cost of day care.

About 75% of the mothers experienced problems with income management. Slightly more of the younger mothers found this to be so than the older mothers (76% and 66% respectively). Of those mothers who were not self-supporting, 86% had problems in this area and 62% of those who were self-supporting agreed. Those with older children (older than one year) found income management more difficult than those whose children were younger than one year old (78% and 65% respectively).

About 71% of the mothers had experienced problems in the area of personal adjustment. Again, the older mothers found this slightly more of a problem than the younger mothers (77% as opposed to 64%). Those with older children were more affected by this problem than those with infants (75% and 60%). About 55 % of the mothers had difficulty in finding suitable living arrangements. This did not vary according to mother's or child's age or financial situation.

Child rearing and care has been a problem for 69% of the mothers interviewed. This is slightly more of a problem for the older mothers and for those mothers with children over one year of age (as would be expected).

About 59% of the mothers have experienced difficulties in their community relations and activities. This did not vary greatly according to mother's or child's age.

CONCLUSIONS

The findings of these studies in many ways constitute a challenge to both public and private Health and Welfare agencies.

Clearly, these mothers are in need not only of social services and adequate financial assistance, but also other community services, including those dealing with health, housing, education, recreation and religion. It is pretty certain that unless these mothers receive such help, their future and the future of their babies is likely to hold continuing poverty, dependence and poor opportunity.

Many of the services now offered to unmarried mothers are spread throughout the community. In addition to the community social agency where she may have made her initial request for aid, the unmarried girl may find herself in contact with a number of authorities: the Department of Welfare when seeking financial assistance; a housing authority, should she apply for a public housing project apartment; hospital clinics and/or private doctors for medical care for herself and the baby; school officials concerning continuing education; and possibly legal authorities regarding the baby's paternity or support. One recommended solution to the problem is a multi-service facility which would provide, in a single setting, personnel of various professional disciplines who could work together with, or on behalf of, the unmarried mother and where appropriate, the putative father. In addition to medical, casework, psychiatric and legal services, an educational program could be offered. Besides regular school courses designed to further the young woman's general education, vocational training, instruction in child care, homemaking and family budget counselling could prepare the woman who intends to keep her child for her new role. Such a multi-service facility would foster close cooperation among the various disciplines concerned with providing total service to the young mother, and would prevent unnecessary duplication. The availability of all these services in one setting might also encourage young mothers reluctant to begin the many different contacts now necessary to use them. Finally, the energy and economic resources of both the unwed mother and the community agencies could be conserved.

The trend in Canada appears to be that more single women will keep their children. We will have to accept this trend and attempt to help our communities to integrate this new one-parent family unit into our Canadian communities.

REFERENCES

[1] Pozsonyi, Judith. "A Longitudinal Study of Unmarried Mothers Who Kept their First Born Children." London: Family and Children's Services of London and Middlesex, 1973. (P.O. Box 848, London, Ontario N6A 4Z5)

[2] Children's Aid Society of Metropolitan Toronto. "Study of Single Parents." Toronto, 1974.

[3] Poulos, Susan. "A Problem Inventory of Single Mothers." Vancouver: Children's Aid Society of Vancouver, 1969.

READINGS

Bernstein, Rose. *Helping Unmarried Mothers.* New York: Association Press, 1971.
A comprehensive guide for the varied human welfare workers who come in contact with unmarried mothers. This book covers the most current practices and methods.

Crellin, Eileen, et al. *Born Illegitimate: Social and Education Implications.* New York: Humanities Press, 1971.
A survey of 650 children in Great Britain born in the same week in 1958 and followed up until age seven.

Hartley, Shirley Foster. *Illegitimacy.* Berkeley: University of California Press, 1975. A multi-dimensional analysis based on cross-national data related to the topic of illegitimacy.

Hopkinson, Angela. *Single Mothers: The First Year.* Edinburgh: Scottish Council for Single Persons, 1976. (44 Albany Street, Edinburgh, EH1 30R).

A study of 116 single mothers who kept their children during the first year of infancy.

Howard, Marion. *Only Human: Teenage Pregnancy and Parenthood.* New York: The Seabury Press, 1975.
The story of three teenage parents who experience school-age pregnancy and parenthood.

Klein, Carole. *The Single Parent Experience.* New York: Walker and Co., 1973.
A guide to men and women who raise children outside of marriage.

Pannor, Reuben, Massarik, Fred and Evans, Byron. *The Unmarried Father.* New York: Springer Publishing Co., 1971.
This study included 222 unmarried mothers and 96 unmarried fathers at the Vista Del Mar Child-Care Service in Los Angeles. The focus is on the social-personal-psychological characteristics of the unmarried father.

Pierce, Ruth I. *Single and Pregnant.* Boston: Beacon Press, 1970.
An advice-giving book to the single girl who finds herself pregnant. Sources of help for such girls are included in the appendix.

Rains, Prudence Mors. *Becoming an Unwed Mother: A Sociological Account.* Chicago: Aldine Atherton, 1971.
This study examines the actual situation of unwed motherhood, as opposed to the causes and pathology of deviance.

Schlesinger, Benjamin. *One-Parent Families in Canada.* Toronto: University of Toronto, Faculty of Education, Guidance Centre, 1974.
A booklet which gives a good overview of Canada's single parents.

———. *The One-Parent Family: Perspectives and Annotated Bibliography.* Toronto: University of Toronto Press, 1978, 4th ed.
An annotated bibliography of 750 items related to single parent families and six essays.

FILMS:

1 *Phoebe*, N.F.B., 28 minutes, black/white, 1964.
A teenage girl becomes pregnant.

QUESTIONS, ACTIVITIES AND PROJECTS

1. *Marsha, a 17-year-old girl, finds herself pregnant and is deciding whether to keep her baby. In small groups brainstorm the alternatives that exist for Marsha. a) Evaluate the various alternatives. b) Which alternative would you personally choose? Why?*
2. *Research what help your community offers to young unmarried mothers who choose to keep their children. Social service agencies and religious organizations are two possible sources of information. Write a short report on your findings.*

4B

Female-headed Separated Families

INTRODUCTION

In Canada it is estimated that about 125 000 families live as separated female-headed families. Separations may not be permanent arrangements. There is no way of knowing how many couples manage a reconciliation and resume living together, nor is there any way of knowing how many continue on in suspended marriage. Some become tired of this state and finally use their abandonment as a ground for divorce.

But whatever the circumstances of separation, the marriage is still technically intact and the facade of matrimony is therefore maintained. The husband's obligation to support his family keeps on, if he can be found and put to his duty again. Because he now maintains a separate domicile, however, the expenses of the two households may cause him to shirk on those of the first. Also, since marriage is merely in hiatus and not yet dissolved by divorce or death, alimony, annuities or insurance policies do not become due the forsaken wife. Her economic status may be difficult to determine so welfare authorities often hesitate to take her under care. The spouses may not, of course, re-marry unless they divorce, and their sexual relations with any others is adulterous.

When there is a separation it is most often the father who is absent from the home. Since the father is usually the family breadwinner, this means that when he leaves, the mother must go to work.

These mothers who must go to work are often handicapped in their earning power by lack of training and skill. In our culture, planning and decision-making about matters of family living and child-rearing are usually joint responsibilities. When these responsibilities are completely thrust on the mother, along with the fact that she is likely carrying a heavy emotional burden, she is apt to be quite overwhelmed.

TYPES OF SEPARATION

What are the main categories of separation? The first type is separation as a divorce preliminary. When the decision is made to divorce, because the husband and wife decide they cannot bear to live together, they separate while proceeding with a divorce. The second type of separation is the separation as a substitute for divorce. Here the couple cannot or will not divorce, but are unable to live together. The conflict for this couple is resolved by temporary separations which may become very long separations.

Separation may come about by the desertion of one of the spouses. Desertion, like separation is not officially recorded unless the deserted parent, usually the mother, applies for public assistance or for a court order.

FACTORS CONTRIBUTING TO SEPARATION

A study of 30 separated women, completed at the Faculty of Social Work, University of Toronto, found that most of the women mentioned financial difficulties, and disagreements about financial matters, as one of the factors, and with many, it was the most important factor, creating the marital disharmony which led to separation. The sample were white, lower middle class, predominantly Protestant, high school educated, Canadian born, urban background women. Many of these separated women felt that their husbands' immaturity was demonstrated around financial matters. They claimed that their husbands were inadequate in their roles as the earners in the home. Failure to bring home sufficient money to support families was repeatedly mentioned as a disruptive factor in family life. Exorbitant credit buying and unrealistic spending to indulge the flamboyant or grandiose tastes of the marriage partner were put forth as a major source of irritation for a number of the group.

A few of the spouses of our subjects insisted that their wives work outside the home to augment the family income. This was against the wishes of the women who felt work outside the home was detrimental to their roles as mothers and homemakers. In contrast, there were other female subjects who resented the fact that their spouses did not wish them to have employment outside the home.

Many of the women felt that their spouses were lacking in personal stability and that this was a main contributing factor to the separation. Several of the spouses had needed psychiatric treatment. Several of the wives had complained that

emotionally immature reactions were precipitated by the first pregnancy.

Incompatibility, poor sexual adjustment, alcoholism, promiscuous behavior and gambling were other factors mentioned as contributing to the separations.

Most of the separated females tended to blame their spouses for the separation. Often the apparent causes are symptoms of underlying causes. Often, too, it is easier to identify the faults of the partner in the unhappy union, than to see one's own contribution to the faulty relationship. Some, however, pointed out that they were partly responsible for the separation.

MARITAL DIFFICULTIES AND COMMUNITY RESOURCES FOR COUNSELLING

Exactly half of the separated group of women made efforts to save their marriages when they were experiencing difficulties, through counselling services. Some of the group attempted to involve themselves and their spouses in marital counselling provided by family service agencies. Some went to mental health clinics, others went to private psychiatrists and others sought marital counselling from ministers.

Several of the group went to the family court over problems of inadequate support. The family court attempts counselling as part of its service. One subject tried to save her marriage by approaching a family service agency in order to attempt to relinquish her child because she felt that the child was jeopardizing the marriage. Another woman was involved in a treatment program for her husband's alcoholism.

Most of the treatment was unsuccessful, in any complete sense, because in many instances spouses refused to cooperate. Despite this limitation many felt that they had received some help for themselves but that the marriages were beyond saving.

POSITION IN THE COMMUNITY

A third of our separated group of women felt that, essentially, their position in the community was no different from that of the divorced or widowed parent. They felt that "all single parents have the same problems of adjusting, facing reality, bringing up children alone, and earning a living," to quote one of the members of the group.

About half of the separated group felt that they were in a worse position than either the divorced or widowed. One of the female subjects described her separated status as follows:

> I am in an anomalous position. I don't belong to anybody. I am a social misfit. It weights heavily against meeting anyone with a view to re-marriage. I am not anything. I am just a woman that is not living with her husband. The separation paper is not worth anything—only an agreement. I would like it to be finished and be free of him. I am nowhere and I don't see getting out of it. He does not want a divorce; he does not want to remarry.

There were references to feeling that they were "neither fish nor fowl," implying that they felt they had no status socially or legally. Several subjects actually posed as divorcées feeling that this status was preferable.

SEPARATION AND CHILDREN

Very few of the children were prepared for the separation. Some of the women felt that the children were too young to understand what was going on, and therefore it was futile to do much by way of preparation. Some stated that the children were aware of the strife between mother and father and had probably overheard plans to separate. One mother reported that at the time of her husband's leaving, the children who had not been prepared for the event, screamed and yelled for him not to go.

A large majority of the separated single parents stated that the separation of the parents had a negative effect on the children.

Worry over the incompleteness of the household, and the consciousness of differences from other families were reported as factors which disturbed the children. Many of the children would have preferred the difficult marital situation, with both mother and father together, to the separated state of the parents. Children reported feeling embarrassed with their friends over the fact that their mother or father was missing from the home. Very young children, it was reported, were very confused about the missing male parent. They had heard of him, but they did not recall ever seeing him.

Many of the separated women remarked on the supposed effects of the missing father on both sons and daughters. Some feared that their daughters had become too attentive to males in the environment; others feared that their daughters had resentful attitudes toward the missing fathers, which carried over into their relationships with other men.

Various symptoms of emotional disturbances, which were attributed to the separations, were reported. Nightmares, crying spells, disturbances in eating and sleeping and disturbed relationships between the children and the remaining parent were considered to be reactions to the separation. Others reported that school adjustment had been affected. While half of the separated women stated that their children had no problems in school, the rest of the group mentioned various difficulties experienced by their children. The problems in school that were referred to were low productivity and poor grades, and disruptive behaviour in the classroom. Nervousness, restlessness and difficulties in concentrating were also mentioned. One child was frequently ill with minor complaints, which appeared to be of a psychosomatic nature, and was frequently absent from school.

Several of the separated female single parents felt their children had actually improved since the separation. There seemed to be less tension, and communication had improved between mother and child.

DIFFICULTIES IN CHILD REARING

Over two-thirds of the women reported that difficulties in child-rearing had increased since the separation. The remaining women felt that there were no particular areas of child-rearing that had become more difficult.

Many of the women found the total parental responsibility for the children a worry and a burden. One mother found it difficult to supply all the attention the children required and she complained that she could never be free of them. Another mother was "anxious about whether or not one parent could ever supply all the love and security a child needed." Making all the decisions around children's affairs bothered some of the mothers, and others felt that they missed the authority of the father in disciplining the children. A number of mothers felt that the whole area of child-rearing was more difficult simply because it was now no longer a shared responsibility. A few mothers complained that the sheer drain on their energies, because of employment outside the home, prevented them from having sufficient energy left over for their child-rearing responsibilities when they got home from work. Some of the mothers singled out sex education for boys as troublesome.

There were several separated mothers, who stated that there were no increased problems in child-rearing, because they felt that the presence of the father prior to the separation actually complicated child-rearing. In these situations, the parents contradicted each other and this made for increased difficulties with the children. One of these mothers stated that her husband was away from home much of the time before the permanent separation, and he had not been much involved in child-rearing. She was used to managing the children on her own.

A few of the mothers who had others caring for the children while they worked found there were a few conflicts around differences in methods of child-rearing between these persons supplying day-time care and themselves.

THE ABSENT PARENT

Approximately half of the separated single parents stated that their children did ask many questions about the absent parent. Most of these questions were about the whereabouts of the absent parent and if and when he was returning home. Other questions were about why most families had both a mother and a father and their family did not. One child wanted to know such specific things as where his father went to sleep, where he was working and where he had his meals. One mother said that her child asked, "Is daddy in heaven or where is he?" This mother said that she had been unable to handle these questions, and had not encouraged them. Another claimed that her daughter did not ask questions about her father. She stated, "My daughter misses not having a father, rather than missing him as a person." Another mother said about a daughter whose father visits regularly, "She doesn't ask any questions about her father, but remembers every detail about what they do on visits."

Other women said that very little had been asked by the children about the missing parent and they seemed to have been satisfied with the answers they had been given.

One half of the separated women stated that they did make a point of talking with the children about their absent fathers. Some felt that their children were too young to have any meaningful explanation given to them.

Most of the separated parents in our sample did attempt explanations to the children about the absent parent. One mother reported that she explained things this way, "Sometimes people couldn't always get along and be happy together. Both of us love you, but I am better able to look after you." This same mother expressed her opinion about explanations to children this way, "Children should have the truth told to them, in keeping with their age. They comprehend more than we give them credit for." She felt that children should never be lied to, or have their questions evaded. Some of the parents of younger children felt that their children were too young to comprehend the real reasons for the absence of the father, and supplied temporary fictitious reasons. Some of these were that the father was away from home on business or that his car had broken down in another city, and he was unable to return home.

Some of the women explained directly to the children that their fathers were irresponsible or very immature and cared for no one but themselves. Still others were careful to explain to the children that while they, as adults, could not get along, nevertheless each parent still retained a love and concern for the children. Others did not prevent their own antagonistic feelings toward the absent spouse from being conveyed in their explanations. Some admitted that they found the whole subject so disagreeable that they discouraged questions or gave evasive and unrealistic answers.

SOCIAL LIFE

Most of the separated single parents stated that their social lives had become more unsatisfactory and constricted since they had become separated. Only a few of the separated group felt that their social lives had actually been improved since they had become separated.

Several of the women felt that social life, in connection with their churches, was organized around couples' clubs or young peoples' groups, and they now felt out of place with both of these groups. One woman said that she was so fearful that people would gossip about her, that she would not talk to any men on the street. This tended to make her isolate herself and this resulted in making her more frustrated and nervous and hard to live with.

The women who claimed that their social life had improved since becoming separated stated that they had led, during their marriage, very restricted social lives. Several of these claimed that they had literally no social life at all when living with their husbands.

CONCLUSION

Separation appears to be increasing among North American families. We have presented some selected findings of a small sample of separated female-headed families in Toronto, Canada. A separation affects the whole family. It is hoped that the "helping professions" (social work, psychology, law, medicine, etc. . . .) can help these families face their varied problems.

READINGS

One in a World of Two's. National Council of Welfare. Ottawa: 1976. (Brooke Claxton Building, Ottawa, Ontario K1A 0K9).
  A report on female-headed families in Canada.
Women in Need: An Annotated Bibliography of Low Income Women. Canadian Council on Social Development. Ottawa 1976. (55 Parkdale Avenue, Box 3505, Station "C", Ottawa, Ontario K1Y 4G1)

Women in Need: A Source Book. Canadian Council on Social Development. Ottawa 1974. A valuable source of information on women in need in Canada, including female-headed families.

Schlesinger, Benjamin. *One-Parent Families in Canada.* Toronto: University of Toronto, Faculty of Education, Guidance Centre, 1974.
A booklet which gives a good overview of Canada's single parents.
_____. *The One-Parent Family: Perspectives and Annotated Bibliography.* Toronto: University of Toronto Press, 1977, 4th ed.
An annotated bibliography of 750 items related to single parent families, and four essays.

FILMS:

1. *Laurette*, N.F.B., 19 minutes, black/white 1969. The problems of a single parent.
2. *Mrs. Case*, N.F.B., 14 minutes, black/white 1969.
   Another single parent and her family.

QUESTIONS, ACTIVITIES AND PROJECTS

1. *The author comments that in the family situation that he investigated few of the children were prepared for marital separation. Ask a guidance counsellor, marriage counsellor or social worker to speak to your class about the ways a child can be prepared for marital separation. Summarize the points that are presented.*

2. *Investigate the community and family resources that could provide a substitute "role model" to compensate for the missing parental figure (one example is the Big Brother Association).*

4C

Children and Divorce

INTRODUCTION

DEPENDENT CHILDREN AND DIVORCE, 1975*		
Dependent Children	**Number of Divorces**	**Percent**
none	21 458	42.4
1	11 523	22.7
2	9 985	19.7
3	4 643	9.2
4	1 904	3.8
5	1 098	2.2
TOTAL	50 611	100.0

—The average number of children per divorce was 1.17 (in 1974 it was 1.22; in 1972 it was 1.15).

—The total number of dependent children involved in divorces in 1975 was approximately 58 527 children.

—Divorce in 1975 involved 101 222 adults and 58 527 children for a total of 159 749 persons.

* Statistics Canada: Vital Statistics. Volume 2, *Marriages And Divorce* 1975. Catalogue 84-205, July 1977.

". . . I could say that I'm trying to bring up my kids the right way, and it's a pity they haven't got a father; but they're much better off without him", stated a recently divorced woman, as I interviewed her about the effect on children of divorce. As I look through my notes of other interviews, I came across the following notation about another divorce—

"Her main practical worry is what will she do next school-year when her daughter won't be able to use nursery school as a day-care service. She's too far from the day-care centre. She has no friends in the apartment building where she lives, nor any nearby. She fears getting a private home to care for the child after school, for fear the person won't be responsible. She has no idea what she'll do, and is beginning to feel panicky.

"She has never given her daughter much explanation of the finality of divorce, and more important, she has not told her that her father has remarried and has a daughter by that union. When she really thinks about it she knows her daughter should be told, but fears the knowledge would hurt the daughter too much. She thinks she'll wait until her daughter is older—she doesn't know how much. Actually, she's quite worried, and doesn't know what she should do."

Since the divorce rate is highest in the first few years of marriage, its victims tend to be predominantly younger children, who are the most vulnerable to disharmony in the family and fear more for their own basic security when parental disharmony becomes pronounced and persistent.

The legal event is undoubtedly much less traumatic to all involved than the emotional divorce which has inevitably preceded it. We recognize that many "intact" homes involve much more discordance than homes broken by divorce. But while the divorce may clear the air and reduce strain on the child in the long run, it also operates as an acute stress in itself since it is a major change for the young child. During the divorce period the child experiences a disruption of regular experiences with two parents, and may be uncertain of what will become of him/her in spite of the best reassurances. What happens to the young child during this period? Obviously, there is a wide range of divorce experiences which will have all types and degrees of effects on children.

It is difficult to separate the effects of divorce from those of the prolonged trauma and strain preceding it. The child's reactions also depend upon such factors as age, sex, extent and nature of family disharmony prior to divorce, each parent's personality and previous relationship with the child, the child's relationships with siblings, as well as the emotional availability of all of these important people during the divorce period and the child's own personality strengths and capacities to adjust to stresses such as separation in the past. Furthermore, in any study of children's reactions to divorce, it is important to recognize the considerable difficulty in differentiating between the impact of several factors: the direct impact on the child of the strife around the divorce; the immediate reactions of the child to the loss of a parent; the impact of the divorce on the remaining parent, reverberating in the child; and the impact, probably some time later, of the loss of a parental model.

Studies of children of divorced parents in nursery schools show that:

1. To the majority of children of this age divorce has a significant impact and represents a major crisis. There is often an initial period of shock and acute depressive reactions.

Sex differences were noted. Boys showed more dramatic changes in behaviour, characterized by the abrupt release of aggressive and destructive feelings.

2. Since children show the immediate effects of divorce with an inability to overcome anxiety and depression through play, it is important to identify and work with these children. It may even be argued that the school has an obligation to intervene at this time in order to prevent reactions from going underground thus preventing future disorders. This is especially so because often key relationships in the family are temporarily disrupted. The father may have moved away and the mother may be emotionally unavailable to the child. Thus, the teacher may be even more strongly thrust into the role of an interim parent substitute.

3. A mental health consultant may be able to pick up signs and symptoms of the behavioural changes from the teachers, to assess the severity of these and to advise the teacher. The consultant may also be available to discuss with the parents how to cope with the effects on the child, and to emphasize the importance of school for the child during this period.

SOME MISTAKES DIVORCED PARENTS MAKE REGARDING THEIR CHILDREN

Some divorced mothers and fathers make what is usually the mistake of having their children live half a year with one parent and the other half with the other. Divided custody rarely works out well. It is more sensible for everyone if a child lives with one parent and spends weekends or vacations with the other.

Similarly, parents often err by permitting one child to live with one parent and another youngster with the other. A 19-year-old boy who remembers living with his unremarried father in such a sticky situation, now says, "Gee, the divorce was bad enough, but I really missed my kid sister who lived with my mother. I never had a sense of family feeling."

Still another common fault is fighting over visiting regulations. Some bitter divorced parents go so far as to "kidnap" their children from each other.

Many divorcées make the legally entitled visits of their ex-husbands so difficult that they unwittingly hurt their children far more. Their "rules" can be incredibly petty. One vindictive woman limits the number of phone calls her former spouse can make to their daughter, who is always eager to talk to her father. But whenever he phones, the mother generally tells him that the girl is "busy", "sick," or "doing homework."

Other vengeful women refuse to allow their ex-husbands into their homes, requiring that the children be picked up and returned on the doorstep. Still others have a maid or a sitter hand over the child like a hostage on a nearby street corner, or on some other neutral territory away from the marital battlefield.

An absent parent's worst visitation mistake is breaking promises or dates. Too many fathers cancel their regular visits with their children abruptly without notice. This is to be deplored—if it isn't a real emergency. It is wiser to inform a child ahead of time and make an alternate date. Children depend upon an absent parent's visits and feel rejected when they are suddenly cancelled.

Other fathers visit their children at such inopportune times as during their son's scout meeting or a young child's nap or mealtime. Experts suggest brief frequent visits for the pre-school child and longer ones, such as weekends and during vacations, for the older child. On birthdays, at graduation and during holidays, children naturally want to have both parents present, even though this isn't always possible.

Many indulgent "Sunday" fathers try to buy their children's affection. They go overboard in giving their absent children too many presents and in taking them to overexpensive places in an attempt to compensate for the quiet family values they no longer can offer. Instead of acting like Real Fathers, which occasionally requires saying "No", too many of these men are Benign Visitors. It only makes a mother's discipline harder if a child of divorce taunts her, "Daddy always gives me presents—why don't you?"

HOW PARENTS CAN MINIMIZE CHILDREN'S GUILT AND FEAR

The first thing to do, according to the psychiatrists and social workers who deal with these problems every day, is to tell the children about the divorce in as reassuring a way as possible.

Whenever possible parents should get together and tell the child calmly. Try not to have him/her find out during an angry quarrel. And don't leave it for the child to learn from others outside the home. Have a full discussion of what it means and stress that it will not mean the end of contact with the parent with whom the child is not going to live. Encourage an expression of feelings. They will be there anyway and it's best to have them out in the open where they can be recognized and dealt with.

Some helpful things parents can say to children in this situation: "Your father and I can no longer live together happily, but that doesn't change the feelings either one of us has for you. Even though he doesn't live with us he will continue to love you and he will never stop being your father."

"What has happened was between Mother and me and had nothing to do with you—you had no part in our unhappiness or our decision to divorce."

Let the child ask questions and try to answer them fully. The less he/she has to wonder and be uncertain about, the less fear there will be. There's nothing wrong with saying, "We don't know about that, we haven't decided yet, but we will do our best to work it out in the way that will be best for all of us."

The attitude in telling the child, even more than the particular words used, is the first demonstration of what the divorce will mean and what life will be like afterward. The child should be reassured that despite the parents' differences with each other, they are still united in their concern for the child. And remember that young children will have to be reassured again and again that they will still be loved and taken care of.

When a child shows no reaction to a crisis like divorce in the family, parents can be misled into thinking an adjustment has been made, when in truth the child hasn't even begun to come to terms with it. This attitude may be a defense against accepting the reality of a painful situation or the child may be hiding destructive thoughts and wounded feelings that will only come to the surface at some later time, when they will be all the harder to deal with. Helping the child come to terms with the situation now, however difficult it seems, can save anguish later.

CONCLUSION

Many adults involved in divorce who have children of any age, seem to forget the vulnerability of their children as they go through the difficult stages of divorce. In trying to work out some of the guilt, accusations, self-blame and shame resulting in divorce, the adults overlook the fact that children can feel the same emotions as their parents. We have to protect children in a divorce from getting involved in the negative and sometimes cruel tug-of-war that ensues when parents decide to part.

We can help many children of divorce in a positive way to go through the trying days of separation and ultimate parting of their parents by including them in many of the decisions related to the divorce, and by avoiding using them as "pawns" in the game of life.

READINGS

Canada Law Reform Commission. *Divorce*. Ottawa, 1975. The views of the Commission related to divorce in Canada.

Canada Law Reform Commission. *Studies on Divorce*. Ottawa, 1975. Two research papers on divorce, and two working papers. The topics include children of divorcing spouses, maintenance and divorce and reform of the divorce act.

Kronby, Malcolm C. *A Guide to Family Law*. Toronto: New Press, 1972. A helpful guide to Canadian laws related to divorce and separation.

Schlesinger, Benjamin. *One-Parent Families in Canada*. Toronto: Faculty of Education, Guidance Centre, 1974. A booklet which gives a good overview of one-parent families in Canada.

Status of Women Advisory Council. "Study Paper on Divorce" by Marcia H. Rioux. Ottawa: 1976. An examination of divorce in Canada and implications for women.

Zuker, Marvin. A. and Callwood, June. *The Law is Not for Women*. Toronto: Pitman, 1976. The legal rights of Canadian women, including divorce.

FILMS

The Admittance, NFB, 43 min, black/white, 1968. The story of a 30-year-old divorced woman.

The Appointment, NFB, 15 min, colour, 1977. A film on marriage and divorce.

QUESTIONS, ACTIVITIES AND PROJECTS

1. *In a crisis situation in the family, such as divorce, it may be that both marital partners are too emotionally involved to assist the children in their adjustment to the new situation. Under these circumstances it is often advisable to have a family counsellor work with family members. Invite a guidance counsellor, marriage counsellor, social worker, minister, priest or rabbi to class. Ask him/her to role-play a counsellor who is assisting a family undergoing a divorce situation. During the presentation, note the techniques the counsellor is using to help the family work through the problem. Have the counsellor clarify his/her reasons for using the techniques.*

2. *What rights do you think that children should have in a divorce? Investigate the status of children's rights in a divorce in your province.*

4D

SINGLE PARENT FAMILIES

Weekend Fathers

Benjamin Schlesinger
Katherine Tasios Dominic

With the increasing divorce rate in Canada and the United States, we are finding more and more weekend or part-time fathers in the family constellation. Wives were granted custody in eighty per cent of divorces involving dependent children in Canada in 1976. Husbands received custody in fifteen per cent of these cases.*

THE STUDY SAMPLE

Nine part-time fathers were interviewed. They had been part-time fathers for an average of 3.5 years, and had an average of two children with an average age of 10 years. They all resided in Metropolitan Toronto.

GENERAL FINDINGS

One of our findings was that those fathers who settled custody in court had not accepted the court's decision and were still struggling to get custody of their children. They still hoped that the role of a part-time father would be a temporary one and that one day, either the court would reverse its decision, or the children would decide to leave the mother and return to

*Source: Statistics Canada: Vital Statistics—Vol. 2, Marriages and Divorce 1976. Catalogue 84-205, July 1976.

them. Those fathers who had settled the custody of their children out of court had accepted their roles as part-time fathers as being permanent ones. It is important to note that those fathers who settled out of court appeared to have more frequent visitation rights and spent more time with their children during summer vacations. The fathers in the former group see their children every other weekend and are not permitted to call their children during the week; the fathers in the latter group have practically unrestricted weekly visits and most of them have telephone contact between visits with their children.

Both groups of fathers were concerned and spoke about "the best interests of the child"; the only difference lay in their perception of their ex-spouses as a parent. The ones who settled in court felt that they were the better parent and the children suffered by being with their mothers. The fathers who settled out of court felt both they and their ex-wives were "good" parents and felt the children were going to be "in good hands."

PROBLEMS ABOUT VISITING

Most fathers were very careful not to antagonize their ex-wives for fear that the ex-wives would retaliate by keeping the children away from them. Some fathers mentioned that they feel, many times, that the term "father by permission of the mother" reflects their own situation.

One father experienced difficulty throughout initial visits with his seven-year-old son. The child was very hesitant in going with his father on a visit because he was afraid he would not be returned to his mother. The father felt that it was the mother's way of preventing the father and son from maintaining a close relationship; he felt the mother was "brainwashing" the child.

Another father felt that whenever his ex-wife was angry with him, she would make excuses such as sickness of a child, or a child's involvement in other activities, as a way of preventing him from seeing the child. This father was not permitted by the mother to enter her house, so, when the child was sick it was impossible for him to visit the child; he misses his children so much between visits that he often parks his car in front of the school yard and watches his children from a distance. There was another instance in which the father and his son arranged to meet during the week in a restaurant, just to talk, and someone saw them and reported it to the mother. Soon afterwards, the court issued a warning to him "ordering" him not to deviate from his visiting privileges.

Some of the fathers felt that the mothers did not want to let the children spend time with them because of fears that the children might want to remain with the fathers.

Another father initially felt very guilty about "breaking up the family." As a result, he could not face seeing his children and his ex-wife, so he limited himself in his visits to the children. He had a very hostile relationship with his wife. His son, just after the separation, started seeing a psychotherapist because of misbehaviour in school and the father felt responsible for this. It took him several months before he started seeing his children regularly.

In another case, the father took the child on a visit and would not return the child because the partings were becoming too painful. The police came to his door soon afterwards.

Most fathers initially were not allowed to enter the ex-wives' premises, and some are still prohibited from doing so. Therefore, they must wait outside to pick up the child.

It is apparent to the fathers that the mother has a great deal of power by being able to prevent the father from seeing the child. Threats and counter-threats of suits are a common occurrence. Generally, fathers claimed that they must be very careful in dealings with their ex-wives; as one father stated "whatever little time I have with my kids is better than nothing."

EFFECTS OF VISITS ON SOCIAL LIFE

The majority of fathers stated that having definite days set up, not only gave structure to their children's lives, but also to their own. This helped them to structure their social life so that it would not interfere with the time they would spend with their children. One father found his social life was suffering because of weekly weekend visits. It is important to note that the father emphasized that he looked forward to spending time with his child, but due to his work requirements, the only time he could socialize was on weekends. Those fathers who had free access to their children expressed comfortableness in calling their children and letting them know that they had something to do on a particular day and would not be able to see them and they did not feel rejected when their children called them to cancel a visit because of some other engagement. They did see their children consistently at least twice a week.

One father mentioned that his social life is very rich, he dates several women, and that this creates some difficulty for him when his 14 year old son asks him about his involvement with women. He feels that he is in a "double-bind" situation; when he tells his son, the son appears to have difficulty accepting the fact that his father dates many women and when he is vague on the subject the son exclaims, "How can you expect me to be open with you when you are not open with me?"

Several fathers said that they did not have much of a social life.

Of all the part-time fathers interviewed, one was living in a common-law relationship. Some fathers expressed interest in meeting someone of the opposite sex but were hesitant about settling down again. Others did not express interest in forming a serious relationship.

FEELINGS ABOUT VISITS

All the fathers stated that they looked forward to visits with their children. They felt that the quality of time spent with their children was greater now than before the separation. Most of the fathers felt that having a special time set aside allowed them to spend the time with their children without interruptions and that this led them to "get to know" the children better. Most felt closer to the children now than during the time they were married. Some fathers felt that during their marriage they had frequently taken out their frustrations with their ex-spouses on their children and this affected the kind of relationship they had with their children. Since these frustrations have been alleviated, the quality of their relationships with their children had changed.

It appeared that the fathers had better relationships with their eldest child; they stated that it is easier for them to communicate and share interests and feelings with them.

For most fathers, including those who had been part-time fathers for longer periods of time, parting after each visit was very difficult and painful. One father said that each Sunday he felt "down" after dropping his son off. The most difficult time for the fathers were holidays in which, under normal circumstances, the whole family gathered together. It is a very lonely time for them. Some celebrated the holiday with the children on the date of their visit. One father, for instance, said to his children, "you must be the luckiest kids in the world, you have two Christmases.

Fathers, immediately after the separation, experienced a strong fear of losing their relationship with their children, and with time, they appeared to become much more confident in their role as part-time fathers.

FEAR OF LOSING THEIR RELATIONSHIP WITH THEIR CHILDREN

A great many fathers experienced a tremendous amount of guilt for not spending as much time with their children before the separation. They were afraid that the children would experience the separation as a desertion on their part and that the children would not want to have anything to do with them. Also, the conflict with their ex-wives continued and they thought that their ex-spouses might attempt to antagonize the children against them.

They were also afraid that there would be another man in their ex-wives' lives and that the children would begin to identify more with this man than their natural father. For the two fathers whose ex-spouses remarried or were living with another man, initially it was a worrisome and painful period for them. One ex-wife insisted that the children call the stepfather "dad" which caused some confusion to the children.

In order for the fathers to alleviate their own guilt and make sure that the children would maintain their relationships, they felt they had to "bribe" their children. They were buying presents and providing constant entertainment during visits. They wanted to let their children know how much they loved them and felt lost as to how to show them. Both fathers and children did not know how to behave in their new roles. The fathers became like a "weekend Santa Claus."

During this stage, fathers tried to make things go as smoothly as possible and were afraid to discipline the children. They fantasized that had they disciplined the children, they would not come back for the next visit. With time, both fathers and children became more secure within their new roles, and moved to a second stage.

It appeared that those fathers who settled out of court moved to the next stage sooner than those fathers who settled custody in court. Some fathers in the latter category seemed to be still in the first stage after two to three years of separation.

During this period, the fathers and children began to behave more naturally when they were together and they were more relaxed with one another. There was less emphasis in providing entertainment and stress was placed on spending "just some time together." The fathers felt secure that the child had a special relationship with them.

FINANCIAL SUPPORT

All fathers paid financial support for their children. Payments of support were very important to the fathers. Paying support generally gave them a "psychological" feeling of providing for their children. Some felt it gave them a right to visit their children.

Three out of nine fathers felt that their support payments were too high in proportion to their earnings. One father, for instance, felt that even though he became a student, he still had to pay the same amount of money in spite of the fact that he had no income from work (his ex-wife was employed).

For one father, it was very important that his children know that he was providing for them; he made cheques personally payable to his children with notes of affection attached to them but the court stepped in and prohibited him from doing this. He wanted the children to know that he cared for them very much and that it was not the court that was supporting them.

CONCLUSIONS

At this time, we have very little information on the coping patterns and father-child interaction of the weekend father. The challenge to family counsellors and family life educators is to make this relationship a positive one, and to reduce stress as much as possible so that the children and their part-time fathers will benefit. We need to bring the fathers out of the "shadow" into the light, and the children from a strained relationship into an easy one.

READINGS

Atkin, Edith and Rubin, Estelle. *Part-Time Father*. New York: Vanguard Press, 1976.
Egleson, Jim and Egleson, Janet. *Parents Without Partners*. New York: E. P. Dutton, 1961.

Hetherington, E. M., Cox, Martha and Cox, Roger. "Divorced Fathers" *The Family Coordinator*, 1976, 25, 417-428.

Palmer, Sally. *Parents and Children in Divorce.* Ottawa: National Health and Welfare Canada, 1969.

QUESTIONS, ACTIVITIES AND PROJECTS

1. If you, as a weekend father, could only spend a few hours a week with your child or children what activities would you wish to pursue? Consider activities relating to the developmental level(s) of the child (or children).

2. Discuss how you, as a weekend father, would want to be involved in your children's
   a) school work
   b) school clubs
   c) summer activities
   d) plans for post-secondary education
   e) discipline

4E

SINGLE PARENT FAMILIES

Motherless Families

Benjamin Schlesinger
Rubin Todres

According to the 1976 census, 94 990 families in Canada were headed by a single father.[1] The motherless family is on the increase in Canada; in 1976 almost every tenth family was a single-parent family, and 17% of them were headed by men only. The latest American data, for the year 1976, indicate that there were almost 1.5 million motherless families in the U.S.[2] A recent survey of the literature by Benjamin Schlesinger[3] reveals few studies in North America on motherless families, since the focus has been primarily on the female-headed one-parent family.

In the last decade fathers have been increasingly expected to assume a more active child-rearing role, due in part to the growing awareness of the value of the father's parental influence. Coupled with this trend is the increase in the number of mothers who are deserting their husbands and children, for short periods of time or permanently. Recognizing these community trends, the courts have begun to award custody of children to the male parent more frequently.

It certainly can be argued that the stability of the family is as much affected by a man's rearing children alone as it is by a woman's. In these days of greater emphasis on equal treatment of men and women, it makes little sense to give a mother the choice of working or staying at home with her children, but to deny that choice to the father. Society's traditional attitude that a mother's place is in the home and a father's place is in the work force has no bearing where there is only one parent in the family. Ideally, the community would offer such help—day care, homemaker services, part-time work—to enable both men and women to work and to spend time at home with their children. Until that utopia arrives, the law should extend to male parents the same benefits granted to females.

THE CANADIAN STUDY

At the end of 1974, with a group of social work students in a research course, one of the authors of this article completed a study of 72 motherless families.[4] It was decided to obtain a sample by asking for volunteer participants. Seventy-eight subjects responded to media publicity and to appeals to single-parent groups in the city.

Highlights

Of the 72 participants, 24 were separated from their wives, 17 were divorced, 15 had been deserted, 15 were widowers and one had not married. These men had been caring for their children alone for periods of 3 months to 10 years, with the average about 3 years.

The average age of the men was 40; the youngest was 24 and the oldest 65. These single fathers were well educated: 85% had completed high school, and of this number 70% had some higher education. Almost all were employed; average income was $11 500. Children living with the father numbered from one to five, with an average of 2.1. Ages ranged from 1 to 23.

The Effect on the Children

Most fathers described the breakup of their family as an emotionally charged event. They said that the breakup was upsetting for their children, and that there were noticeable changes in their behaviour, including resentment toward the parents. Some fathers said their children were too young at the time to understand the change in the family and therefore showed no reaction. Others said there was no difficulty because the children had been prepared for the mother's absence.

Many of the fathers reported that communications among family members had improved. It was the researchers' impression that many fathers appeared to have suffered more than their children (in the areas of sleeping, eating, peer relationships, work, play and physical appearance).

Life Style

Who performs the role of the mother-housekeeper in the motherless family? The fathers in the study were responsible mainly for preparing breakfasts and suppers during the week. Household chores, such as washing dishes, were done mainly by the father or were shared with the children. General housecleaning was mostly the responsibility of the father. In almost every instance, fathers and children ate together. Nearly half of the fathers said that when a child was sick they stayed home with the child. The fathers also took major responsibility in consulting the child's school teacher and attending to medical problems. Housekeepers were usually employed, especially in families with young children.

Social Life of the Fathers

At the time of the study, three-quarters of the fathers were dating, most of them at least once a week and the majority found their relationships satisfactory. The women friends were brought to the homes, where they met other family members and participated in family activities. Most of the children encouraged their fathers' social activities. Thirty of the fathers said they would like to remarry. In noting the advantages of remarriage, most stressed companionship, someone with whom to share potential responsibility, and providing the children with a mother. Almost all the fathers knew the whereabouts of the mothers, most of whom were fairly close by. About half of the fathers said they sometimes saw the mothers.

Community Assistance

About one-third of the fathers indicated that they had needed financial assistance after becoming single parents. Of those who applied for bank loans, credit or mortgages, most were granted such aid. Most of the fathers said they had needed help or advice from other people since becoming single parents, and almost all had sought and received such help—most commonly about job and family.

Two-thirds of the men felt there were differences in the way single fathers and single mothers were treated by society, principally in financial help, the system of justice and society's attitude.

The most frequently mentioned concern was the financial burden of rearing and maintaining a family alone. Money problems included the costs of housekeepers and day-care centres, and the maintenance of an adequate standard of living. Among the issues raised was the lack of government supports; many felt that "there should be a father's allowance." The men also felt that it was easier for women to acquire welfare assistance; they sensed discrimination against fathers who considered it necessary to stay home to care for their children. The fathers also said that society in general seems to believe that men are unable to rear a family appropriately by themselves.

As an indication of social stigma, some men complained of difficulty in acquiring new friends, and some reported they were no longer accepted by their families and friends after becoming single parents. These comments may explain why a significant number of the fathers complained of acute loneliness. Many felt unwelcome in groups, and an inability to "fit in." Some pointed out that other parents often were reluctant to have their teen-age daughters go to father-parented homes unsupervised. Relationships with married couples also presented difficulty. Many respondents said they were treated as a threat to the security of the marriages of their male friends. A large number commented on the difficulty in hiring housekeepers when the latter learned there was no wife in the home.

Some of the fathers expressed doubt that their children were receiving appropriate parental care and attention. Disciplining the children was a problem for many fathers. Some thought that available social services were geared to women rather than to all single parents and that it was difficult to locate appropriate services. A small number were dissatisfied with the help they were able to get from social workers or agencies.

CONCLUSIONS

On the basis of this small exploratory study of motherless families, which to our knowledge was the first in Canada, the following comments can be made:

1) There is little research on motherless families in North America. The only large study of this type available was completed in Britain.[5]

2) The social security system is primarily geared to fatherless families. It is essential to examine the financial, social and psychological needs of the motherless family, and to eliminate some of the legal barriers to constructive help to them.

3) Child-rearing patterns in motherless families at various stages of the growth of children (infancy to adolescence) should be studied, as well as the differences between child-rearing patterns in fatherless and motherless families.

4) Family laws should be reexamined, with a view to rectifying some of the inequalities related to fathers who want to look after their own children, as sole parents.

5) Better statistics are needed to monitor the increasing phenomenon of motherless families—such data as the age of the children, when these families become motherless, how long fathers remain single parents, how many remarry, whom they marry (another single parent?), how many such families come to the attention of social agencies and if they are found in public housing projects.

6) The social work literature should be increased. Those who work with motherless families should discuss treatment methods, work with self-help groups and

the child-rearing, social, sexual and coping patterns of the families. There are no doubt ethnic and social class variations related to motherless families.

REFERENCES

1. 1976 Census of Canada *Families by Family Structure and Family Type.* Catalogue #93-822, Bulletin 4-3, May 1978.
2. Department of Commerce, U.S. Bureau of the Census. Current Population Report, Population No, Characteristics Series P-20 #323. Marital Status and Living Arrangements, March 1977, Washington D.C.
3. Schlesinger, Benjamin. *The One-Parent Family: Perspectives and Annotated Bibliography,* Fourth edition. Toronto: University of Toronto Press, 1978.
4. Todres, Rubin, editor. *A Study of 72 Motherless Families in the Metropolitan Toronto Area.* Toronto: Faculty of Social Work, 1975. The first Canadian study related to motherless families.
5. George, Victor, and Wilding, Paul. *Motherless Families.* London: Routledge and Kegan Paul, 1972.

READINGS

Schlesinger, Benjamin. *One Parent Families in Canada.* Toronto: University of Toronto, Faculty of Education, Guidance Centre, 1974.
A booklet which gives a good overview of Canada's single parents.
———. *The One-Parent Family: Perspectives and Annotated Bibliography.* Toronto: University of Toronto Press, 1978, 4th ed.
An annotated bibliography of 750 items related to single parent families and four essays.

QUESTIONS, ACTIVITIES AND PROJECTS

1. *Traditionally the courts have awarded custody of young children to the mother following a divorce on the assumption that the mother is best suited to have guardianship of the children. Some contemporary fathers are questioning this viewpoint. Invite a lawyer who specializes in family law to class to outline the conditions whereby the children may be placed with either parent.*
2. *It has been suggested that our Social Services are biased against fathers who are single parents. Examine articles in newspapers, magazines and journals for evidence of this bias. Share your findings with the class.*
3. *Interview a father who has custody of his children to discover how single parenthood has affected his lifestyle.*

4F

THE WIDOWED

So much attention is given to today's high rate of marriage failure in North America that "single parent," to many people, means only a divorced or separated parent. But with less publicity, death continues to take its toll, as it has from the beginning of time: every year thousands of families are left fatherless or motherless. Surviving spouses are single parents, too.

In Canada according to the latest statistics available (1971) there were 213 657 widowed families, of whom 47% had as their head a widow or widower under the age of 55. These families had a total of 247 000 children living at home, nearly half of whom are under the age of 14.

THE ADJUSTMENT PROCESS

While the big problem facing divorced or separated parents is how to get along with an ex-spouse, the chief concern of widows and widowers is how to get along without one. Here is the main difference that distinguishes almost all the special problems of single parents who have been widowed.

For example, in the months and years that precede a marital breakup, mother and father frequently build up such strong antagonism to each other that divorce, despite all its attendant difficulties, comes as a relief. Death, on the other hand, often strikes suddenly, leaving the widowed to-

tally unprepared to cope with single parenthood. And even for those who have been forewarned by long illness or disability, it is not always possible to adjust to the loss before it becomes an actual fact.

Sometimes parents who have lost a partner through death seem to have an easier time of it than parents who are divorced. Unlike the divorcee, the widow obtains social support and has a well-defined role to play. In other words, she can mourn outwardly. And her friends and relatives need not be in conflict about helping her—it is the "right" thing to do. Much the same is true of the widower; in no literature where he appears with his motherless children is he likely to be the villain of the piece.

Until recent years, as a matter of fact, the widowed parent was generally considered to be the responsibiltiy of his or her family. Relatives were under social pressure to contribute to the bereaved woman's support or at least to help ease her emotional adjustment, and it was understood that the female relatives of the family would care for the widower's children.

In many groups, despite the "atomization" of today's family, this still holds true. But in all too many others, the widow or widower is so far removed from the relatives—emotionally and geographically—that nothing more than long-range sympathy can be expected from them. He or she must learn to cope with the problems of widowhood alone.

Sometimes a long illness precedes death, and the bereaved partner learns gradually to face the inevitable prospects of being widowed. For many husbands and wives, however, the inevitable adjustment is just postponed by a long illness: right up to the last minute, they hope that the ailing partner will, somehow, get better. And all too frequently, in families where the children are still growing up, death strikes suddenly, without warning, without any chance for adjustments.

It may take two years or more to become reconciled to bereavement, and the working out of grief seems to proceed uneasily, by contradictory impulses, isolating the grief-stricken in a struggle that they cannot share. Grief, by its nature, seems to yield very reluctantly to consolation. The profound discouragement of the bereavement tends for a while to devalue all relationships except that which has been lost, so that the widowed, instead of turning to their children, parents, or friends with all the more affection, become, at times, almost indifferent toward them. Moreover, there seems to be a need to mourn the dead, to show how much the loss has meant, and consolation must wait until this tribute has been paid. Hence it is difficult for friends or relatives to help the widowed overcome their grief. Sympathy may only aggravate distress: exhortations to be practical and look to the future seem glib and insensitive, solicitousness seems officious—the comforters seem to fuss ineffectually outside a conflict that they cannot understand.

But, if relatives and friends cannot do much to ease the pain of grief, their practical help is invaluable. It is useful at any time, and especially valuable to a widowed mother who must be relieved of part of her household routine if she is to earn a livelihood for herself and her children. Not that the nature of these services changes so much in widowhood: she probably received the same kind of help, for the most part, when her husband was alive. But now she depends upon it more. Only in certain household jobs, and practical advice, does it seem that a brother, a cousin, or a son may, in the most literal sense, sometimes take the dead man's place. If the nature of the help her relatives give her otherwise changes very little in widowhood, this is partly because at all times it provides insurance against just such hardship.

SOCIAL LIFE

On the whole, widowhood tends to impoverish social life. A widow can take little pleasure in entertainment, feels awkward with her old friends, loses the only strong tie with her husband's family, and has moods in which her lonely struggle to master grief, her apathy and repudiation of consolation isolate her even from her own family. These tendencies are often reinforced in cases of financial stress. The widow has less money to spend and less time, too, since she is more than ever dependent on her earnings. Perhaps there is also a sense of failure in misfortune, however undeserved, and the more so when the misfortune involves poverty.

Occasionally a friend arranges a meeting with a widower ("Just right for you, dear")—as if widowhood were the only thing the two need have in common—or a husband brings a bachelor from his office to join a dinner party attended by a widow. The match-making is well-intentioned but so obvious that it is often a kiss of death for any friendship that could develop between the two.

But there are men—oh yes! There is the good friend's husband, so helpful and attentive. "Joe would have wanted me to take care of you," he says, with an anything but brotherly squeeze. Or, "Mary asked me to stop by some night and see how you're getting along." Many widows are particularly bitter on this score. "One of the most disturbing things that I had to cope with was the advances, verbal and physical, from men I knew well. The first few times it happened I went home crying. These were men who were my husband's friends; their wives were my friends! It was quite disillusioning for me."

Eventually, however, the widow wards off the wandering husbands; friends and relatives remember her less frequently; perhaps she finds a job that brings in some money and fills some of the empty hours. Life may settle then into a pattern that promises anything but excitement and new acquaintances in the future.

It may be difficult to avoid "the widow's rut" in a small town. But in large towns and cities, where there are more people and more to do, a widow may seek activities that bring her new experiences and new acquaintances. Dance classes, adult education classes, a regular job, and volunteer work all fall into this category. "The important thing to remember," warns a mother of two girls who lost her husband nine years ago, "is to be interested in the activity for itself, as well as for the people it will introduce you to."

From population statistics it would seem unlikely that there would be strong similarities between the social problems of the widow and the widower. For every marriageable man over 30 years of age, there are some four or more marriageable women. A man has greater social freedom: he can more easily initiate a friendship. He has greater mobility: he can seek companionship with women his own age or much younger. And a widower is usually in a better financial position than the widows of his community.

But statistics never tell the whole story.

While it is true that the imbalance will get the widower more invitations to dinners and parties, they are usually the same kind of invitations that the widow receives in fewer numbers—"I know a nice girl that I'm just dying for you to meet!" As an "extra", a man is less uncomfortable than a woman, to be sure, but the fifth-wheel feeling is still there. "When my old friends invite me to parties, their wives always come over and dance with me. I don't know whether they dance with me because they want to or because they pity me." The widower, too, may get a shocking new view of some of his friends' wives: "I hear complaints, 'My husband does this,' 'My husband doesn't do that.' They sound so dissatisfied. I get so discouraged; I feel that I will never marry again." And although the man's ability to get around freely may seem highly desirable to a woman, he is likely to consider it a questionable advantage. "Where can I go? To a public dance? To a resort hotel? That's a bachelor's life. I'm a family man, and I'm not used to it any longer. The single people who go there don't have children. They are not interested in my kind of life, in my home and family problems." With baby-sitters to hire, with his children at home waiting for him, the widower cannot—and usually does not want to—go gallivanting. His need, like the widow's, is to meet mature, congenial men and women who may themselves be single parents. He wants an integrated social life that will provide adult companionship for himself, family outings for him and his children, and, possibly, opportunities to consider remarriage with a woman who will not only be his wife, but who must also be a substitute mother for his youngsters.

FINANCIAL PROBLEMS

On the average, a family that is "widowed" earns less than when it was intact. In widowhood, money takes on a different significance from what it had before. The fact that there is less money than before, or that the sum left by the husband is the end of all financial help from him, becomes a second deprivation. It is bound up in the widow's sudden loss of someone to lean on.

Money's meaning may get all out of proportion. The widow may cling to every penny as to a life preserver. Or she may spend it like water in an effort to buy back the social status she has lost by not being a married woman. She may feel that she must go out immediately and get a job. She most certainly will resent remarks of friends who remind her how lucky she is compared with widows less comfortably situated. She will seek advice about how to invest her money and then not follow it.

If there was any oddity about the way the husband left his estate, or if he left very little, this fact will get mixed up in the widow's thinking about him. She must justify any mistakes he may have made in order to keep her image of him as a good provider.

What a widow with money problems—and the wealthiest have them—must do is to take time and attempt to evaluate what she wants her life to be like and show she can best get the things she wants. She must live within limits prescribed by her assets, personal and financial, but drastic curtailment of her standard of living in order to save everything for the children's college education would probably be a mistake. Selling her possessions may be necessary, but she should not take such a step until her emotions have calmed a bit and she can realistically evaluate the choices open to her. For this, she will probably need competent advice from a banker, lawyer, trusted friend, or professional adviser of her husband's. If none of these is available, family service agencies can provide some financial counseling.

A job cannot cover a widow's grief or end her loneliness. It cannot substitute for renewing social contacts and may, indeed, be just a dodge to avoid beginning to go out among people again. It cannot be the only source of satisfaction in life. It cannot all by itself give a former married woman the status she has lost.

There may be no doubt that money must be earned. If so, the widow who has never worked, or who has not worked in a long time, may find need for vocational counseling to discover the fields in which she is best suited. She may also need training or retraining, and a vocational guidance counselor would be well up on what facilities are available in the community.

The widow left with young children or with adolescents has some very special problems. The rebuilding of a shattered family life demands an answer to the basic question of how to be a parent alone, how to give the children what they need and still let the mother have a life of her own.

Here again the recently widowed mother should be encouraged to maintain the status quo for a time. Young children react to death with fear for their own safety. They may feel abandoned and helpless. Keeping them in the same home and doing things in pretty much the same way can reassure them. In the case of adolescents, who are in an unsettled developmental stage anyway, death of a father is a truly serious upheaval. Another big change in their lives would be a further blow to stability.

Once the first period of grief is past, the widow must consider how she can balance her needs as a person and what the children need from her. If she can think about it realistically, she will remember that no one can "make up" to a child for the loss of a father. Likewise, children cannot be expected to offer their mother her sole emotional support. A widow must learn neither to depend on her children too much nor to live exclusively for them.

If a widow has grown children, the pressure to move into their home is often great. Often the children will want to take over completely and do all the planning for their mother. A widow should not be pushed into making a hasty decision about where to live and what to do with the rest of her life. She needs time to consider the many choices available to her.

A STUDY OF WIDOWS AND WIDOWERS

Our study in metropolitan Toronto related to the one parent family gave us additional insights into the problems faced by widows and widowers.

We asked the widowed what were some of the difficulties they had to face after their spouse's death. All the widowed mentioned loneliness.

One of them exlaimed: "Loneliness! I still haven't got used to it. You can be alone in a big crowd. However, I am now beginning to come out of it. A year ago, if you had come for this survey, I wouldn't have been able to talk about it. It has affected my work to some extent."

A widow stated: "Everything! I found managing the household finances difficult, as my husband had looked after them. Household repairs were another problem. I had difficulty deciding whether I was making the right decisions, as we had always decided everything together. I relied completely on my husband. We did everything together. Suddenly, I had to do everything alone."

Another widow commented: "Loneliness was the most difficult problem. One is totally unprepared. Depression has been a problem also, but I have been able to cope." A further comment was: "Coming back home to my parents made life most difficult. They tended to pity me and be angry about my predicament. You get used to thinking and saying "we," and it

was hard to say merely "I" again. This took some time. Income is not a problem because I earn nearly as much as my husband did before he died. I only have to pay a small amount toward housekeeping expenses. Loneliness was a real problem, with other people trying to be kind, only making things worse."

A 45-year-old widow told us: "The most difficult problem was loneliness—living in the house alone without him. I was very upset, and although I was a very healthy woman, I lost weight and my blood count went way down for the first six months after his death. I was just numb. I didn't even realize I was sick."

A younger widow whose husband died when her child was a few months old explained that she was very bitter at first: "Why should one adult life be taken and a baby's given?" She felt this was hard on the child and was guilty for having such thoughts and yet she rather resented the child for living when her husband had died. She knew this was not "fair nor logical" and it took her a year to "figure things out" and accept the loss.

Several of the widowed mentioned financial difficulties, as well as problems around making decisions. Many had trouble sleeping at night and would put off going to bed as long as possible. A few widows mentioned losing interest in housework and cooking and more or less letting things "slip". A 27-year-old widow summed up her feelings as follows: "I feel that with the separated and divorced, however painful the breakup, you are at least prepared for it, but with the widowed you are totally unprepared for what happened. At least you don't want to be put in the state you are put into."

The effects of the loss of a parent on the children showed up to a certain extent in behaviour patterns. How the children accepted and reacted to the loss varied with their ages. Many of them were young and did not remember the deceased parent. One widow discussed the reactions of her small sons as follows: "The younger boy was just a baby . . . and didn't know what was going on. The older one was very upset . . . He would not make any reference to his father for four or five months. Now he comes in from play and clings to me for no obvious reason, but I know it is connected with his father."

Another widow told us about her own children's reactions to the sudden loss of their father: "I think they adjusted very well, perhaps because they were so young (three, six, and eight years at the time). I pointed out that they were not the only ones that this type of thing happened to. The eldest (a son) took it the hardest. He was very despondent and nervous for about a year. There was a loss of security. They wanted me around all the time for about a year. They were very solicitous where I was concerned. They wanted to be close to me and were always looking to see if I was there. My son was a bit frightened if I was not there or feeling well. He had frequent nightmares for about a couple of years."

One mother described her five-year-old daughter as being in a "fog" for two or three years after her father's death. Her teacher in grade 1 felt that she was lost in a private dream of her own, feeling different because she did not have a father.

A 15-year-old boy reacted as follows to the death of his father: "He cried only once, but he still does not talk about his father or do anything on the hobby he and his father had together. He has no other deep relationship with an adult male."

Nine children were reported to have had difficulties at school since the death of a parent, and six of these had failed a grade, which was felt to be related to the loss of the parent. Most children seemed to seek out another person of the absent parent's sex for substitute identification,

such as a grandparent, uncle or aunt, teacher, parent of a friend, or neighbour. One mother noticed her children's over-attention to any man who was around, and another mentioned her five-year-old daughter's hugging a complete stranger in the supermarket. Another mother summed up the situation as follows: "They feel the lack of a father very much, as he was very affectionate . . . They feel something is missing in the household. I think that they lack the male voice of authority in the house . . . My son missed the compatibility that there would be between father and son. They feel the absence of love between parents . . . They also miss the fun we used to have together, as we did things as a family. I have also noticed that the girls are particularly demonstrative with their uncles and seem to jump all over them."

Our study showed, too, that children's conception of death is often puzzling. It seemed that the younger children were concerned about practical matters. For example, a three-year-old boy wanted to know whether his father was warm and whom he was living with now. Four-year-old twin girls asked their mother a lot of questions about heaven, such as, "Do they have beds in heaven? Will Daddy get wet when it rains in heaven?" A five-year-old girl asked her mother, "Did he go back to God because he didn't love us? If God took him away, why can't He give him back?" Parents agreed that such questions are difficult to answer. Sisters, aged six and ten years, wanted to know, "What sickness did Daddy have? Will we get it?" Other sisters, aged four and six years, pray for their father every night and believe if they pray hard enough he will come back. One seven-year-old boy whose mother had died said one day that God wouldn't take his daddy because He would not be "that cruel".

Most parents attempted to tell their children the truth about their spouse's death. One widow told her children that their father was in heaven and could not come back but that they would meet him there someday. She ran into trouble when the children wanted to know why they could not go there and meet him now. Another widow had explained that her husband had gone to heaven, but children on the street told her daughter that he was buried in the ground. This mother was able to explain that the body was in the ground but the spirit in heaven. The majority of parents felt that they had been able or would be able to explain death to their children. A number felt their religion had helped them in this area.

We enquired about any particular areas of child rearing that had become more difficult since single parenthood. One widower mentioned sex education for his daughters as having created a problem, and two thought that shopping for clothing for the girls was difficult. Comments from the widows varied from one who replied, "Everything," to five who felt they had not found any areas any more difficult. Twelve widows mentioned problems with discipline. One felt that at times she was too lenient and at other times too hard, and that it was difficult to find the "proper level of strictness". One widow felt that the greatest difficulty was not having her husband there to plan with and to talk over activities, problems, and hopes for the children. Three widows considered sex education a problem. Two had explained this to their sons, but felt their husbands would have done a better job, and one widow was dreading having to tackle the subject.

CONCLUSION

Sociologists have long recognized that the disruption of marriage by death of one partner has profound repercussions for the widowed spouse, their family, and the community. Certainly a rapidly growing population of elderly women, an ever-mounting proportion of whom are widowed, would call for a systematic study of their lives, problems, and modes of adaptation. Knowledge of the variations in successful adaptations to widowhood status would have pragmatic consequences for educating and preparing individuals and families for dealing with this common experience with better understanding and insight.

READINGS

1. Beck, Frances, *Diary of a Widow*, Boston: Beacon Press, 1965.
2. Marris, Peter, *Widows and their Families*, London: Routledge and Kegan Paul, 1958.
3. Rich, Louise, *Only Parent*, Philadelphia: J. B. Lippincott, 1953.
4. Rogers, J., Vachon, M. L. S. and Lyall, W. A. L. *Community Contacts for the Widowed*, Toronto: Community Contacts for the Widowed, 1976.
5. Schlesinger, Benjamin, *The One-Parent Family: Perspectives and Annotated Bibliography*, Toronto: University of Toronto Press, 1978. Fourth edition.
6. Start, Clarissa, *On Becoming a Widow*, New York: Family Library 1973. A report on setting up a self-help group for widowed persons.

FILMS

Antonio, NFB, 28 minutes, black/white, 1966.
The Yellow Leaf, NFB, 29 minutes, black/white, 1956. The problem of an elderly widow.

QUESTIONS, PROJECTS AND ACTIVITIES

1. Consider the following statement: "The average North American woman can anticipate facing approximately 18 years as a widow." Divide into small research groups. Each group will research and plan a class presentation on possible preparations during marriage which might assist a woman in one of the following areas, should she be widowed:
   a) financial independence
   b) emotional security
   c) social acceptance
   d) raising small children
   e) guiding adolescent children

2. The adjustments which divorced and widowed families must make often lead to a high level of stress. Suggest ways adjustments might differ for family members in these two different situations. Consider such factors as emotional reactions and financial difficulties.

5A

RECONSTITUTED FAMILIES

Husband-Wife Relationships in Reconstituted Families*

INTRODUCTION

During the past few years, there has been a sudden interest on the part of family sociologists, marriage counsellors, and the public media in the area of remarriage. The terms "blended families", or "reconstituted families" have been invented to describe the growing phenomenon of second marriages in Canada and the United States. In Canada about 18% of the yearly marriage rates are second marriages (Wakil, 1976), in the United States this figure reached 30% in 1974 (Reingold, 1976).

We completed a study of 96 couples, of which one partner at least had been married previously, in Metropolitan Toronto, Canada in 1975 and 1976. Volunteers were obtained by advertising in the newspaper, and were predominantly white, Protestant, and middle-class in terms of income, education and housing. They were comparatively young in age, with high-school or higher education. Most women in the group were homemakers; 22% of the men were professional—the rest occupied white-collar positions. About 40% had earned income of $4 000 to $8 000; 50% had $10 000 to $20 000;

and the group showed a trend towards home ownership and home rental as opposed to apartment-dwelling.

PATTERNS OF REMARRIAGE, 1975

Who Married Whom in 2nd Marriages in 1975.

Bride	Bridegroom	Total No. of Unions
Widow	Single	1 795
Widow	Widowed	3 614
Widow	Divorced	2 047
Divorced	Single	9 942
Divorced	Widowed	1 595
Divorced	Divorced	9 775
Single	Widowed	1 406
Single	Divorced	12 126
		42 300

Four Largest Combinations of Second Unions in Rank Order—Canada 1975

Bride-groom	Bride	Percentage of 2nd Unions
1. Divorced	Single	28.6
2. Single	Divorced	23.5
3. Divorced	Divorced	23.1
4. Widowed	Widowed	8.5

Source: Calculated from data in Vital Statistics: Vol II—Marriages and Divorces, 1975.
Cat. #84-205—Annual—July 1977.

---

* I am indebted to Edythe Jacobson, M.S.W., for her help in formulating some of the content of this paper.

OPINIONS ABOUT THE MARITAL RELATIONSHIP

In responding to the questions whether the present relationship differed from the previous one, a widowed male replied:

I have never asked myself this question—I am not looking for comparisons—they are two different people, not to be compared—I have put the past in the past and now live a different life in the present.

The other responses all indicated that inevitably you make comparisons, it is only human, although you might try not to. You can try not to dwell in the past, and the best way to do so is to sort out the previous marriage, to do grief work, whether the loss was through divorce or death. Compare mentally if you must but be wary of comparing verbally, especially in areas which you know your spouse is sensitive.

Here are several comments of men and women on their new marriage and new mate:

—It's a full marriage—kids, debts, heartaches. There's more emotional togetherness in this marriage.

—He makes me feel adequate. We bring out the best in each other.

—I feel like somebody now. When I do something for my wife she appreciates its.

—My present husband is interested in me as a person. I am treated as a woman and a mother, not a useless vessel.

—I have more outlets for self-expression, both as an individual and as a couple.

—I am an adult now—I was a child then.

OPINIONS ABOUT SUCCESSFUL REMARRIAGE

In identifying what made up a successful remarriage, the respondents indicated that emotional compatibility, agreement on life style and goals and companionship were most important. Ultimately they spoke of maturity. Maturity was variously described as knowing what is important to oneself, what one wants, needs, and values; not expecting perfection; understanding; knowing the importance of compromise; the ability to trust each other; the ability to make use of the experience of the first marriage to grow as a person; and the ability to grow together in the relationship.

Our respondents indicated that a resolution of one's past was vital and led to an intimacy and openness in a relationship.

In remarriage you have a better chance of knowing why you're getting married than you did the first time. You can learn from the past and become more questioning. Especially be able to answer the question, "What makes me think this will be better than the last one?"

The experience of the first marriage is useful in many different ways:

—In a second marriage one may recognize danger points and talk them out before they become magnified.

—One can have some perspective on the relationship in terms of its workability and value in small things.

—In remarriage there is more of an appreciation of the benefits of marriage.

What does a remarriage require of persons? It requires self-knowledge, patience, acceptance and ability to enjoy. "My wife was previously single and I must accept and enjoy her enthusiasm and feelings—for example, she is very upset when a cake falls."

Previously divorced persons were asked to give their advice to a person who is divorced and planning to remarry. A majority of replies warned against not knowing your reasons, and moving on the basis of insecurity.

— Don't think anybody is better than nobody.
— Don't marry to prove you can get another husband.

Honesty and self-knowledge was ranked as a prerequisite. Many persons urged that you make sure you are not marrying the same person, that you are not being led by false feelings, that you are not expecting marriage to solve your individual problems. Finally, discuss the first marriage, find out why it was unsuccessful and analyze yourself as honestly as you can. To summarize, from a divorced male, "Don't try in a remarriage to prove the battles you lost in the first marriage."

THE MOST DIFFICULT FACTORS OF ADJUSTMENT IN REMARRIAGE

The respondents identified the most difficult factors of adjustment in a remarriage. While some of these are universal to any marriage, there is a complicating threat in remarriage. The most significant problem was that of working out a state of togetherness and partnership after having experienced (at least on the part of one person) a process of union, loss and separation. The couples spoke of learning to depend on one another, to trust and be responsible. They also mentioned combining two fairly set environments, and changing one's use of time. In short, the newly married must think as a couple, instead of as separate individuals. Compromise, giving without resentment and recognizing the other's personality are all necessary.

Many people mentioned the previous marriage as an important factor. Several responses showed residual pesonality damage carrying over from the first marriage. This was especially so for the divorced, but also true for the widowed. Re-

spondents reported a fear of failure and consequent sensitivity and insecurity around what was expected. These people talked about a need to overcome previous inconsistencies and rejections, both in themselves and in terms of having been subject to such from the previous spouse. This fear of failure leads to other fears: a fear of disagreements, a fear of making comparisons, a fear of falling unwittingly into previous patterns, a fear that the present spouse will show the same faults of the previous spouse and a tendency to look for these. Related to these fears and insecurities is what many respondents saw as a difficulty communicating directly and clearly. This process is hindered by operating at a defensive level and on the basis of assumptions, and a fear of opening up because of old barriers from previous marriages.

Finally, the "Invisible Third Party" emerged as an area of concern. The previous partner had meaning to the person who was married, to his current spouse and to their relationship. How this meaning is interpreted is vital. The fact that one's partner loved another before creates jealousy, resentment and worry. It does not necessarily cause insecurity, but especially in the initial stages of the relationship, it can draw out a person's insecurities. Moreover, often there is love (in case of widowed person) for the deceased mate. There can also be natural idealization, which creates jealousy and an impossible kind of competition. The majority found themselves comparing, either favourably or unfavourably, their former spouses and stressed how unwise this was. As in the case of any marriage there is the impulse to run when doubts emerged, and when the person was previously married, there is the impulse to run back to the previous spouse, or if he (she) is deceased, the wish that this could be possible.

ADVICE TO SINGLE PEOPLE ENTERING A REMARRIAGE

The previously unmarried were asked to advise those single persons planning to enter a remarriage. Many urged that the single person learn about the first marriage, "Find out, analyze, know, talk about reasons and feelings." Several personal qualities were noted as essential. These included sensitivity, tolerance and maturity.

—The remarried person has to learn to trust again. The previously unmarried has to be aware of the bruises that remain and try not to take things personally.

—You must have a greater ability to give because you are second and others reinforce this.

—Find out what you can about the married person. Have a trial marriage if possible. Don't live in the past.

One person advised to accept the first marriage as part of the spouse's life, and urged that you share, but share only as much as he/she wants to share. As well, it was pointed out that if you get the intimate details about the first marriage it might lead you into competition, which is a considered risk.

There are advantages and disadvantages in a remarriage where one partner is previously single. As one person put it: "There is only one set of memories to be laid aside." The previously single is not encumbered by a sense of loss and failure, and can therefore help the spouse, and can be more objective. On the other hand the previously married person has advantages in terms of concrete experience. The previously married can predict routine hazard areas, knows that fights are normal and everything is less of a crisis. He/she is more understanding, knows what to expect, is more sensitive and patient. "Once you've lived with a person you learn less inhibitions, more willingness to share and find real partnership." This can lead to conflict in that the previously married is free from illusions, while the previously single might have some remaining. It is not easy for anyone to give up illusions:

My husband came into this marriage prepared to work at it. I didn't know you had to.

Within this context, the majority of our people felt that it was more difficult to be the previously unmarried partner than the previously married.

Exposure to any experience, and particularly marriage, provides an understanding which can only be conceived by living the experience.

Those who felt it was more difficult to be the previously married person pointed to the lack of resolution of the previous marriage and the concomitant insecurities this brought. The previously married feels obligated to prove the marriage will work, regardless of who was responsible for the failure of the first. He may be more anxious, more skeptical; or he may overcompensate. He has to get deconditioned from the previous marriage.

There is always the feeling that if things don't work out the way your spouse expects, you wonder if he's thinking, "Here we go again."

In responding to the questions on involvement of friends and relations in planning remarriage, a good number of persons felt that it was necessary and helpful to discuss the decision with family and friends, if only to open up with these people.

Seek the advice of honest friends and take it seriously. You need support and friendships, but do not make your decision on the basis of what they say.

The respondents showed a tendency to strive for equality and independence within sharing when discussing financial matters.

I believe in complete honesty between partners about their financial positions and resources—I don't believe in having little secret hoards of money.

The women were especially strong in saying that they should have independence in terms of financial sources.

We should share the responsibility of running the home. Each partner should have personal money to spend without accounting for it.

CONCLUSION

Finally, what emerged forcefully when discussing all areas was the exhortation to know yourself, what you need, want, can change and what you're willing to work for. "A second marriage is more realistic, more thinking", said one man. One divorced woman significantly did not talk about "the right man," as a good many respondents did. She spoke of finding a man with whom she could live and build a life. The theme was not pessimism but a kind of mellowed determination.

READINGS

Bear, Jean. *The Second Wife.* New York: Doubleday, 1972.
An advice-giving book on how to live in a "second" family.

Duberman, Lucile. *The Reconstituted Family.* Chicago: Nelson-Hall, 1975.
A study of remarried couples and their children.

Maddox, Brenda. *The Half-Parent.* New York: M. Evans, 1975. (Toronto: McClelland and Stewart)
Living with other people's children in reconstituted families.

McCormick, Mona. *What the Literature Reveals About Stepfathers.* La Jolla, California: Western Behavioral Sciences Institute, 1974.

Reingold, Carmel Berman. *Remarriage.* New York: Harper and Row, 1976.
What it is like to live in a "second" family. Taken from interviews.

Rossevelt, Ruth, and Lofas, Jeanette. *Living in Step.* New York: Stein and Day, 1976.
The reality of remarriage is discussed, including children in a second union.

Schlesinger, Benjamin. *The One-Parent Family: Perspectives and Annotated Bibliography.* Toronto: University of Toronto Press, 1975.

———. "Women and Men in Second Marriages", in S. Parvez Wakil, ed., *Marriage, Family and Society: Canadian Perspectives.* Toronto: Butterworth and Co., 1975, pp. 317-334.

———. "Remarriage as Family Reorganization for Divorced Persons," in L. Ishwaran, ed., *The Canadian Family.* Toronto: Holt, Rinehart and Winston, 1976, pp. 460-478.

———. *Remarriage in Canada.* Toronto: Faculty of Education Guidance Centre, 1978.
A booklet describing remarriage in Canada. Has a good bibliography.

Step Family Foundation Newsletter. *Step Family Foundation.* 11th Floor, 333 West End Avenue, New York, N.Y. 10023.

Stepparent's Forum. Westmount, P.O. Box 4002, Montreal, Quebec, Canada H3Z 2Z3.

Wakil, S. Parvez. *Marriage and Family in Canada.* Calgary: Journal of Comparative Family Studies, 1976. (Monograph).

Westoff, Leslie Aldridge. *The Second Time Around.* New York: Viking Press, 1977.
Interviews with various people in second marriages.

QUESTIONS, ACTIVITIES AND PROJECTS

1. *Prepare a chart like the one below to indicate the ways a marital relationship can improve "the second time around."*

Areas	First, troubled marriage	Second, successful marriage
a) Expectations of marriage b) Communication skills c) Problem-solving skills d) Maturity e) Job security		

2. *Using the chart in the Introduction to the Variety of Family Forms (page 8), discuss the adjustments that the various kinds of reconstituted families might have to make.*

5B

RECONSTITUTED FAMILIES

Children in Reconstituted Families

In Canada, in 1975, the percentage of second marriages was 15% of all married persons during that year, or 59 028 people. The average ages of Canadians at the time of the second marriage was 34.9 years for divorced women, 38.3 years for divorced men. We do not have, at this time, any accurate figures relating to how many children were brought into these reconstituted families.

A few years ago, with a group of students from the University of Toronto, Faculty of Social Work, we interviewed 96 couples in marriages where at least one partner had been married previously. These remarriages involved 198 children.

From these interviews, we have selected responses which most typically reflect what happens in various forms of reconstituted families.

WHAT HAPPENS IN RECONSTITUTED FAMILIES

A previously single woman married to a widower with children, who had a baby girl of her own from the new marriage stated, "The girl who had previously been the youngest was no longer so, and she felt a degree of rivalry. She, however, was given more responsibility and had to learn to do a few things for herself."

A divorced man married to a widow with children, and who now has one child of the new union, said, "The children had their set ways and I had to observe how they treated their mother and learn how to approach them without hurting their feelings."

A widower married to a widow where both brought in a total of six children claimed there was no problem in the children's adjustment because, "We prepared them. We went on dates with the children and without them. I talked to the children about the problems in life without a mother. The children knew I wasn't marrying just for them, but wanted a wife. They adjusted quite well and quickly."

A divorcée married to a single man felt that her 14-year-old son had adjusted easily because "My husband treated my son as an uncle would, because the boy already had a father."

A single man married to a widow with one daughter felt that, "Security for a child in remarriage is a problem. It takes a long time for a child to trust and accept the new parent as part of the family."

Many parents recognized that there were difficulties in adjustment that children had to make in areas of sharing a natural parent, trusting and accepting the new parent's personality and ways and fitting into the new family system with siblings. However, a gradual adjustment period was indicated as being the usual pattern, with this period of "getting to know one another" starting very often during the courtship. Frankness and honesty when discussing areas of concern with the children was given a high value. Many respondents realized there were differences between the biological parent and new parent that took time to adjust to, so that competition of the stepparent with this other parent was not deemed wise.

According to respondents in the interviews, many children do not compare the natural parent and corresponding stepparent. However, adults were answering on behalf of the children, so this is not a certainty. Approximately 70% of natural and new parents said there was no comparison made, whereas by contrast, divorced mothers more often thought that children commonly made these comparisons.

A widow married to a single man reported that her children compared their biological father and their stepfather at first. "My daughter would say, 'My Dad would let me do that', but this didn't last long, as my husband discussed it with her."

A divorced man married to a divorced woman where both brought in children, said, "I suppose they do compare at times, but I know they care for me and are happy. This is all that matters."

A divorced woman married to a divorced man who did not bring in his own children said, "There is a marked difference in personalities between the former and present father. They cannot fail to notice the difference and are confused at times when they want to remain loyal to their own father, but they appreciate what their new father is trying to do for them. The boy especially has trouble as the divorce was a traumatic experience for him when he was nine years old."

A single man married to a widow commented, "On trips to the park or at Christmas time, they would talk of their dad. At first this bothered me, but I don't mind it now."

A widower who married a single female made the point that "The age of the children is a significant factor, but love is the ultimate solution. As soon as the children discover that the way to be loved is to love, there is little reason or opportunity to compare."

A divorced woman with one son, married to a divorced man with no children, stated, "My son sees his own father two weeks each summer when he is wined and dined. The real father is younger and bends over backwards to impress his son. My present husband doesn't buy my son's affection as his own father does."

PROBLEM AREAS IN STEPFAMILY RELATIONSHIPS

We will examine specific problems expressed by the adults in view of their particular role and status.

Widowed fathers had to help their children accept their mother's death. They found it difficult to make the children feel loved and wanted while dividing their time between them and their new wife. The children had to adjust to the stepmother's habits and ways of housekeeping and the fathers had difficulty promoting cooperation within the household. Sometimes children would pit the father against the new parent. Helping children accept and respect the stepmother and maintaining fair discipline were not easy tasks.

Widows reported difficulty dividing their time between the children and their new husband. The children sometimes resented the stepfather because they felt disloyal to their deceased father. The change of name, discipline from two parents and adjustment to new surroundings were other areas of contention.

Divorced stepfathers cited the problem

of adjusting to increased activity in the home, especially with teenagers and could not readily accept their habits. They were concerned about the amount of involvement with the children, excercising discipline and showing affection. Some found it difficult to accept the children emotionally, and they had to cope with their own jealousy and occasionally with manipulation by female children. Winning their status was a gradual process. On a practical level, they were worried about increased costs.

Among divorcées, negative community attitudes and interference from relatives (especially grandmothers) posed a problem. Mothers were concerned about privacy; they were afraid the children would get on their husband's nerves and wanted them to be more independent. Some expressed difficulty with discipline and maintaining neutrality and wanted to open communication channels between children (especially teenagers) and spouse. There was a need to assuage the children's fear of a break-up, and to cope with their upset after visiting their natural father. Cooperation with housework and financial considerations, including the children's disregard for the value of money, were further areas of conflict.

Single men expressed fear of stepping into a ready-made family, citing acceptance by children, coping with the first husband's resentment and the children's visits with him as problematical. They were uncertain about exercising discipline, giving affection and gaining the children's trust. Sibling rivalry, adjustment to children's eccentricities, competition between stepdaughters and their mother for attention and trying to offer equal time to stepchildren and their own children were added strains. Their own identity (whether the children called them Dad, Mr. or used first name) and giving up luxuries like travel were other "instant family" adjustments.

Single women joining an existing family faced the problem of discipline (especially of older boys), establishing new house rules and promoting cooperation within the household. They had to accept that the children's habits and behaviour would not meet their expectations, and face their own feelings about wanting their husbands to themselves. Sometimes men and their children formed alliances against the new wife. Their own role was ill-defined, with comparisons made to the natural mother and grandmother, and feelings of resentment from the children. Additionally, they worried about the stepchildren's feelings toward new children.

These problems are most common in the early stages of adjustment. In time, trust and understanding generally develop. As one mother said, "They now consider him more of a father to them than their own father." Said another, "It took about six months for the child to accept sharing the new father with men."

Sometimes the new unit is seen in a favourable light compared with the former one. One father noted, "My first wife played favourites, but now the children are loved fairly and kindly." Of course age is an important factor and remarriage can fill an immediate need, as one father explained. "It didn't take my son long as he was only four years old at the time of remarriage, and he was starved for maternal attention."

We have presented some findings about the feelings of parents and stepparents in blended families. A further step would be to interview the children, to find out their feelings about living in a second family.

READINGS

See list of readings at the end of chapter 5A (page 66).

QUESTIONS, ACTIVITIES AND PROJECTS

1. *Plan a series of questions for an interview with a child in a reconstituted family. Use the questions in an interview, taping or recording the answers. Indicate the sex and age of the child, and describe the reconstituted family that he or she now belongs to.*

   a) *Summarize the particular needs and adjustments of the children in this reconstituted family.*

   b) *What help was offered to these children? What additional resources could have been used to counsel or assist the child during the period of transition?*

2. *If you are personally familiar with a remarriage situation, comment on the adjustments that you have experienced or observed with regard to*

   a) *sharing living space*

   b) *relationship with stepparent*

   c) *relationship with non-custodial parent (birth father or mother not living in the remarriage)*

   d) *relationship with the original and with the new extended family—grandparents, cousins, aunts and uncles*

   e) *parental financial concerns*

   If you are not personally familiar with such a situation, discuss your own ideas about these kinds of adjustments.

6
Satisfactions in Family Life: Some Comments

INTRODUCTION

It is quite common today to have almost daily headlines dealing with the breakdown of North American family life. We are bombarded with statistics which indicate that more families are dissolving than are forming. We are told that family life is boring, unattractive, a prison and stifling. We are urged to pay homemakers for their work, and to point out to our children the pitfalls of marriage.

"Committment," "permanence," "working things out" in family life is left to history we are told, not to the 1970s. When I approached a local T.V. station to put on a few shows dealing with "healthy" and "satisfied" families, I was told that this is not "dramatic." It is of interest that a large number of programs on television today feature a single parent and the children as models of modern family life rather than intact families. Is it possible that the media writers and decision makers are projecting their own sometimes disorganized lives onto the screen and magazines assuming that this is the norm today?

THE SETTING

During the summer of 1977 I was teaching in family life institutes in Newfoundland and Nova Scotia. My students were all teachers, primarily in separate school settings (Roman Catholic).

As part of my seminars I asked the 180 teachers to indicate their satisfactions and dissatisfactions in family life, and, in Nova Scotia, my class of 30 teachers interviewed 150 families in Cape Breton, Nova Scotia to find out about their satisfactions and dissatisfactions. Both settings are primarily rural.

DISSATISFACTION IN FAMILY LIFE

The teachers in Newfoundland found some of the following dissatisfactions in family life in their communities: there was drinking in families, high unemployment and no privacy in small communities. Parental neglect, not enough social agencies to help families and isolation from the extended family were other problems. There was lack of communication between parents and children, husbands who have had to leave home to find employment and no family life education.

The teachers in Nova Scotia, replying to the same question, reported the following: arguments among family members, individuals being taken for granted by other family members, seeing children leave home, mothers receiving no appreciation from other family members for doing ironing, mending, cleaning and the monotony of keeping house.

SATISFACTION IN FAMILY LIFE

Some of the following statements illustrate the satisfactions which families have.

"From the beginning of our marriage it has seemed like a miracle that anyone as wonderful as my husband could think I was worth sharing a lifetime with. He comforted me when I lost my parents, and encouraged me to fight my battles for myself."

"We were a poor but happy family of 15 children. Every one can remember days of eating only oatmeal porridge, bread and molasses. On the other hand, we can also remember when Dad would save those last few pennies to buy our treat for the week, or sitting around a wood fire as Mom sang to us."

"My husband's attitudes towards my working have undergone a complete change as he has come to realize that I am a more interesting, happier, self-satisfied person because of my job. It also relieves him of the responsibility of sole provider, especially in case of business failure or his sickness."

"Each weekend is usually the scene of a large family gathering, with children, and sons and daughters-in-law and my own brothers and sisters. Our parents still hold a vital part in all our lives and their grandchildren's lives. They are usually included in the making of decisions by my brothers and sisters (8 children)."

"My mother is proud of her family and we are proud of each other. But most of all we are proud of her for she gave up much in order to keep us together as a family and to help us become the self-sufficient happy adults we are."

"Yes, happiness means different things to different people. To some it may mean contentment, peace of mind, concern, loving, caring, etc. To me, happiness means anything one has, does or experiences which makes the heart feel good."

In Newfoundland the teachers listed some of the following attributes as part of a satisfying family life.

- Extended family ties, close permanent neighbours, roots and peaceful surroundings in a small community.
- Close friends, pride in being a mother, companionship, going to church and outings together.
- Love and interest of family members and caring people in community.
- People helping each other, church activity, a feeling of belonging.
- Fulfillment, security, love, acceptance, people who care, joy and being good models for children.

Our Nova Scotia group added other qualities of satisfied family life, which included:

- The relationship I have with my husband and children, and my father-in-law.
- Sharing with my husband the joys and sorrows of raising children.
- The security of knowing that you've got people that love you and care for you.
- Love, peace and happiness, friendship.
- Sharing experiences with my husband, the close associations with my family, a visit from my son and daughter-in-law.
- The personal growth that has been possible through marriage.
- Experiencing success and failure together, raising my children and watching them grow up, living together in harmony.
- Being fortunate in having a healthy family.
- Rejoicing when a family member is successful and when family members work together.
- Being accepted as an equal in spite of my shortcomings.
- Having a husband who loves me and needs me and makes no secret of it.
- The love we have for each other and planning for the future.

I was deeply moved by two unsolicited statements among the many which I received during the summer. The first, from a wife: "I really enjoy the very close relationship my husband and I have built up over the years. I like the fact that we have worked as a team to support ourselves and our two children. I get satisfaction from being able to function as an individual apart from my family through my teaching job.

"I enjoy the feeling of belonging to an extended family unit and the fact that our children will know their grandparents. I am satisfied knowing that I can love and trust my husband without fears of having these used as weapons against me. I also like the fact that unreal expectations are not placed upon me. I do not have to be Mrs. Efficient, I can let things slide when I am tired and whenever it is needed my husband pitches in. I am satisfied because we have fun together and we can communicate our feelings to one another. I am committed to our relationship and will continue to try to build upon and improve it."

The second, from a husband: "I feel that my family gives one another the companionship we need. My wife gives me the mental and physical stimulation needed. She also fulfils my emotional needs. We are a very nuclear family and enjoy working this way. Even if we are a nuclear family we have time to extend to grandparents and adopted relatives that I feel are impor-

tant. I feel that our family is growing as a family. I take pride in our material accomplishments. My wife has helped as a working mother. I don't mind helping her. I also realize that she works damn hard, possibly harder than I do."

CONCLUSION

It was gratifying to me to find among this group of teachers a positive outlook on family life. It was also refreshing to find that they found satisfaction in their families and in the family life of their communities. We should not underestimate the tremendous amount of health and sanity in families today. It is time that we publicize this fact and support these families in their day by day existence. It is also time that family sociologists, social workers, and other professionals in the helping professions focus some of their time and talents on examining the phenomena of satisfied families. I am sure that we can learn a lot from them.

READINGS

Bane, Mary Jo. *Here to Stay: American Families in the Twentieth Century.* New York: 1976 Basic Books, Inc.

FILMS

Coming Home, NFB, 84 min, colour, 1973.
A full length film of looking at a home visit on the part of an older son.

QUESTIONS, ACTIVITIES AND PROJECTS

1. *Identify what you have personally experienced as being the most rewarding elements of living with your family. How can these experiences be offered by groups other than the traditional nuclear family?*

2. *Brainstorm in small groups to compile a list of the responsibilities that members of a family have within the family unit.*

    (a) *In chart form, compare how family members can maintain their individuality and still contribute to the family unit.*

    (b) *What changes might occur in a family member's status and role(s) when new members are added to the family unit? Consider the addition of babies, grandparents and other relatives.*

3. *Erik Erikson, a well known psychologist, has defined one of the tasks of the adolescent as that of establishing a unique identity apart from the family unit. Comment, in your notebook, on your own "identity conflict" at this time.*

II
MARRIAGE

Introduction

According to the 1976 Census of Canada, 10 593 155 Canadians were married.* Thus 46% of our total population was married. If we take only the population over the age of 15, about 60% of Canadians are married.

MARRIAGE DEFINED**

Marriage is a socially legitimate sexual union, begun with a public announcement and undertaken with some idea of permanence; it is assumed with a more or less explicit marriage contract, which spells out reciprocal rights and obligations between spouses, and between the spouses and their future children.

This definition rests on four subsidiary terms which, in turn, require definitions on their own. They are "socially legitimate sexual union," "begun with a public announcement," "with some idea of permanence," and "marriage contract."

SOCIALLY LEGITIMATE SEXUAL UNION. This is a sexual union which is not "against the law." The married couple will not come in conflict with social norm, or be punished, for having sexual intercourse.

Since marriage, by definition, involves a socially legitimate sexual union, a married couple does not have to be discreet about the fact that they are having sexual intercourse. Perhaps they do not announce to the world "We are having sexual intercourse," but they say "We are married," "I'd like you to meet my wife," "This is my husband," and so forth. And the terms "married," "wife" and "husband" imply—to all except little children who have not yet learned the facts of life—that they are having sexual intercourse, or that they may if they want to.

BEGUN WITH A PUBLIC ANNOUNCEMENT. Nearly always, marriage begins with an elaborate ceremonial, which may include feasting, fancy dress, processionals, perhaps religious observances of some kind, and large-scale financial outlay by either the groom, the groom's parents or the bride's parents. At the very least, bride and groom announce their marriage to "society"—to kinfolk and neighbours, perhaps to the state and law court, or to God (as in the Christian church wedding).

WITH SOME IDEA OF PERMANENCE. Marriage, as opposed to other possible kinds of sexual unions, is not supposed to be a temporary arrangement. It is not a one-night affair, or a short-term contract (of six months, or two years or five). It is supposed to last "til death do us part," or at least " 'til death or divorce do us part."

ASSUMED WITH A MARRIAGE CONTRACT. Getting married means taking on obligations. Some of these obligations may be very specific and formalized; others are not. In some societies the marriage contract is highly legalized. If writing

*Statistics on marriage in Canada can be found in Tables 1 and 2 in the Appendix.

** I am indebted to William H. Stephens for ideas related to the definition of marriage, as presented in his book *The Family in Cross-Cultural Perspective*, New York: Holt, Rinehart and Winston, 1963.

is known, the marriage contract may be drawn up like any other legal document. In such highly legal marriage contracts, there are usually lists of specific offenses against each spouse; any major offense is punishable by divorce or by fine, or by some other sort of penalty. The marriage contract may state who gets what in case of divorce: who gets the children, how the property will be divided. The marriage contract often contains financial agreement; a certain amount may have to be paid to the wife's father before the marriage is fully "legal." Recently many couples are describing the features of equal partnerships in their marriage contracts.

Aside from the specific terms of the marriage agreement, there are other implicit obligations a person assumes when he contracts for marriage. He/she agrees—however implicitly—to play the spouse role that society deems appropriate. Depending on what society it is and what the particular cultural requirements are, the groom may implicitly agree to give economic support to his wife, to help his father-in-law, to teach and discipline his children and not to philander. The bride may agree (implicitly) to cook, clean house, carry wood and water, mend and do other various personal services for her husband, to be an acquiescent sex partner, to care for the children, to help with the farm work and so forth. These implicit, informal, extralegal parts of the marriage contract may also have "teeth" in them; breaches of the implicit marriage contract may also bring punishment in terms of community disapproval or, at the very least, family quarreling and dissension.

Marriage, as a socially legitimate sexual union, differs from extramarital sexual unions in that it imposes obligations in return for sexual gratifications—the obligations of the marriage contract. In an adulterous sex encounter, or during ceremonial sexual license, or in a permissive sex relationship people do, at times, get their sex "free." But in marriage, sexual gratification is not free—even though it may seem to be. Marriage, to which sex satisfaction may be a major inducement, is fraught with obligations—to the spouse, to children, perhaps to the spouse's relatives and, at times, even obligations to the state or the church.

Of course, there is the reverse side of the coin. When you get married, other people become obligated to you too—your spouse, perhaps your spouse's relatives, your future children. Perhaps the essence of social living is obligations: obligations you owe to others and obligations other people owe to you. When you get married your obligations are widened and enhanced—you become "more social", in a sense. You assume more social ties. There are now more people with whom you are interdependent.

Also, marriage often means a shift in social obligations. It adds new obligations, but it may weaken previous reciprocal obligations between the newly married person and parents and other blood relatives. This is usually the case in our own society, but we seem to be a bit extreme in this regard. We look at mate selection and marriage from the perspective of teenage girls.

With a life expectancy in Canada of 74 years for women and 69 years for men, it is still surprising that one quarter of the brides and 7% of the grooms marry under the age of 20 years. It is estimated that the chances for a break-up of a teenage marriage in Canada are twice as high as those marrying between 20-24 years, and three times as often as those marrying between 25-29 years of age.

We examine mate selection and teenage marriages in Canada in this section.

7
Mate Selection and Marriage: A Female Perspective

INTRODUCTION

In Canada, in 1976, there were 193 343 marriages. In these unions, 25.5% of the brides were under the age of 20, while 7.2% of the grooms fell into this age group. Although the average age for first marriages is 22.5 for women and 24.9 for men, many, as we can see, plan and get married during their late teens.

In our society, part of the function of dating is that we begin to select our future mates. As the 17-year-old girl or boy moves from group-dating to individual dating, to "going steady," to engagement and marriage, she or he is constantly building up an image of the "ideal" mate. Many may not be so conscious of this type of "selection procedure," but with each date one asks, "What good and not so good qualities does this person have?" Thus, a "catalogue" is established, and we begin to sort out from our many boy-girl relationships the characteristics we like and dislike in a future mate.

I was able to learn much more about this topic when I gave a series of lectures on dating, courtship and marriage to a group of 120 eighteen-year-old girls. I asked my students to write a one-page reply to the questions "What Do I Want in a Mate?" and "What Do I Want out of Marriage?"

WHAT I WANT IN A MATE

As we begin to think about the potential future man or woman we want to marry,

we frequently build up an "ideal" picture. This "ideal" is usually never reached in actual life, but let's look at what one girl feels.

Following is a description of my ideal man. The ideal man should be a person with respect, intelligence, faith and love.

He should have respect for himself as well as others, including his wife. He should treat her as an equal in all respects—in intellect, as a female, as a close friend and as a lover. As far as intellect goes it would be more ideal to have a person of a slightly higher intellect so as to have someone to look up to and ask advice of. As to respect for wife as a female, he should understand her role as a woman—a wife, mother and lover. As a friend he should be someone who is always there when he is needed and should be willing to understand, advise, praise and criticize you. He should be willing to listen to and share one's joys and problems.

His intelligence should be adequate to suit his wife. As well as intelligence he should have social poise and manners in order to be able to conduct himself desirably at the right times. A generally jovial disposition would also be desirable.

The man must have faith in himself. To be secure in one's convictions and goals in life is to me the greatest mark of any human being.

The ultimate quality I desire in a man is love—love for the individual, for himself, for others and for life. To live is to love and to love is happiness. Happiness given and received is my ultimate goal in life.

Can a man combine all these qualities and can we expect this ideal combination in a marriage? There were many girls who listed the desirable traits they would like to find in their future husbands. I have gathered them under headings. The girls would like:

1. A man several years older than themselves.
2. One with a certain degree of maturity.
3. One with a sense of responsibility who will accept the institution of marriage, be able to support a wife, family and a home and to keep a stable and well-paying job.
4. A man with intelligence. Not merely someone with a university education, but a worldly man, who is well-read, and knows what's going on and can intelligently converse with almost everyone.
5. One who possesses social graces and a certain amount of sophistication.
6. Someone attractive, with certain strong facial features, and soft, dark, straight and fairly long hair, of slightly thin physique without bulging muscles. He should dress in conservative tweeds, brogues, dark socks, striped ties with an occasional touch of silk and carry a thin black umbrella on cloudy days.
7. A basically clean and tidy person.
8. A man with an appreciation of culture—art, music, literature, etc.
9. A man deserving of one's love.
10. One who is perfectly compatible in bed.

Some other qualities looked for by many of the eighteen-year-old female students were:

1. Honesty. A man who makes a woman feel secure. A woman should not have to wonder about what he is doing, where he is, etc. Truthful and straightforward communication makes the close relationship of marriage workable.
2. Tenderness. The ability to say "I love you" once in a while, and to express his love in different ways.
3. Courtesy. A man should show consideration for his wife as he does for complete strangers. He should have good manners which are not forgotten when alone.
4. Understanding. A man should know the times when something is really important to his wife and the other times when it is not. He should understand her moods and temperament and know how to cope with them.
5. Loyalty. A husband should not criticize his wife in public. If he must do so, do it when the two are alone.
6. Fairness. A husband should be just, and not make his wife feel inferior.
7. Good father. A husband should like children. He should enjoy playing with them and teaching them. He wouldn't mind getting up at two o'clock in the morning with a sick child.
8. Masculinity. A masculine man has faith in himself and his competence. He doesn't mind helping his wife with the housework every so often. He should be able to pick up after himself.
9. Potential. A man doesn't have to be wealthy. He should be able to support his wife without her working. A man should be greatly interested in his work.

What seems to emerge from these

thoughts is that a girl would like a man who loves her, cares for her and respects her; a man with whom she can carry on an intelligent conversation; one who is masculine and who at the same time can show tender and warm feelings. The question we would ask is are these hopes and expectations fulfilled in later marriages?

WHAT I WANT OUT OF MARRIAGE

Security is one requirement:

I want the kind of security that comes from being loved and from loving someone. If we have children, I want security in the form of a nice home and a steady income—but for the sake of the children more than for myself. I do hope to have children, and someday to feel pride in my husband and in myself for having raised them to be fine people. I want to know the kind of joy and happiness that come only from being part of a closely knit family group, a family that is happy to do things together, where each member is independent enough to do things and have interests of his own.

The roles in marriage are also discussed:

I want a happy marriage. To me this means that not only is my mate a lover but also a companion. I want to be treated as an equal partner in the marriage and know about the household finances, etc., but I would also like my husband to be like a "master." That is he would take care of major things. I would also like to feel secure, both financially and emotionally.

As far as the husband in marriage is concerned:

Marriage to me symbolizes compatibility with my husband, enjoyment of sexual relations, love and concern for each other, social acceptance for both of us, and a moderate income to cover the rising cost of living. Through him

I would know and experience happiness, a desire to live and love, and above all a sense of security and belonging.

Some of the girls listed some of the things they wanted out of marriage:

1. A kind, gentle considerate husband.
2. A family in which communication among its members comes naturally.
3. A home that is situated in an open area, as opposed to city life.
4. A family that thinks of itself as a family, not just relatives living under the same roof.
5. A marriage that will last "until death do us part."
6. Watching children grow up and helping establish them in their chosen professions.
7. An opportunity to travel, i.e., vacations.
8. Children who develop a strong character and a high moral code of conduct.

I think one has to be careful not to brush away these wishes as just expressions of "square" girls and as starry-eyed, idealistic, security-seeking, middle-class pronouncements of life today. The qualities which our students listed are in my opinion very important ingredients in a marriage, and are the basic important bonds which hold marriages together and through which a marriage grows and is cemented over the years of family life. There is nothing wrong in wanting a happy, warm, compatible, loving and considerate marriage.

By the way, studies of marriage indicate that, in most cases, "like marries like;" thus we find that similar backgrounds in education, race, religion and economic status still play a most important part in whom one marries.

A MARRIAGE CHECK-UP

It helps in many marriages to have a marriage check-up once in a while, and Dr. Clinton E. Phillips and Mrs. Erma Pixley of the American Institute of Family Relations suggest the following questions which husband and wife might beneficially discuss together.

A. Communication

1. Do we have enough time and quietness for talk together? If not, how can we remedy the situation?
2. How much are we listening to each other, even though our interests and opinions may vary?
3. How often are we talking over our problems without dealing in personalities?
4. In what ways are we attempting to establish interesting, objective conversation with our spouses?

B. Love

Married love is a growing experience in which all the factors in marriage play a part.
1. In what ways do we honestly try to please each other?
2. Are we comfortable with each other, even when there are problems or when we don't agree?
3. In what ways do we show that we are as truly concerned for the well-being of our mate as we are for our own?
4. How much and what kind of companionship do we enjoy together?
5. How do we express feelings of warmth and tenderness and appreciation toward each other?

C. Finances

1. Do we need to look for a better way to handle our finances?
2. Are we living within a flexible budget?
3. If not, how can we modify our budget?
4. What compromise has each of us made on ways of spending money?
5. If there is still disagreement, in what areas? Can we adjust our differences or "agree to disagree"?

D. Sexual Adjustment

1. Does sexual intercourse bring us pleasure and a feeling of unity and fulfilment?
2. If not, should we plan to see a counsellor or get other help?
3. Are we both comfortable in the fun and play part of our sexual association?
4. To what extent are we aware of individual variations and differences in each other's sexual needs and responses?
5. How do we make adjustments to and allowances for male-female differences in sexual needs and responses?

E. Temperament

1. Is either of us struggling for power, trying to "manage" the marriage? If so, it's hard on love. Are we "misers with criticism and spendthrifts with praise"?
2. Is either of us frequently depressed?
3. If so, can we trace the cause and do something about it?
4. Is each of us growing in maturity sufficiently not to expect his mate to meet all his emotional needs?

F. In-Laws

1. How can we make more creative use of our in-laws?
2. Do we keep pleasantly in touch with them?
3. Can we listen openmindedly to their advice and then act as we think best?
4. How has each interpreted his spouse to his family and vice versa in a positive manner?

G. Recreation and Social Activities

1. Are we enjoying optimum recreation with each other and with friends? (Some couples have too much recreation and some not enough.) If not, talk over together what you can do.
2. Are we interested in some community activity? If not, what could we try?

3. What things do we do separately so that we can come back to each other with new things to talk about?

H. Our Emerging Family Pattern

1. In what ways have we created a new family pattern, not bound by the patterns of former homes?
2. How have we clarified and accepted our respective roles as husband and wife?
3. What more could each of us contribute to the life of his mate?
4. Toward what definite family goals are we both working?
5. Do we remember birthdays and special occasions?

It can even be helpful prior to marriage to go over this inventory to examine one's own values related to a future marriage.

READINGS

Back, George R. and Wyden, Peter. *The Intimate Enemy.* New York: Avon, 1970.
How to fight fair in love and marriage.

Blood, Bob and Blood, Margaret. *Marriage.* New York: Free Press, 1978, 3rd edition.
An excellent textbook on marriage.

Clarkson, Adrienne. *True to You in My Fashion.* Toronto: New Press, 1972.
Interviews of 13 men about their marriages.

Kieran, Dianne, Henton, June and Marotz, Ramona. *Hers and His: A Problem Solving Approach to Marriage.* Hindsale, Illinois: Bryden Press, 1975.
An examination of courtship and marital relationships in Canada and the U.S.A.

Mace, David and Mace, Vera. *We can Have Better Marriages if We Really Want Them.* New York: Abingdon Press, 1974.
A hopeful, positive view of marriage today.

Mair, Lucy. *Marriage.* London: Penguin Books, 1972.
An anthropologist in Britain examines marriage.

Stephens, William N. *Reflections on Marriage.* New York: Thomas Y. Crowell, 1968.
Sixteen selections on marriage.

QUESTIONS, ACTIVITIES AND PROJECTS

1. (a) *List the qualities of your "ideal mate."*
   (b) *Write a self-analysis giving reasons why you have chosen certain qualities as being of primary importance.*
2. *Make a collection of audio-visual materials such as cartoons, popular songs, and/or pictures, to illustrate that people today marry because of:*
   (a) *society's expectations*
   (b) *loneliness*
   (c) *desire to improve one's status*
   (d) *the wish to legitimatize sexual relations.*
3. *Work in groups of 4 or 5. Write a one-page description of your ideal mate. Do not indicate your own gender or the gender of your mate. Do not sign your description. Exchange your description with another group member. Through discussion determine which qualities appear to be generally desired. Are the descriptions easily identified as being written by a male or female? If so, what are the clues? Do males and females seem to want different qualities in a mate? If so, try to determine why the differences exist.*
4. *Plan a series of questions to help you discover what makes a couple's marriage a successful one. Include questions about their expectations of a mate and of*

marriage and how these expectations were realized, as well as questions prob-
ing the reasons for their successful marriage.

(a) Use your questionnaire to interview a couple (or person) you feel has a
happy marriage.

(b) Share your findings with the class.

(c) Compare the characteristics the couples identified as being necessary in a
mate with those you identified in your own list in question 1.

(d) Write a short report summarizing the findings of the class.

8
Teen-age Marriages

INTRODUCTION

Recently, a teen-age wife was sitting in my office. Beverly wanted help in sorting the difficulties of her year-old marriage to Jim, age 19.

> We've had a lot of trouble. We weren't ready for responsibility. We shouldn't have married so young. We should have waited until after high school, at least. We thought we were in love, and we would get married and have a good time. We had a very poor idea of what marriage was. We thought we could come and go, do as we pleased, do or not do the dishes, but it isn't that way.

In the early years of Canada's history, marriage at a young age was the common pattern. Early childbearing was a practical necessity then, when one's life expectancy at birth was only about 50 years. With today's life expectancy at 74 years for a woman, the desirability of having children early is less apparent.

A hundred years ago, a girl was likely to marry a man whose family had always lived in her community and with whom she had been somewhat acquainted, even from girlhood. The families of the two might easily have been friendly for years. Today, many teen-agers are rushing blindly into early marriage with little or no acquaintance with each other, their families or their backgrounds. In many cases, the girl is expecting a baby prior to the marriage.

The survival rate of many of these young marriages is very low. The divorce rate among couples who married before the age of 19 is about three times as high as among couples who married after the age of 20.

Our confusing Canadian marriage laws may have partly influenced this trend. In New Brunswick, a girl can marry at age 14 and a boy at 16 but parental consent is required for anyone under 18. In Quebec the minimum age for marriage is 14 for a boy and 12 for a girl, but anyone under 18 requires parental consent. Ontario allows marriage below 16 with parental consent, plus a medical certificate stating that the union is necessary to prevent illegitimacy of the expected baby. Saskatchewan has an age limit of 18 and Alberta and Prince Edward Island of 16 for marriage with parental consent. A medical certificate of pregnancy as well as parental consent is required for girls below 16 to be married in Alberta and Prince Edward Island. While in Saskatchewan a court order is required along with parental consent for individuals below 16. In British Columbia, girls from 16 to 19 need parental consent, and under this age need court approval.

The United Church of Canada in its deliberations recommended that in view of the high divorce rate in teen-age marriages, a minimum legal age for marriage without the consent of parents should be 21 years for both bride and groom. With consent, the minimum age should be 17 years for girls and 18 years for boys.

Another 17-year-old, Susan, who is sorry now that she rushed into marriage, told me:

I would have waited to finish high school first. It has tied me down so. I've had no fun since I was married. I can't go to dances. I don't feel right there. The same is true about other school activities. I guess I thought he was the only one in the world. I was badly mixed up. I thought marriage was like the movies, a bed of roses.

SOME REASONS FOR EARLY MARRIAGES

What are some of the reasons for this rush into early marriage? From my experience and work with teen-agers I have come to the following conclusions.

One reason behind early marriages is the idea of "romantic love." This idealization of the relationship between the sexes may blind young people to the demanding realities of family life. According to the picture created by many movies, books, popular music and many TV and radio programs, life begins and ends when boy meets girl. They fall in love and live happily ever after with a "love mate." When young people are caught up in fiction, negative aspects of the boy-girl relationship are ignored. The realities of marriage are not considered.

Sex experimentation and illegitimate pregnancy lead some young couples to marry. Young people who have been forced into marriage may consider an unhappy marriage and divorce more socially acceptable than unmarried parenthood. Typical of this category is Rose, age 18, who in her own words tells her story:

I did not know anything about sex. We could not discuss it at home. One day I went joy-riding with a few boys and we had a drink. Joe, my boyfriend, wanted to teach me all about

sex, and I guess he did. I found myself pregnant. We got married quickly after that.

Studies of teen-age marriages show that about one-third of all teen-age marriages are due to pregnancy.

Escape from an unhappy home life is also a reason for many of our young marriages. Joy, age 17, told me:

My home was not a home. Dad drank a lot, and Mom had to work day and night to keep things going. With three younger brothers and sisters, I had no quiet at home. I couldn't take the beatings, and no one cared about me. When I met Dick, I felt that for the first time someone cared for me. We ran away and got married. It's better than home.

Unfortunately, a quick marriage does not solve the problems which have been mounting up at home. Young people who feel that "all will be well" once married are only fooling themselves. They find that frequently the same problems that they had at home are present in the new marriage.

"Everyone is doing it" is frequently another reason. The experience of seeing so many friends marrying at an early age may bring about a snowball effect, and young people feel that they may as well join the modern trend.

Teen-agers today are walking on a tightrope. They are not accepted as adults, and yet they are not looked upon as children. They are in a confused state as far as their role in society is concerned. Many of them feel that an early marriage will bring about recognition, a place in the community and responsibility. Somehow, many have the view that all you have to do is get married, and your neighbours will treat you as an adult. Dorothy, age 19, expressed this when she said to me, "I'm somebody now. I am Mrs. Jones, and I get a family allowance cheque each month for one-year-old

Jimmy. I am a housewife. I feel responsible. I'm not a kid any more."

THE SCHOOLS AND TEEN-AGE MARRIAGES

Teen-age marriages also present a problem to our school authorities. School superintendents in 45 cities in North America were asked to discuss their policies on married teen-agers in their schools. In some areas, married students used to be excluded from high school, and now the P.T.A. has recommended separate schools for the married high school students. Other cities often send married students to evening school instead of to regular schools.

Married teen-agers are in a difficult position in regard to schooling. On one hand, they need education in order to get ahead in the world of work; on the other hand, the school authorities feel they are a disturbing influence in the high school world. A teacher recently told me, "We had a married couple in Grade 11, and they always talked about sex to the other students and got them all upset and bothered. We had to ask them to leave school."

The married teen-age girl finds it more difficult than the teen-age boy in school, especially if she is pregnant. Most of the teachers and principals to whom I talked felt that there is no place for a pregnant teen-ager, married or not, in the classroom. They felt that she should be immediately expelled. Some were lenient enough to state she should be asked to leave half-way through her pregnancy.

How can the schools help the married teen-ager? My own experience suggests the following:

Encourage discussion about sex and marriage in the home and at school, so that our youngsters will have a realistic preparation for marriage.

With the help of parents, churches and clubs, special guidance courses should be set up to discuss dating, marriage, and family living. Many churches have made strides in this direction with pre-marital courses given by various experts in medicine, home management, religion and family life.

Make literature available in our school libraries which would include marriage preparation, marriage and some of the hazards of teen-age marriage.

If a teen-age marriage occurs, help the couple to stay in school. They will need all the education they can get, so that they can manage their future life in relative financial security.

In the case of pregnant teen-age wives, they should be encouraged to see a doctor and, if needed, get help from a Family Service Agency if no immediate family is available. Allow them to remain in school as long as possible.

Do not rush to censure teen-age marriages. Rather, ask why did this particular girl or boy marry? Help them with adult advice, support and experience, and do not cast them out of their group in school, neighbourhood and family.

PARENTS AND TEEN-AGE MARRIAGES

It is also surprising how many parents push young boys and girls into marriage. They will delude themselves that the children are ready, or they hope marriage will "steady" them. There is, if not encouragement, a lack of discouragement. A mother who knows perfectly well that her daughter can't cook an egg will smilingly allow her to be married. Sometimes parents will go to the marriage-licence office and lie about the children's ages for them.

I recall a recent case of marriage between a boy of 18 and a girl of 17. The two had started dating when the girl was 11, with full parental approval. The two became formally engaged when the girl was under 14. When she was 17, the marriage took place, a big wedding with all the trimmings. It was about six weeks for disillusionment to set in; both the girl and boy were completely unprepared for marriage. The boy was accustomed to falling asleep on a sofa and having his mother undress him and put him to bed; he expected his bride to follow this comforting routine. But she herself had been an indulged child and could think of marriage only in terms of being petted and being made much of. When she became pregnant, he discovered it was boring to spend time with her; she wanted to stay home and be treated with the deference that she believed due in her condition. He found a girl friend to sustain him during his wife's pregnancy. The couple divorced in a year and a half, a divorce described as a shock to all their relatives.

Why do many parents push their young daughters into early marriage? Some parents seek social status for themselves through their children's popularity. It is a mark of prestige to have a daughter who is much in demand. A mother whose child spends a good deal of time alone or with a single girl friend may feel second best. Thus she will actively seek popularity for the child by permitting her to date earlier.

One mother recently told me, "My neighbours envy me. The boys just flock to our house and I feel young again. Ruth looks so pretty dressed up, and she goes with the best company."

Parents want their children to have "all the fun and advantages" they themselves missed. Often a mother who felt herself less popular than others in her own youth is desperately afraid that her child will have the same painful experience. Thus she will push her child into mixed social activities to give her a good start.

At a recent meeting, a mother confided in me, "I grew up in the depression. It was a difficult time. My family was poor but now we have made a lot of money and I am giving Margaret anything she wishes. I do not want her to feel sad, poor or get hurt as I did in those difficult times."

Many mothers want to relive the carefree days of youth through their daughters' experiences. Many women are unwilling to face the harsh reality that their own youth is behind them. With the prospect of oncoming middle years too painful to contemplate, they look back, instead, where there is fun once again in dates—this time their daughters'. Such mothers will pepper their daughters with questions about which boy dates which girl, help arrange parties, fret about their daughters' social success. The young girl, knowing she has her mother's approval, finds her a willing listener and even an accomplice in her romantic problems.

I also feel that many parents are encouraging earlier dating. Dating, dancing and occasional kissing and petting are commonplace among 11- and 12-year-olds today. A mother became recently quite upset when her 11-year-old asked her if she "could kiss the boys good-night." Mothers are the principal helpers in this rush for "socializing." Dancing classes, special wardrobes, boy-girl parties are all part of the early rush which leads to early marriages. The excuse you hear from mothers of 12-year-olds is, "times have changed" or "our children are growing up faster; we may as well go along." But early growing up can cause trouble. What happens when kissing and dancing become "kid stuff" to the 15-year-old girl? By the time these experienced children have reached their teens, they have covered the field and are ready for nothing less than marriage. In the parents' need to have the daughters grow up quickly, they make them old before their age. One 17-year-old girl told me, "I have had everything—trips, nightclubs, the latest fashions and hundreds of dates. I am bored with life. What else is there to do? I might as well get married." A sad note on which to start a marriage.

It is not easy to be a parent of teen-agers, and there are no easy answers to the problems of early marriage. And yet we have to continue to ask the questions—"What's the rush?" "Why do you want to get married at such an early age?"

READINGS

Duval, Evelyn Millis. *Why Wait Till Marriage?* New York: Association Press, 1965.

Sokol, Jeanne. *What about Teenage Marriage.* New York: Julian Messmer, 1961.

FILMS

The Game, NFB, 28 minutes, black/white, 1966.
The boy meets girl game.

The Invention of the Adolescent, NFB, 28 minutes, black/white, 1967.
An historical presentation of the problems of adolescence.

QUESTIONS, ACTIVITIES AND PROJECTS

1. *Discuss the positive and negative aspects of teenage marriage.*
2. *Write a reaction to the United Church's recommendation that the minimum legal age for marriage without consent of parents should be 21 years for both bride and groom.*
3. *Write a case study of a couple you know who married while in their teens. Indicate any problems they may have encountered as a result of their youth. Consider areas such as money, in-laws, pregnancy, social life and recreation. If they did face problems, describe how they dealt with them. Share your case study with the class.*

III

FAMILY
PROBLEMS

Introduction

In this section we report on four major Family Problems in Canada: Child Abuse, Wife Abuse, Alcoholism and Family Life, and Multi-Problem Families. They are selected among the varied family problems in our society since they constitute problems faced by a substantial number of Canadian families.

CHILD ABUSE

Child abuse is a new term for an old problem. Maltreatment and neglect of children has always existed. Some of their manifestations are still condoned. Society's tolerance of ill-treatment has lessened in recent years to the point that intervention to prevent such behaviour is now of urgent public concern.

It is a complex problem that takes many forms, some of which are very difficult to detect. However, there are three main categories of abuse: physical, emotional and sexual.

Child neglect is sometimes considered abuse. It may be physical or emotional or both, but it usually differs from abuse by being an act of omission rather than commission. Abuse and neglect can be considered as parts of one problem viewed from different perspectives.

There are infinite variations in the types and seriousness of abuse. Excessive shaking of a small child may seem minor, but can result in brain damage. Extreme abuse can result in the death of a child.

Emotional abuse may range from habitual humiliation to the withholding of life-sustaining mothering. Sexual abuse may occur as an incident with mild conse-quences or as rape. No single definition can cover all types of abuse and treatment must vary from case to case.

Children are usually completely at the mercy of adults. There are laws that offer some protection, but they are not well known and are considered by some people to need revision.

Abusers and the Abused

Child abuse is not confined to families whose members are economically deprived, educationally disadvantaged, mentally ill or drug or alcohol-addicted. That may sometimes appear to be the case, because abused children from these groups come more readily to the attention of authorities.

In three-quarters of the reported cases, the child's parents are the abusers. The remainder are substitute parents, brothers and sisters, siblings, relatives and temporary guardians.

A child of any age may be the object of physical, emotional or sexual assault, although cases involving infants are the ones most often seen. Statistics indicate that among children under 13, there is not much difference between the numbers of cases involving girls and boys.

Over the age of 13, there are more cases involving girls than boys. Greater differences may be seen in the type of abuse and the reasons for it, regardless of the age or sex of the victim.

There is evidence to suggest that certain children are more vulnerable than others. For different reasons, in different situations, one child may have characteristics that make him more likely than another to be the victim of abuse.

Number of Cases

No one knows how many cases of abuse occur annually in Ontario. A Child Abuse Registry was established in 1966 by the Ministry of Community and Social Services in Ontario to receive and compile reports of abuse from Children's Aid Societies. The number of cases reported to it by the societies increased from 407 in 1970 to 1045 in 1977. The total number of cases between 1970-1977 was 5040.

Since reporting procedures are not uniform the actual number is in doubt. It is probably substantially higher, since the statistics reflect only cases of verified physical abuse reported by the Societies.

Deaths officially attributed to child abuse by the Supervising Coroner of Ontario from 1970 to 1977 was 47. This number does not include S.I.D (Sudden Infant Death), or "crib death" as it is sometimes called. It is not known whether any deaths now attributed to that phenomenon are actually the result of child abuse.

WIFE ABUSE

For centuries violence toward wives has been considered acceptable as evidenced by such popular sayings as, "Certain women should be struck frequently, like gongs" and "A woman, a dog and a walnut tree, the more you beat them the better they be." Wife beating is part of the history of Western civilization. In the Middle Ages men were exhorted from the pulpit to beat their wives to kiss the rod that beat them. The deliberate teaching of domestic violence, combined with the doctrine that women and children by nature could have no human rights, had taken such hold by the late Middle Ages that men had come to treat their wives and children worse than their beasts.

Conflict between husband and wife, and within this broad category of conduct, physical violence between partners, is neither a new nor a rarely encountered phenomenon. Beatings, kickings, extreme verbal abuse—many women suffer such abuse every day at the hands of their husbands and boyfriends. Usually it is coupled with child abuse and stems from alcoholism. Because of the sanctity of the home, the women are usually unable to get relief from this situation from the police and the courts.

The whole issue of the "battered wife problem" has recently been brought specifically to public notice by widespread publicity, magazine articles, radio and television programs and the efforts of voluntary groups seeking to improve current provisions for women who are victims of violence at the hands of their partners. Unfortunately, all too often popular treatments of social problems are couched in simplifications and generalizations which tend to block knowledge and full understanding.

ALCOHOLISM AND THE FAMILY

Alcohol is the most widely-used psychoactive drug in our society and the drug that induces harmful dependence in the greatest number of people.

In Ontario, about 80% of the population over the age of 15 drink some alcoholic beverages. There is good evidence that many more young people of high school age use alcohol than use any other drug, with the possible exception of tobacco. Of the people who do drink, about 85% drink no more than an average of three pints of beer or their equivalent a day; these people are probably in no danger of becoming alcoholics as long as they do not increase their alcohol intake. Those who now take more than three drinks a day but are not alcoholics may or may not, as individuals, be in some danger of becoming alcoholics in the next few years: the dividing lines between low-risk drinking and high-risk drinking, and between high-risk drinking and alcoholism, are not clear cut. However, about 3.5% of the Ontario drinking population, or some 120 000 people, are clearly alcoholics by any definition.

THE MULTI-PROBLEM FAMILY

These families constitute the lengthy records in social agencies, the numerous visits to medical and psychiatric hospitals and the population of the worst slums of our cities. They are the people for whom many members of our community have given up all hope, effort and intensive service. They make up the families who are known to us from generation to generation as dependents on welfare, charity and hand outs. Unemployment, delinquency, illegitimacy, family breakdown, alcoholism are all part and parcel of most of these families. We stood back for many years, closed our eyes

and allowed the families to sink deeper into the slums of the body and mind. We felt that we could do nothing for them, that they were the lost cause.

Only within the last 15 years have we in Canada begun to examine this area of social welfare. We are at the stage of exploring and identifying the characteristics and needs of these families and implementing some projects to work directly with these families on a concentrated basis, and to attempt to arrest this generational pattern of dependency.

We have considerable knowledge about the causal factors which seem to influence the growth of multi-problem families in our Canadian communities. We will briefly review the social and psychological factors which have been found to be almost universally accepted by professional persons interested in this area of human concern. Canadian studies are reviewed in this section.

9
CHILD ABUSE

INTRODUCTION

Child neglect and abuse are not new phenomena in our society or in any society. The problem of the abused or battered child is a phenomenon common to every community. It dates back to ancient times when a father had power of life and death over his children, to the era when children were sold into slavery or were maimed and mutilated to make them the objects of pity so as to attract more generous alms giving.

We live in a civilization which is essentially family oriented and child centred yet we find that children are still victims of destructive parental behaviour. The term "child abuse" as used here will refer to a limited range of potentially damaging behaviour toward children. This limited range is characterized by any situation in which a child is non-accidentally physically attacked by an adult. The forms or types of abuse inflicted on abused children are a negative testimony to the ingenuity and inventiveness of people.

Until 1960, there was little social research or professional literature published dealing with the physical abuse of children. In recent years, however, several major studies relating to abused children and their families have been initiated.

The "battered child" syndrome takes its name from the fact that the child's injuries are the result of twisting, throwing, knocking around or some other form of "battering" by the abusive person. The injuries include bruises and one or a combination of fractures of the arms, legs, skull or ribs. In many instances poor skin hygiene and some degree of malnutrition are also evident. X-rays of the child often reveal other fractures in various stages of healing, indicating that such abuse has been repetitive. Abuse of this nature is most severe, sometimes fatal, and is most often inflicted on children who are too young to speak, thereby ruling out their explaining how the injuries occurred. While it is strongly suspected that the parents either inflicted the injury, or know how it happened, they are most reluctant to volunteer any information.

Accurate figures regarding incidence of this type of abuse are difficult to come by. Physicians' suspicions may not be aroused because parents may shop for medical care after each injury of their child from different hospitals and doctors, fail to get treatment at all or fabricate stories to account for the injury, blaming an ex-caretaker, a relative or a jealous sibling.

It is often difficult to identify the battered child. Abusive acts perpetrated by the children's own parents or substitute parents usually take place within the home where the sole witnesses are members of the immediate family. Aware of society's standards, the abusers do not readily admit to abusive practices. If the child is too young to speak, there is no complainant; if the child is old enough to speak for himself, his listeners may come to conclusions based on subjective feelings instead of seeking the facts in the situation. The credibility of the child's story is also affected by the child's immaturity. Thus the principal basis for identifying the problem has had to be the judgment of the professional person. Judgment is an essential factor but it cannot substitute for objective criteria.

In 10% of the cases of child abuse, professionals have found that long-term separation of parent and child is the only way to assure the child's physical safety. For the remaining 90%, however, treatment can be offered to help parents understand and redirect the anger that is usually at the base of their abusive behaviour and to help them improve their overall care of their children. The treatment is based upon our knowledge of the dynamics that cause adults to strike out against their children.

Child abuse in Canada is found in rich families and poor families, in families with one child and in families with many children, in families with one parent and in those where two parents are present. It occurs among all racial and economic groups, and among the employed and the unemployed.

HISTORY OF CHILD PROTECTIVE SERVICES

In Canada, the United States and England the movement for the protection of animals actually preceded the movement for the protection of children. The first protection law was enacted in New York in 1893. This came into effect because of a nine-year-old girl, Mary Ellen, who had been grossly abused and chained to a bed. The woman who found her in this condition tried to enlist aid from clergymen, lawyers and police courts only to discover that no state or municipal law existed under which the parents could be charged with cruelty to their own children. With the help of the Society for the Prevention of Cruelty to Animals a conviction was secured on the grounds of "cruelty to a human animal" and public interest in child cruelty was aroused.

John J. Kelso was the first person to do something about the cruelty, abuse and exploitation that a large number of Canadian children were experiencing. A Toronto newspaperman by occupation, Kelso had been engaged in writing about and taking action in child protection work since 1886. As elsewhere, the children's protection movement started out combined with protection for animals. In fact, the first response on the part of the Toronto City Council to this dual movement and the establishment of the Toronto Humane Society in 1887 was securing a drinking trough for horses. Some people argued against including children in humane societies saying that dogs and cats would not get adequate protection.

On July 3, 1891 at a public meeting in Toronto a Children's Aid Society was organized, the first one in Canada; Mr. Kelso was elected President. The administration, financing and staffing was carried out by interested citizens as a Christian duty, not for material gain. In 1893, the Children's Protection Act provided for the establishment of Children's Aid Societies. They considered themselves law-enforcing bodies rather than social agencies and emphasized punishment of parents and guardians. The underlying concept was that people have a personal responsibility for their social plight and can control themselves and their actions to remedy the situation. In the second decade of the twentieth century training and professional education in social work became available, thus providing trained staff in the child welfare field.

CHARACTERISTICS OF ABUSING PARENTS

Abusing parents lack the confidence and

trust to develop satisfying relationships with others largely because they did not receive adequate mothering as infants. Thus the abusing parent tends to lead a life which is described as alienated, asocial or isolated. Later life experience then serves to compound the feelings of rejection, inadequacy and loneliness.

Usually only one parent actually attacks the child. Marital partners tend to protect the abusive parent from disclosure or prosecution by denial or obvious facts. One parent is the aggressive actor; the other is a passive under-study. The child often becomes the scapegoat for his parents' conflicts. The abusing parent in many cases views his victim not as the child he/she really is, but as an adult.

The following typical reactions and attitudes of abusing parents have been observed after child abuse has occurred. The parents:
—do not volunteer information about the child's illness or injury;
—are evasive or contradict themselves regarding the circumstances under which the child's condition occurred;
—show irritation at being asked about the development of the child's symptoms;
—are critical of the child and angry with him for being injured;
—give no indications of feeling guilt or remorse regarding the child's condition;
—show no concern about the injury, treatment or prognosis;
—often disappear from the hospital during examination or shortly after the child is admitted;
—tend not to visit the child in the hospital;
—seldom touch the child or look at the child;
—do not involve themselves in the child's care in the hospital;
—do not inquire about the discharge date or ask about follow-up care;
—ask to have child home only when interrogation has frightened them;
—show concern not about the child but about what will happen to themselves and others involved in the child's illness or injury;
—maintain that the child has injured himself;
—act as though the child's injuries are an assault on them;
—fail to respond to the child or respond inappropriately;
—give no indication of having any perception of how a child could feel, physically or emotionally;
—constantly criticize the child;
—show no concept of the rights of others;
—are preoccupied with themselves and the concrete things in life;
—are often neglectful of their own physical health;
—exhibit violent feelings and behaviour and in interviewing reveal that this was a pattern in their original family;
—reveal in the interviewing that they are concerned about having been abandoned and punished by their own parents and are longing for a mother;
—show overwhelming feelings that they and their children are worthless.

The mother is most frequently the abuser in pre-school children, whereas the father is usually the perpetrator of abuse against older children. On the average the parents tend to be in their mid-twenties or early thirties. The serious abuse is caused by one of the child's parents or a substitute parent (step parent, common-law parent, foster parent) but it can also be caused by a sibling or relative. Many studies report that when persons outside the immediate family household are suspected, the baby-sitter is frequently identified as the perpetrator.

The abusers represent all socio-economic classes and levels of education and come from various cultural, religious and racial groups. Most of the studies of abusing parents over-represent the poor, because the well-to-do families can more easily conceal the problem. The well-to-do have minimal contact with social service agencies and go to private physicians who may believe their explanation since they appear to be respectable, socially important people.

They are parents who reject their children and are primarily concerned with their own feelings and pleasures. Mothers in this group show an inability to love their children or to feel protective toward them. They feel threatened, fatigued and frustrated by their demands, and express their resentment in cruelty toward them.

They are parents who, surprisingly enough, are exceptionally meek and dependant. They are unassuming, unusually reticent about showing their desires and unaggressive in their daily contacts with the outside world. Generally, they want to be told what to do and when to do it. They appear to depend on someone else simply to get them through life itself.

Within the family, these parents were found to be unconsciously competing with their children for the love and attention of their mates, a significant clue. An individual's fear that a husband or wife prefers the affection of a child can arouse acute jealousy which, in turn, can trigger a vicious assault on the "rival." The child-beater, however, is rarely if ever aware of the real reason for his or her action.

They are parents with deep-seated feelings of hate and aggressiveness. They are angry, sometimes at the world in general, sometimes at specific things. The anger simmers constantly, betrayed by bitingly critical comments about friends, neighbours, relatives and in negative attitudes toward virtually everything and everyone.

This basic angry feeling probably stems from childhood experiences in their own families. Many of these parents come from homes where love was absent, where lashing out at other members of the household in a hostile manner was acceptable behaviour. One wonders how parents from such a home can be loving and understanding to their own children when they have experienced nothing of this.

Not all incidents of abuse have one set of factors, so that some parents may be quite normal, but merely follow a culturally acceptable child-rearing pattern, perhaps in a somewhat exaggerated manner due to stressful situations or to chance. North American society approves of a certain measure of physical force as a legitimate educational and socializing agent, although this may vary to some extent with social class and ethnic group.

CHARACTERISTICS OF ABUSED CHILDREN

The victim is usually a pre-school child and frequently is an infant, especially in the case of severe abuse. The infant is at a disadvantage in that he/she is solely dependent on parents for satisfaction of basic needs and therefore is more demanding of parental attention and time. Also, the infant is restricted to the privacy of the home and cannot verbalize or walk away.

The following typical forms of behaviour of abused children in the hospital were observed by some investigators. The children:
—cry hopelessly under treatment and examination;
—cry very little in general;
—do not look to parents for assurance;
—show no real expectation of being comforted;

—are wary of physical contact initiated by parents or anyone else;

—are apprehensive when other children cry and watch them with curiosity;

—become apprehensive when adults approach some other crying child;

—seem less afraid than other children when admitted to the wards and settle in quickly;

—seem to seek safety in sizing up the situation rather than in their parents;

—are constantly on the alert for danger;

—are constantly asking in words and through their actions what will happen next;

—are constantly in search of something: food, favours, things, services;

—ask, "When am I going home?" or announce, "I'm *not* going home," rather than crying "I want to go home";

—assume a flat "poker face" when discharge home is mentioned or taking place.

Although most abused children are assumed to be innocent bystanders some investigators suggest that a few of these children may contribute to their own abuse, since their behaviour is considerably more provocative and irritating to a caretaker than the behaviour of other children.

But even if the child does not seem to be particularly provocative or irritating, he/she is singled out for abuse. The child may remind some parents of a significant person in their past who was troublesome or rejecting. The child may remind parents of themselves in the past so that the self-hatred is displaced onto the child. A cranky baby, one who cries a great deal, eats poorly and occasionally gets sick may be more likely to incur the wrath of these "needy" parents. One child may be singled

out for abuse because he/she is illegitimate or unwanted or was an extramarital child. The child may have been born at a time when there were many crises present within the family—marital strife, financial problems or the absence of one spouse.

DEALING WITH CHILD ABUSE

Punishment of parents through criminal prosecution does not correct the fundamental cause of the abuse. If we recognize the mental, physical and emotional inadequacies of these parents then we must also recognize that prosecution does not change their behaviour.

With few exceptions these parents are not sadists. They do not take cruel delight in mistreating children. They more accurately can be described as people who can't help themselves. They have a low level of frustration and tolerance, with hair trigger controls which any irritant can set off into emotional violence. Many were themselves victims of parental neglect or abuse and their behaviour as parents is a reflection of what they were exposed to as children.

What these parents need is help and treatment. They need services to guide and counsel them toward accepting their responsibilities as parents. They need services which will help build up their damaged personalities and give them the strength and stability to successfully live up to parental roles.

The fact of child abuse is an anomaly in our enlightened age. We live in a civilization which is essentially family oriented and child centred; in communities which talk of respecting the rights of children; and in a society which expresses dedication to the concept that the welfare of children is of primary importance. Yet we find that children are still victims of destructive parental behaviour. What is more alarming is the fact that with all our vaunted know-how, communities, for the most

100 Family Problems

part, have failed to provide effective measures to meet this profound problem. The present massive interest in the plight of the battered child leads one to hope that widespread concern will be translated soon into social action to provide services calculated to meet the needs of children in great hazard at the hands of parents and at the mercy of a well-meaning but misguided public.

RECOMMENDATIONS TO COMBAT CHILD ABUSE

The Calgary Child Abuse Committee has made certain recommendations which apply to the Canadian scene.

Coordination of community efforts. Coordination must be achieved by all professions and groups interested in child abuse if preventive and treatment measures are to be successful.

Modification of provincial laws. Community action may be necessary to urge establishment of central registries for reporting and documenting child abuse and neglect.

Parent and public education. Prevention of future abuse can only be achieved when citizens understand and accept the concept of responsible child rearing. Parent skill classes should be held in junior and senior high schools, in prenatal classes, and in adult education classes.

Professional education. Schools responsible for the education of all professionals working with children and families should have mandatory course content on effective child rearing and the problem of child abuse.

Predictive programs. Programs for prediction of high-risk parents should be instituted in prenatal and obstetric departments and programs for the development of good parenthood should be fostered for these parents.

Rehabilitation programs. To be effective, any treatment that is developed should be highly visible to the public through the use of the media, information packages and public presentations. Treatment efforts should be closely coordinated with those of protective services and the legal system. Supportive programs (such as day-care centres and homemaker services) must be seen as adjuncts to the treatment process.

Rehabilitative, Family-Oriented Programs. It is a matter of concern that many people still consider punishment of the abuser as the prime deterrent. Recent evidence to the contrary suggests that the best rehabilitative family-oriented programs can, in 80% of cases, rebuild a safe family environment. This evidence must be publicized to document the necessity for treatment programs.

Much can be done on a limited budget by concerned citizens willing to work together on behalf of the abused child. It is the responsibility of every community across Canada to develop and implement appropriate programs to this end.

READINGS
Bakan, David. *Slaughter of the Innocents.* Toronto: CBC, 1971.
Five talks on child abuse given by the author on CBC radio.
Bakan, David, Eisner, Margaret and Needham, Murray G. *Child Abuse: A Bibliography.* Toronto: Canadian Council on Children and Youth, 1976. (1407 Yonge St., Toronto, Ont. M4T 1Y7).
A comprehensive bibliography dealing with child abuse.
Dickens, Bernard M. *Legal Issues in Child Abuse.* Toronto: Centre of Criminology, University of Toronto, 1976.
A discussion of the legal issues involved in child abuse in Canada.
Greenland, Cyril. *Child Abuse in Ontario.* Toronto: Ministry of Community and Social Services, 1973.
A report dealing with child abuse in Ontario.
Hepworth, Philip H. *Services for Abused and Battered Children.* Ottawa: The Canadian Council on Social Development, 1975.

A summary of available services in Canada for abused children.

Report to the House of Commons. *Child Abuse and Neglect*. Ottawa: Standing Committee on Health, Welfare and Social Affairs, 1976. (Printing and Publishing Supply and Services, Canada, Ottawa, K1A 0S9).
The committee hearings dealing with child abuse in Canada.

Schlesinger, Benjamin. *Child Abuse in Canada*. Toronto: Faculty of Education, Guidance Centre, 1977.
A booklet giving an overview of the child abuse problem.

Child Abuse and Neglect—A Canadian Newsletter
Child Abuse Advisory Committee
Family Resource Centre
Alberta Children's Hospital
3009-3351 S.W.
Calgary, Alberta T3E 2T8
A newsletter which summarizes provincial action related to child abuse.

Van Stolk, Mary. *The Battered Child in Canada*. Toronto: McClelland and Stewart, 1972.
A pioneer effort in dealing with child abuse in Canada.

AUDIOTAPES:

Available from CBC Learning Systems, Box 500, Station A, Toronto, Ontario, M5W 1E6

The Abuse of Children
David Bakan, professor Psychology, York University, in a series of five talks on child abuse (now called the "battered baby" syndrome) in which he related this phenomenon to infanticide as a practice which has at different times carried sacrificial, pathological and (at all times) deeply symbolic significance. Cat. Nos. 160 to 164: five talks, each 30 minutes.

Children And The Law
A documentary describing some past and present legal attitudes towards the rights of children under the law. Cat. No. 811: 30 minutes.

QUESTIONS, ACTIVITIES AND PROJECTS

1. *Prepare a class bulletin board of services available in your community to assist families with such problems as*
   a) *child abuse*
   b) *wife abuse*
   c) *alcoholism*
   d) *other serious family problems*
2. *Think of a crisis situation in your family to which you reacted emotionally or violently.*
   a) *What factors contributed to the stress of the situation?*
   b) *What assistance did you receive from others to help you through the stressful experience?*
   c) *Looking back on the situation, how would you handle it today, in a more rational manner?*
3. *Research the local newspaper and current magazines for articles on child abuse. Have the class analyse the articles to discover the possible causes of a particular family problem. On the basis of these causes make a list of possible solutions to the problems.*

10
ABUSED WIVES

"A woman married, is like a pony bought to be ridden or whipped at the master's pleasure."

—Old Chinese Proverb—

INTRODUCTION

Ever since the formation of the institution of marriage the problem of abused, battered and neglected wives has existed. One hundred, even fifty years ago, the wife was regarded as the property of her husband. He had a right and possibly the duty to beat her. Despite the fact that this problem has occurred for centuries it has tended to remain hidden and has not been a source of concern for society. Most battered wives have not made their plight known to relatives, friends or authorities. They feared the stigma or the breakup of their family. Many kept silent due to feelings of futility, shame and hopelessness.

What is new today is that many wives are refusing to be treated as a piece of property. They're no longer putting makeup over their bruises. They're leaving and they're talking. Their stories are shocking.

Nobody knows just how many battered wives there are in Canada, but we can tell you a bit about them. Their ages range from 20 to 60, and they come from every economic background. The myth that wife beating is restricted to the lower-income family is just that—a myth. Tied by their economic dependence to a violent man, they see no escape. Often, the more affluent the life style, the more frightening the thought of leaving becomes. These women are too ashamed to seek outside help.

They probably don't even tell their closest friends. They seldom have any idea of the help that's available to them, so whether they live in a run-down flat or a two-car suburban home, they put up with their lives.

SOME FACTS ABOUT WIFE ABUSE (1976)

- it is estimated that there are 50 000 battered wives in Metropolitan Toronto
- in Vancouver 800 battered wives sought help in an 18 month period
- about 25% of all homicide victims in Canada are women
- from 10-30% of all police calls in Canada are related to family disputes, second only to motor vehicle accidents
- in most shelters for women in Canada, 75% of the women have fled home because of wife abuse
- we have almost no research in Canada on wife battering
- there are very few convictions in Canadian courts for wife abuse
- wife abuse takes place in all kinds of families from rich to poor

THE ABUSED WIFE: WHY SHE STAYS AT HOME

Richard J. Gelles (1976) has recently examined why abused wives stay at home. In a review of the literature and Gelles' own study it appears that the reasons for remaining at home are:

1. Some wives have a history of marital violence and thus stay.
2. Some wives have a negative self-concept.
3. Some believe they can reform their husbands.
4. It would be an economic hardship to leave.
5. The children need the support of the mother.
6. Many women doubt that they can get along alone.
7. Women feel that they will be unable to work if they leave.
8. The less severe the violence, the more she will tend to stay home.
9. If she experienced violence as a child, she is inclined to stay home.
10. The fewer the resources a woman has, the less power she has, the more she is entrapped in her marriage, the more she suffers without calling for help.

THE VIOLENT HUSBAND

In examining the characteristics of the violent husband, we found the following trends in the literature:

1. Men use violence as "power" and part of masculine aggressiveness.
2. Some men were spoiled in childhood and expect the wife to serve them. When this does not happen violence follows.
3. Some husbands want to dominate their wives, and the only way they know is through violence.
4. Some men may resent competition for the children by the wife.
5. Violence may represent sexual satisfaction for some men.
6. Some men learned in their childhood that you get things done by violence.

They were beaten by their own parents.
7. Dissatisfaction at their jobs is projected on the wives through violence.
8. Some men have "Jekyll and Hyde" marriages. To outsiders, these men appear as stable, solid citizens or "the perfect family man." At home, they are violent husbands.
9. Excessive use of alcohol, unemployment and poor housing may trigger off violence on the part of the husband.
10. Some of the male's violence may be an attempt to "get through to the wife."

THE COMBAT ZONE AND SETTING

The violence among husbands and wives appears to take place in the privacy of the home. The typical location is the kitchen, bedroom or living room. It appears that the bathroom is the "demilitarized" zone.

The most frequent time of inter-couple violence is in the evening or late evening. These couples are usually isolated from their neighbours.

FORMS OF VIOLENCE

The types of violence used by men includes slapping, punching, kicking, pushing, cutting, bruising, strangling, pulling hair, suffocating, raping and the ultimate—murder. It is of interest that the literature does not report what wives use when they batter their husbands.

VIOLENCE AS LEARNED BEHAVIOUR

The theme of "violence begets violence" permeates the literature of family violence. Violence is a learned behaviour. Those children who experienced violence during their own childhood tend to repeat this pattern in their adulthood, either as victims or abusers.

CHARACTERISTICS OF WIFE ABUSERS

From our examination of the literature on wife abuse, which is at present in its infant stage, we found the following characteristics listed for wife abusers. One has to caution the reader that there are other categories which may develop as we examine the problem of wife abuse in depth.

1. Projection of blame for marital strife

To varying degrees, the abusive mate will project blame for the conflict leading to violence. He may state that he would not have to get drunk if his wife were not such a nag, or that he would not have to get angry if only she would do what she is supposed to do. He denies the need for counselling because nothing is wrong with him. In some instances, he allows his mate to receive counselling but will often forbid her to seek outside assistance because, he reasons, she would have no difficulties if she would turn to him.

2. Disallowance of autonomy

Central to the abuser's sense of well-being is a strong and unyielding need for his mate to conform to his definition of her role within his system. If she deviates, his sense of equilibrium is upset. Because his mate must conform to his expectations, her autonomy as a separate person with a will of her own is greatly compromised. The abuser experiences or expects to experience his mate as someone to depend on, someone to depend upon him, a possession or an extension of his ego.

3. Mate as a symbol

In addition to the lack of autonomy, the abuser does not relate to his mate as a person in her own right but as a symbol of a significant other person. For example, it is as if she is expected to respond as his mother responded. The transference is particularly strong when the abuser becomes enraged. The abuser may set his wife up to respond to him in a rejecting or hostile manner, then state that she provoked him to attack her physically.

4. Adherence to expectations of marriage

Related to the two latter characteristics described above is the abuser's rigid adherence to his expectations of a marriage. The expectation may be the same as his parents' marriage or its opposite. Expectations of role and behaviour of the mate are strong and will not be compromised. He demands change within his mate to meet those expectations; it is not *his* ideals or behaviour, but those of the mate which must be modified.

5. Attractive characteristics of the abuser

Several authors have noted, and most professionals have found, that the wife is often reluctant to leave. Several factors contribute to her desire to remain in the relationship. Three major factors are: frequency and severity of abuse, having been a victim of violence as a child and degree of her power and resources. In addition, low self-esteem, a sense of shame, fear and love for the abusive husband must be considered. Love for the abusive mate is not necessarily masochistic. The abuser is not totally vicious; he can and often does offer warmth, protection and a sense of security.

6. Lack of intimacy

In abusive relationships, lack of mutual giving and receiving pleasure, low-self-esteem, the inability to accept and project positive aspects of self, depression and vulnerability are present in varying degrees.

Sex as a part of intimacy is often the clue to the problem. Battered women often describe their sexual relationships as distasteful because sex is imposed upon them, because they are criticized for their performance or because their own satisfaction is of little or no consequence to their mate.

FIVE TYPES OF RELATIONSHIPS IN WIFE ABUSE

A British psychiatrist, Dr. M. Faulk, has outlined five types of relationships in wife abuse.

1. *Dependent passive husband:* In this type of relationship, the husband gave a good deal of concern and time to trying to please and pacify his wife. She was often quarrelsome and demanding. Wife abuse came as an explosion, after a period of trying behaviour by the victim. There was often a precipitating act by the wife which brought on the abuse.
2. *Dependent and suspicious:* In this type of marriage, the husband had a long history of being unduly suspicious of his wife's fidelity. The husbands were controlling and jealous, but they would not leave their wives despite their suspicions. This situation built up an intolerable tension which led to a violent outburst, often preceded by increasing violence.
3. *Violent and bullying:* These men used violence and intimidation to solve their problems or gain their end in many aspects of their lives. Sometimes this behaviour was closely linked to alcohol abuse. The offence was often just the last violent incident in a long chain of violent incidents many of which might be quite minor.
4. *Dominating husband:* These husbands had a great need to assert themselves and would allow no insubordination from their wives. They were often quite successful in other aspects of their lives. Their offence might be precipitated by some trivial affair which they interpreted as a threat to their position of power.
5. *Stable and affectionate group:* This group included couples who appeared to have enjoyed a long-standing, stable relationship. The violence occurred at a time of mental disturbance, characteristically when one or both spouses were depressed.

The commonest type of relationship in wife abuse found in his British study was the dependent and passive husband.

SOME RECOMMENDATIONS ABOUT WIFE ABUSE

A major report by Downey and Howell in Vancouver (1976) has some of the following recommendations:

1. All large urban areas should have a *family crisis centre.* Such a centre should be well publicized and should be open 24 hours daily to provide services to wives, husbands and children. The family crisis centres should have three primary roles: *first,* they should provide emergency services. This includes immediate emergency counselling on rights and services available, and help for women to leave the dangerous home situations. Emergency services require close ties with local medical, social, legal and police services. *Second,* they should be responsible for coordinating existing arrangements for families in distress. This requires bringing those in need into contact with lawyer, doctor, health visitor, housing, financial services, clergyman, probation officer, marriage guidance counsellor, child care worker

and so on. *Third,* the centre should develop specialist advisory services, education and publicity programs, group support for women with similar problems, and the recording of data on incidence, treatment and outcome.

2. There should be immediate provision of more transition emergency shelters. Refuges are not considered *the* solution to the problem. But they do provide good temporary relief for women who have been battered and need to remove themselves, and often their children, from violent and dangerous situations.

3. The emotional needs of children of violent homes must be met, especially in the refuge setting. Not only have the children probably been witness to the violence, they have been uprooted from their home. They may be sheltered in an area away from their school and friends, and living in crowded conditions in a totally female environment in an atmosphere of hostility towards their fathers and men generally.

4. Studies involving the husband and other family members need to be undertaken and family dynamics explored. Research into violence, the reasons for its apparent tolerance by wives and communities generally, needs to be conducted. Procedures for recording cases of marital violence need to be developed.

5. Violent husbands need help too. They must be encouraged to seek assistance and should be treated considerately.

6. All health and welfare agency personnel must become fully involved in the identification of family violence.

7. The role of the police is crucial. They help in identifying domestic assault cases, in the enforcing of the law, in protecting the battered wife and in referring the victim to the helping system.

SHORT AND LONG-TERM CHANGES TO COMBAT WIFE ABUSE

Another study in Vancouver by Gropper and Currie (1976) suggests both short-term and long-term changes to combat wife abuse.

Short-Term Changes

a. The development of more transition houses with staff who are aware of women's needs, especially for self-esteem.

b. Research must be done in the area outlined above, concentrating on self-esteem in women and how it is conditioned by societal factors.

c. The development of group resources for violent men so that they can gain insight, responsibility and lose their sense of aloneness.

d. Training programs should be developed for people who deal with battered women, especially doctors, lawyers, police and court workers. This training program should include "consciousness raising" sessions on the role of women in society.

e. Changes should be made to property laws. They should recognize a woman's contribution in her marriage by legislating a 50/50 split of property upon dissolution of the relationship.

Long-Term Changes

a. Society must be structured so that women can play full and recognizably productive roles in Canadian society. This means that:
   —childcare must be provided on a wide scale;
   —more jobs must be provided so that women can work, and these jobs should cover a wide spectrum of trades and professions.

b. Attitudes must be consciously changed

in a number of important areas. This is a long-term process but can be dealt with in some short-term ways. Schools, the media and literature could be encouraged to support the following values:

—cooperation rather than competition
—non-violence
—equal potential of women
—potential of men to be gentle, warm and personal
—inner values (consideration, cooperation) rather than outer values (like beauty or "charm")
—childbearing as a choice rather than a necessity.

CONCLUSION

As for the present, thousands of Canadian women live with pain, embarrassment and shame. They don't enjoy it, but they put up with it because they are trapped by the system and know of no other alternative. Our legal system is too complicated to be of much help and the police are ill trained and often prefer not to get involved. The government doesn't show much interest either, or we would see more funds for establishments where the abused women could go for help.

But it is possible to get out. And for her own sake, and for the sake of her children, the battered wife must get out. First, she has to tell relatives or friends, get proof of her injuries, then report it to the police and leave. While their numbers are too few, there are places where the abused women can turn for help: homes like Interval House and Nelly's in Toronto, Transition House in Vancouver, rape centres, Family Service Associations, community clinics. Organizations like these will offer help, shelter and counselling.

The few transition houses in Canada which offer the battered wife a place to escape their spouses are perhaps the only sure alternative these women now have.

Until the police become more sensitive, until the courts become more sympathetic and until social services become more available, the only option most of the women have is to flee from their husbands. True, the real solutions will spring only from massive social change in the relationships between men and women as well as in the structure of power in society. In the meantime, we can only hope that wives victimized by their husbands will no longer be victimized as well by society's ignorance and indifference. Wife abuse has become one of the latest emerging social problems in Canada. It's time that the screams of Canada's abused wives are heard by all of us.

READINGS

Downey, Joanne and Howell, Jane. *Wife Battering.* Vancouver: United Way of Vancouver, 1976.

Vincent D'Oyley (ed.) *Domestic Violence: Issues and Dynamics.* Toronto: Ontario Institute for Studies in Education, Informal Series #7, 1978. (252 Bloor Street West, Toronto, Ontario, M5S 1V6). The major papers of a conference held on March 11-12, 1977 on the topic of violence between mates, at O.I.S.E. Contains a good bibliography on "Battered Wives" (pp. 229-248).

Faulk, M. "Men Who Assault Their Wives", in Maria Roy, ed. *Battered Women.* New York: Van Nostrand, 1977, pp. 119-125.

Gammon, Mary Alice Beyer (ed.) *Violence in Canada.* Toronto: Methuen, 1978. A collection of 15 articles related to violence in Canada. Part Two, deals with domestic violence (pp. 77-134).

Gelles, Richard J. "Abused Wives: Why Do They Stay?" *Journal of Marriage and the Family,* 38 (November 1977), 659-668.

Gropper, Arlene and Currie, Janet. *A Study of Battered Women.* Vancouver: Ishtar Women's Resource Centre, 1976.

Marsden, Dennis and Owens, David. "The Jekyll and Hyde Marriages." *New Society,* May 8, 1975, 333-335.

QUESTIONS, ACTIVITIES AND PROJECTS

1. *List family situations that make you angry.*
   (a) *Identify how you express your anger in these situations.*
   (b) *Categorize the ways you deal with your anger as being constructive or destructive.*
   (c) *At what stage can one deal with anger to prevent a violent explosion.*
   (d) *Indicate the ways that anger can be used constructively in problem-solving.*
2. *Evaluate a crisis centre for abused wives which is part of the bulletin board you assembled on community services (page 101), using the criteria listed on pages 105-106. If there is no such centre in your area, find out what agencies an abused wife might call on for assistance.*
3. *Invite a speaker from a crisis centre or family agency in your community that assists the abused wife to talk to your class.*
   (a) *Have him or her discuss the author's premise that "violence is learned behaviour" (page 103).*
   (b) *From the discussion draw up a list of ways in which the community can assist family members in dealing with stress in constructive ways.*

11
Alcoholism And The Family

R. Margaret Cork

INTRODUCTION

The family that has an alcoholic member is usually viewed in one of two ways—as the primary cause of his* behaviour or as the martyred recipient of it. In one sense this view has some validity. It is true that the alcoholic's parental family has often played a part in the development of his problem. It is also clear that his current family, be it parental or marital, inevitably suffers the consequences.

In spite of this, the tendency on the part of friends, relatives and others offering help has been to see the alcoholic in isolation from the rest of his family. Understanding or treatment has been provided to one *or* the other, rather than to the alcoholic *and* the rest of the family as a group of interdependent individuals each of whom is affected by the behaviour and personality of each of the others. Insufficient recognition has been given to forces within family life that contribute to drinking, recovery from drinking, stability of family life and instability of family life. Without greater attention to these forces, achievement of sobriety may be limited or unsatisfying and prevention of alcoholism and/or emotional disturbance in the next generation may be impossible.

* It is assumed in this study that the alcoholic is a male. Where the alcoholic is a female, characteristics described are usually applicable.

Clinical studies have suggested that the personalities of individuals who become alcoholics usually are determined by early parental relationships or lack of significant ones. While no extensive research has been done on the family of the alcoholic, much has been done on family life in general which shows that whenever normal relationships among family members are limited or cut off, the lives of all members are affected to some extent. With the addition of continued or repeated excessive drinking, the chances of normal, healthy family life are reduced or even eliminated. Other studies would seem to indicate that while there is no "alcoholic personality" as such, most alcoholics do have certain common characteristics which, together with continued excessive drinking, play a significant part in the deterioration of family life.

COMMON CHARACTERISTICS

These common characteristics, which are often overlooked in our approach to treatment of the alcoholic and of his family, will be found in varying degrees in different individuals. They will be more or less evident at varying stages, and not all of them will be seen in all individuals suffering from alcoholism. However, some of the most frequently observed characteristics— and those which most vitally affect family life—are as follows:

Inability to take appropriate responsibility

within the family. This has the result that budgeting, financial planning, and care of the children are left entirely to the wife, as are household tasks normally performed by the husband. This may lead to growing resentment as well as to removal from the alcoholic of the few responsibilities he may be able to handle. A particularly difficult situation for a wife to accept is one in which her husband cannot take normal responsibility for his home but can nevertheless fulfill a relatively responsible role in his work, his trade union, the church, or the community.

A lack of self-discipline which shows up in impulsive, inconsistent, indulgent, or dominating behaviour toward other family members. This might be tolerated in relationships outside the home, but it is disturbing or damaging to the closer relationships of family life.

An over-dependency which cannot be accepted and responded to by the other family members and which makes it difficult or impossible for the alcoholic to meet the normal dependency needs of his children. In some instances, the alcoholic's dependency needs are so great that he is threatened by the birth of each child. Other alcoholics feel threatened as their children reach adolescence or young adulthood. In some instances, the dependency needs of the wife are as great or greater than those of the alcoholic. In such cases, both partners' needs are constantly unmet, and each may turn elsewhere to find fulfilment—the alcoholic to drinking and the non-alcoholic to the children.

A pre-occupation with himself and his own suffering which makes it difficult or impossible to accept or recognize the normal needs or pain of other family members (such as the hurts of childhood or an illness of the marital partner). Very often, the alcoholic husband and father resents demands made on him. Family members, in their turn, feel growing resentment be-

cause their sufferings are not recognized or dealt with.

A negative attitude toward authority which may prevent his holding a steady job or limit his ability to assume a healthy degree of authority as head of the family. This may result either in lack of discipline or too rigid discipline for the children, with consequent confusion or hostility. Where there is lack of discipline, there may be transfer of authority to other members of the family, usually the mother or an older child, to the detriment of family life in general.

A sense of inadequacy in certain vital areas of family life which distorts marital and parental roles. This is seen most often in the alcoholic's inability to find and keep a satisfying job, to experience normal sexual relationships, to play or work with his children, or to relate meaningfully to friends, neighbours, or relatives.

An unrealistic, immature approach to the ordinary business of living which leads him into extravagant buying and accumulation of unnecessary debts. This limits his ability to provide the necessities of family life and thereby play his normal role in maintaining the home. For example, an alcoholic may buy a new car when his children need shoes. He may leave repairs to the home undone, or he may deprive the family of essential outings and creative experiences.

Limited interests which tend to isolate him and other family members from normal activities. He is often addicted to TV or spectator sports in which little is demanded of him. He may resent the normal interests of his wife and children, often to the point where he forbids their pursuit. If family members, in an attempt to relate to him, limit themselves to his interests, the result may be social isolation for the whole family.

Shallow or superficial ways of relating to people which make it difficult or impossible for him to demonstrate or communicate the love and affection so necessary to the growth of family life. This may create a neurotic inter-dependence among family members as they try to meet the loneliness and emptiness of the alcoholic. The child who does not experience sufficient love in the home may learn to resent and hate people. He thus has limited opportunity to grow into an outgoing, understanding person.

It is easy to see that these characteristics can limit or disrupt family life even more than excessive drinking. They are often the source of marital discord long before drinking has become a really serious problem. When drinking is at its height, they complicate family problems. Finally, they provide a basis for continued difficulty even when drinking is controlled.

Drinking episodes are often merely a crisis or breaking point. They provide something tangible on which all family members can project blame for the disruption in family life. It is the personality of the alcoholic and the family's pattern of reacting to it that seem to constitute deeper and more serious limitations on healthy family living.

FAMILY REACTION

While some studies have indicated that there are characteristic ways in which a family reacts to the existence of an alcoholic member, no one pattern is entirely typical. Each family, as well as each individual member, reacts in different degrees and at different stages in the process. The factors controlling this reaction include the original health of the family, the ages of various members, the family's culturally determined attitudes toward drinking, the family's position in the community, and its degree of financial security. All families, however, do show some similarities in their reactions.

THE MARITAL PARTNER. Before taking a closer look at the whole family's reaction to the alcoholic member, let us consider briefly the alcoholic's marital partner who, in a high proportion of cases, is the wife. Most families might be able to handle a husband's recurring drinking bouts if neurotic characteristics, some of which are similar to those seen in the husband, were not present or did not develop in the wife.

In the popular view, the non-alcoholic wife is a tragic, brave, long-suffering victim of circumstances who is not in any important way responsible either for her husband's drinking or the disruption of family life. However, most wives who have participated in Alanon (Alcoholics Anonymous) or in more structured forms of treatment will admit that they were to some degree disturbed individuals when they married or that they became so later, while drinking and marital strife were developing into serious problems. With help, they have been able to recognize that they had contributed both to the ongoing drinking and—more importantly—to the breakdown of family life. Many wives have also become aware that they can play a vital part in the recovery of the family. In many cases, a wife's new insight and self-understanding have enabled her to help the children to develop more normally even when their father has continued to drink.

DENIAL, FEAR, AND PROTECTION. In the earlier stages of the problem, there is usually a need to deny or hide the fact of excessive drinking and/or family disruption. There is a tendency to blame the family's troubles on external factors and to seek a solution through manipulating the environment. Fears of many kinds and degrees pervade the family members. These include fear of what outsiders will say or think, fear of increased suffering or unbearable financial deprivation, fear of inability to cope with the everyday problems of living, and even fear for one's own sanity.

Most families attempt, at times, to protect the alcoholic member. This proceeds from a genuine desire to help him, as well as from a need to protect themselves (often unconsciously) from the consequences of his behaviour—loss of job, jail sentence, or danger to his life or the lives of others. Family members usually make various attempts to help the alcoholic to control his drinking. Some family members may even react by submitting to verbal or physical abuse.

TWO COMMON REACTIONS. What happens to family life under the impact of such an experience? There are two reaction patterns which appear to be most common. One seems to be composed of a growing, interacting hostility or resentment among all members of the family, with consequent damage to interpersonal relationships. In such cases, a mother may align the children with her against the father, or the children may refuse to give respect and obedience to one or both parents. Some children may indulge in excessive bickering or quarrelling with one another or in antisocial behaviour in the community.

The other common reaction is distortion or loss of normal family roles. This usually occurs because the mother is taking on more and more of the father's role with consequent loss or limitation of her own. Children may also be forced into abnormal roles when they shoulder inappropriate responsibilities such as those of a pseudo-parent to younger siblings. Some are expected to contribute too early to family income. Others are compelled to be unwilling listeners to one parent's criticisms of the other. Some children are so overindulged or overprotected by one or both parents that their normal maturing processes are delayed or limited.

Under such circumstances children, as well as parents, may become increasingly torn by anxiety and conflict and may interact with one another in ways that are destructive to family life. A child may suffer from a lack of a parental figure on which to pattern himself. He may become unsure of himself and may have more difficulty than usual in establishing his own identity. His view of family life and marriage may become severely distorted. In some instances, children may begin to take on some of the characteristics described earlier—irresponsibility, lack of self-discipline, self-centeredness and inability to form relationships essential to normal growth.

HELP FOR THE FAMILY

The importance of helping the *family* becomes clearest when we look at the family life of the recovered alcoholic. A few families rapidly regain their former stability once the alcoholic member's drinking is controlled. Most families do not, however, until attention has been paid to disturbances in each of the members. Families in which the alcoholic cannot use help to control his drinking are another case in point. Even here, family life may often be strengthened or stabilized. Where excessive drinking has led to temporary separation from the alcoholic member, appropriate treatment of the remaining family members may make possible a workable reunion later.

READINGS

Some selected items available from the Education Division, Addiction Research Foundation, 33 Russell Street, Toronto, Ontario M5S 2S1.

Alcohol and It's Effects
Cork, R. Margaret, *The Forgotten Children.*
A report of the author's interviews with 115 children of alcoholic parents. The author's special interest is the study and treatment of children of alcoholic children.
Fraser, Judy. *The Female Alcoholic, 1977.*

MacLennan, Anne, ed. *Women: Their Use of Alcohol,* 1976.

Smart, Reginald G. *The New Drinkers: Teenage Use and Abuse of Alcohol,* 1976.

Pittman, David J. ed., *Alcoholism,* New York: Harper and Row, 1976.
Seventeen selections deal with the problem of alcoholism.

FILMS

Alcohol: How much is too much? NFB 11 min. colour, 1977. The drinking of alcohol and its effects.

The Alcoholic Within Us. NFB 23 min. colour, 1977. The six emotions which are thought to cause alcoholism are shown.

Alcoholism: Out of the Shadows. NFB 30 min. colour, 1977. The problem of alcohol abuse in our society.

Drinking. NFB 21 min. colour, 1976. The short-term and long-term effects of alcohol on our bodies.

Profile of a Problem Drinker. NFB 29 min. black/white, 1957. The case history of a male drinker.

The Summer We Moved to Elm Street, NFB 28 min. colour, 1971. A drinking father and his family.

QUESTIONS, ACTIVITIES AND PROJECTS

1. Write a letter to a newspaper columnist (like Ann Landers) dealing with a problem you, or someone you know, may have with alcohol. Do not sign it. Put all of the letters into a basket. Pull one letter and discuss your response in a small group.
2. (a) Chart the nutritive value of common alcoholic beverages, alongside the nutritive value of 5 non-alcoholic drinks. Analyze your findings.
   (b) Draw a flow chart showing the detrimental effects of alcohol on the human body.
3. Collect or tape record advertisements for alcohol.
   (a) To what age group are these meant to appeal?
   (b) Why are the people in the ads drinking? Can you suggest other reasons people may drink?
   (c) What hidden messages can you find in the advertisement for those who drink the beverage?
4. Invite a member of your local Alcoholics Anonymous organization to your class to discuss how alcoholism affects family members.

12
Multi-Problem Families

DEFINITION OF THE MULTI-PROBLEM FAMILY

The definition used most widely in Canada for the multi-problem family is that a family is considered multi-problem if the following characteristics are present:

1. Failure in functioning of the father, such as alcoholism, criminal acts, desertion, mental illness and the like.
2. Failure in functioning of the mother, such as alcoholism, criminal acts, desertion, mental illness, child neglect and the like.
3. Failure in the functioning of the children, such as criminal acts, mental illness, poor school adjustment and the like.
4. Failure in marital adjustment, such as out-of-wedlock children, promiscuity, severe marital discord.
5. Economic deprivation and grossly inadequate housing.
6. And as a result of three or more of the above-listed, the family has been a chronic or intermittent undue burden to a community for over three years.

This definition thus includes only families who have come to the attention of community agencies because of their many problems.

CHARACTERISTICS OF MULTI-PROBLEM FAMILIES

One of the chief characteristics of both adults and children of multi-problem families is their lack of trust in others. They have few friends and little contact with social groups. They are mistrustful of neighbours, employers, physicians, nurses, school teachers, social workers, public officials and so forth. In their dealings with health and welfare agencies they may express interest in the service offered, but they tend to avoid personal involvement, often failing to carry through on plans that have been worked out with them.

Because of their extreme distrust of people, members of these families have an exaggerated fear of authority. Most people, of course, have some fear of authoritative agencies, particularly courts or other official bodies. Members of disorganized families, however, have a greater and more pervasive fear; they feel threatened even by persons who have limited legal authority and whose approach is non-authoritative. Schools, churches and health and welfare agencies are not only the symbols of community mores and social standards, they also have certain powers that can be invoked.

Members of socially deprived families often have strong feelings of anger, aggression and hostility intermingled with their mistrust and fear. Some are openly hostile and aggressive, while others attempt to hide their negative feelings behind a facade of friendliness and extreme politeness. Often these resentments go back to early childhood, when they were exposed to neglect, abuse or abandonment by their parents. They have a sense of hopelessness which underlies all other feelings. They find temporary escape by going on a drinking or spending spree, by sexual promiscuity, by fighting or by engaging in delinquent behaviour.

Any group of asocial families will include some with various degrees of mental health. Some may have relatively little mental illness; their deviant behaviour is largely a reaction to undue social strain and stress. Others may be psychotic or suffer from neurosis. A large proportion of asocial persons, however, have what are described as "character disorders," the chief clinical feature of which is the arrest of the individual's emotional development. Because of inadequate parental care and guidance in early years, these people retain many infantile attitudes and ways of behaving. In consequence, their responses are more appropriate to the pre-school age of development than to the adult level. They have difficulty in putting off gratifications, have little judgment about money and other practical matters, are selfish and self-centred and tend to get into trouble.

There is increasing evidence that many of the parents of multi-problem families suffered considerable deprivation themselves during the early years of their lives. Many came from broken homes in which one parent, usually the father, had deserted or was imprisoned. Many, as children, had periods of institutional or foster-home placement or were brought up by a series of relatives. If they remained at home, their mothers were often employed and the children received inadequate substitute care. The mothers who had been deserted often entered into common-law relationships, sometimes bearing children by several men. In other words, the parents of the multi-problem family of today often have come from families that had similar characteristics. Case records show that the social behaviour of families sometimes extends through several generations.

The social milieu of many multi-problem families suggests the nature of their psychological problems. Because they suffer such severe deprivation, they develop negative and hostile attitudes. Also, since they are often subjected to rejection by the community, they tend to isolate themselves from their neighbours. The negative attitudes of the community toward these deprived families are likely to be heightened if the families belong to a race or culture different from the predominant one. Although people of minority groups are often subjected to rejection in our society, the rejection is more overt if their standards of living or conduct deviate markedly from those prevailing.

IDENTIFICATION OF MULTI-PROBLEM FAMILIES

In our own capital, Ottawa, a small study of multi-problem families sheds some more light in this area. In 1961, the Welfare Council of Ottawa surveyed a group of 47 multi-problem families. These were large families, averaging 7.2 members per family (Canadian average 3.5), and all lived in housing which was too costly, too crowded or in poor physical condition. The education of the adults was limited to Grade 9 or less, and all were in debt and serious financial difficulty.

The families used 35 health and welfare agencies and had been known to one or another agency for 10 years or more. There was little coordination among the agencies, each agency serving the family not knowing what other agencies were doing with the particular family. Recommendations made in the report include coordination of services to these families.

Vancouver has pioneered in some pilot studies to identify and analyse multi-problem families in a metropolitan setting. In the month of June 1960, 1 407 multi-problem families, active with 14 social agencies, were identified in Vancouver. These families represented 21% of agency case loads and were known by the agencies on an average of 4 years. The families seemed to live mostly in the downtown section, characterized by deteriorated housing, high land value and low rentals. An interesting finding shows that these families were largely of Anglo-Saxon origin and had been residents of the city for generations. Vancouver estimated that about 12 000 to 16 000 people were involved with these families in the course of a year.

The Salter-Jarvis area in Winnipeg, which is approximately 1 km in length and breadth, had a population of 3 000 at the time of the study. In December 1962, 287 cases were being served in the area, the average-sized family being 3.5 members. It was estimated that 1 000 persons were in social or economic dependency, or both. Five agencies had been active in this area for many years but were showing little or no effect on the numerous and complex problems of these people. A large percentage of the 287 cases seemed to be families of the multi-problem type, since they were known by at least 2 to 4 agencies which were simultaneously extending services.

Halifax, Nova Scotia, identified 262 multi-problem families in 1966.

TWO-GENERATION MULTI-PROBLEM FAMILIES IN TORONTO

The study of two-generation families was undertaken in two social agencies in Metropolitan Toronto in 1972 and covered 25 two-generation families, or 50 families. The study revealed a much larger size family in this group of two-generation families than the average Canadian family: the average size in the first generation was 7.2, and in the second generation, 5.3. Most of the second-generation families were still active with social agencies in Toronto.

The two-generation families were confronted by a frightening array of problems, including alcoholism, illegitimacy, marital discord, ill-health, unemployment, delinquency and crime, housing, financial problems and sexual deviation. There were also pronounced problems in the area of care and training of children. Child neglect in the forms of physical abuse, lack of health supervision, lack of parental control and guidance, illegitimacy and desertion were present in most cases.

The problems that stood out sharply in the first generation were those of delinquency and crime, neglect and lack of parental control of the children. In the second generation the most frequent problem was that of unmarried motherhood and illegitimacy.

The study also revealed that two-generation families are mainly located in the downtown section of the city of Toronto, where there is a heavy population concentration. Residential mobility was high in these families, with an average move per family of more than once a year, but largely within the same social milieu.

The data revealed that a high percentage of the children were cared for by social agencies. In the total number of families of both generations, 57.7% of the children were placed with Children's Aid Societies. In addition, in both generations, 38.7% of the children were placed by other means than Children's Aid Societies.

The average number of years a family was served by social agencies in the first generation was 7.2, and in the second generation, 3.8. Many of the problems confronting these families had come to the attention of a number of different health and welfare agencies in Metropolitan Toronto and outside of Toronto.

What emerged from this study was the prospect that if no concerted effort is made in an organized manner to prevent further dependency, the pattern of these families will continue from generation to generation.

FINANCIAL COSTS

Another study calculated the costs for two Toronto multi-problem families. Family "A" had been receiving help from 16 agencies over a period of 17 years at a cost of $53 225, and Family "B" known for 25 years, had used up $61 700 of public and private funds. These costs did not include the price paid in human terms by these families, or the cost of services of the array of professional volunteer workers who had been in contact with them.

VALUES OF MULTI-PROBLEM FAMILIES IN LONDON

A study which examined the values of multi-problem families in London, Ontario in the late 1960s found that there is considerable evidence that these people do have a desire for change. On the whole, they are not satisfied with their lives as they are living them. They largely identify with middle class standards, which they see as desirable, but which they have been frustrated in achieving. In some instances, secondary problems are created by their recognition of failure to achieve the expected. They feel that they are maintaining as good standards as possible, although they are not always satisfied with these. When they are criticized by the dominant middle-class society (through the social worker, public health nurse, etc.), their problems are reinforced rather than alleviated, and they feel their difficulties and differences all the more strongly. Thus, in some cases, apparent lower-class behaviour does not result from their identification with the lower class but from their frustration in achieving more.

The families in London were still predominantly fertile, with the age range of

the men from 21 to 45, and women, 21 to 35. The average number of children was 4.5, smaller than the average in other studies, which is usually 6. However, this group was younger and still growing. That 23.3% of the families had children under 6 years of age demonstrates the need for effective and preventive measures. The greater percentage of the sample were native-born. The occupations of the male heads all required less education than higher-paying jobs. These families would presumably become increasingly dependent economically as technological advances continue. Of the men, 46.6% had an intermittent pattern of employment, 30% a steady pattern, and 16.6% were usually unemployed. Agency records in most cases were incomplete as far as education of the clients was concerned. In the 24 cases were education was recorded, none had schooling past Grade 12. Each family was known to an average of 6.1 of the 12 agencies from whom data were obtained. The average contact was 12.2 years from the date of the first contact to the date of the research.

A STUDY OF MULTI-PROBLEM FAMILIES IN VANCOUVER

A study in 1972 of 100 multi-problem families found that the most characteristic failure of the families was the inability to remain economically independent. Ninety-five families had been in receipt of financial assistance for a period of one month or more. Twelve families were in receipt of assistance by the end of their first year of marriage, and some 34 families by the end of their fifth year of marriage.

Eighty-three of the families were characterized by "a dismemberment of conjugal pair." The first time dismemberment occurred, husbands left home in 59 cases and wives in another 24 cases. Thirty-four families, or 41% of those broken by the absence of a spouse, experienced a second separation. A third separation was recorded for 7 families.

About 14% of first separations were in the category "multiple absences from the home situation"—situations where there was a multiplicity of indefinite desertions which could not be tied down to specific periods of time but were judged to be sufficiently serious to constitute marital breakdown of the same order as a definite and prolonged absence from the home. Of the remaining 71 first separations, only 5 were enacted through formal channels of legal separation or divorce. About 45% represented desertion and 46% separation by mutual agreement.

A mental health problem of the husband was recorded in 63 of the families, compared with a recording in this category for the wife in only 37 instances. About 76% of the mental health problems of the husbands, and 22% of those of the wives, were classified as personality defect and social maladjustment.

Finally, only 23% of the sample did not have contact with Family Court.

The sequence of failure in family functioning began approximately 6 years after marriage with a mental health problem of the husband. This was experienced by 63 of the families. However, 76% of the husbands' problems were associated with alcoholism or heavy drinking.

CONCLUSION

We have yet to learn how to deal most effectively with this type of family. There have been efforts made in London, Halifax, Montreal, Ottawa, Toronto, Winnipeg and Vancouver to find out first the characteristics of the families, and then to attempt to intervene in the generational dependency pattern of these families. While multi-problem families represent only a small percentage of families in Canada, they consume nearly half of the total welfare budgets of our metropolitan areas. More than part-time efforts are needed on their behalf. The total community will have to find ways to break the generational cycle of misery. At the same time it must be recognized that there are families for whom no concentrated efforts will help, and they may have to be supported for the rest of their lifetime. Hopefully, their children can be helped to emerge from the pattern of hopelessness and despair.

There are many areas related to the multi-problem family that have to be examined so that society may take the necessary preventive and social action. As of the present, however, no systematic studies have been directed at describing the general intellectual level, psychiatric impairment or specific medical disability of this group.

Although it is true that multi-problem families receive the most attention from the community, it is not true that they receive the most or even a fair share of its benefits. The basic responsibility for improving the lives of all Canadians rests with the community—its people, institutions, and all else that make up the society in which we live. Every aspect of our lives is shaped and determined by the expectations of the society around us, whether it be family, school, job or friends. This being so, it is our total society that must build a structure and provide an atmosphere that will assure the basic requirements necessary for the welfare of its members. Such things as good housing, adequate schools, education and vocational opportunities, absence of discrimination, health and medical programs—all must be provided before we can judge any group of people to be "hard to reach", "hard core," or "self defeating."

READINGS

Adams, Ian, *The Poverty Wall.* Toronto: McClelland and Stewart, 1970.
An angry book about Canada's poor.

Adams, Ian, Cameron, William, Hill, Brian and Peuz, Peter, *The Real Poverty Report.* Edmonton: M. G. Hurtig, 1971.
Former members of the research staff of the Poverty Committee of the Senate of Canada write their own version of the Poverty Report.

Copp, Terry, *The Anatomy of Poverty.* Toronto: McClelland and Stewart, 1974.
The condition of the working class in Montreal, 1897-1929.

Harp, John and Hofley, John R. (eds.) *Poverty in Canada.* Toronto: Prentice-Hall, 1971.
Eighteen articles discuss poverty in Canada.

Mann, W. E. (Ed.) *Poverty and Social Policy in Canada.* Toronto: Copp Clark, 1971.
Thirty-two selections review aspects of social policy and poverty in Canada.

Ryan, Thomas J. (ed.) *Poverty and the Child.* Toronto: McGraw-Hill Ryerson, 1972.

Various authors discuss the effects of early childhood experiences in conditions of deprivation.

Schlesinger, Benjamin. *Poverty in Canada and the United States: Overview and Annotated Bibliography.* Toronto: University of Toronto Press, 1968.
This book contains 600 annotations and selected essays dealing with poverty.

_____. *The Multi-Problem Family: A Review and Annotated Bibliography.* Toronto: University of Toronto Press, 1970, 3rd ed.
This book contains 322 annotations and essays related to the multi-problem family.

FILMS

Up Against the System, NFB, 20 min, black/white, 1969.
How people on welfare feel about their situation.

The World of One in Five, NFB, 27 min, black/white, 1969.
A fifth of Canadians live in poverty. This is their portrait.

QUESTIONS, ACTIVITIES AND PROJECTS

1. *The author states that "although it is true that multi-problem families receive the most attention from the community, it is not true that they receive the most or even a fair share of its benefits"* . . .

   Work in groups. Appoint one member to write to The Department of National Health and Welfare, Brooke Claxton Building, Ottawa, Ontario K1A 0K0, and your Provincial Department of Social Services, requesting information concerning economic and social benefits available to the multi-problem family, using the following categories:

   (a) Social Services—*health care; public health; family and child welfare; public housing; job retraining; rehabilitation programmes.*

   (b) Social Insurance—*unemployment insurance; Canada Pension*

   (c) General and Social Welfare Payments—*old age security pensions; family and youth allowances.*

   Under what circumstances might these benefits be adequate or inadequate?

2. *What other agencies in your community are involved in the assistance of multi-problem families?*

IV

CHANGING PATTERNS IN FAMILY LIFE

Introduction

This section begins with an overview of decision making patterns in families during the six stages of the family life cycle. It then examines in detail some examples of changes within different stages of the family life cycle.

Adolescent sexuality is looked at via an "alphabet" developed for this paper which focuses on the major issues in the sexual lives of Canada's over 4 million teenagers.

Very little study has been focused on the characteristics of single people. A chapter examines the lifestyles, family and social relationships and attitudes of unmarried women and men. The results deny many of the popular stereotypes of single persons.

In Canada 44% of women over the age of 15 are working women. Of these women 60% are married. Every year more women enter our labour force. Some of the effects of this trend are reviewed. One of the major gaps in Canadian society is adequate child-care facilities for working mothers. We take a look at what's available, and what's missing.

During the early 1970s it often seemed as though society was downgrading the Canadian women who decided to make homemaking their career. We made them feel like second-class citizens, who were "slaves" to their families. Many homemakers felt guilty about staying home, and when we asked "What kind of work do you do?", the answer was usually a timid voice "I'm just a housewife." An article notes that it is time that we recognize homemaking as a career for those Canadian women who choose it.

Another issue in family life today is the question of sex roles. What is "male" and what is "female"? We examine the question of "maleness" as it affects Canadian men today.

Grandparents are important members of the family. More than 8 million children under the age of 19 may each have 2 sets of living grandparents. Very little attention has been paid to them. We look at the contributions which grandparents can make to family life in Canada.

13
The Family and Decision Making

WHO MAKES THE DECISIONS IN TODAY'S FAMILY AND HOW ARE THEY MADE?

One of the central activities of the family has always been the decision making function. In the society of yesteryear most decisions were made according to custom and were usually imposed by the parents on the children. Tradition and precedence determined the decisions, which were not so much made by the young couple as for them.

In a changing society such as our own, decisions are made, not by seeking advice of parents or by appeal to precedent, but by the couple, considering the values at stake. The decisions of today are considered more and more by an increasing participation of the family members. In the "companionship" family, they tend to be made by joint action of husband and wife with the children taking a more active part as they grow older.

In modern North American marriages, the wife and husband seem to take equal parts in deciding important questions. The lead in making decisions is determined by a number of factors. Among these are the area in which the decision is being made and whether it is regarded as more appropriate for the husband than the wife; special competence of one or the other; who displays a greater interest in the decision; the relative tendency of one or the other to dominate in the relationship; and the nature of their dependence upon the other. Naturally, there exist wide differences in the relationships of husband and wife. The relative authority of the spouses in the marriage develops in personal interaction between them which may go back to their dating period.

DECISION MAKING PATTERNS

One aspect of decision making is the type of marital role-pattern of husband and wife. The three types of role patterns are: husband dominant, wife dominant, and equalitarian.

The husband dominant role is often a holdover from the traditional relation of the sexes in marriage. A husband states, ". . . in my home, I am the boss, and what I say goes. No one makes a decision without consulting me. My family knows who is head of our household . . ."

The wife dominant role has emerged in our society with the weakening of the tradition of control by the husband and recognition of the equality of the wife. A wife explains, "I look after all the bills, the children, household matters, and collect the pay cheque of my husband. You could say I run the house, and my husband provides the money . . ."

The equalitarian division of labour entirely disregards the traditional patterns of masculine and feminine behaviour. The couple share most of the tasks to be performed in the house. There is mutual discussion in approaching decisions. "We have frequent family councils. Last year we discussed buying a car. My husband and children and I talked over the type to get, size, and other matters . . ."

It appears that the discussion of decisions play a central role in making for development, equilibrium, or frustration in modern marriage.

FAMILY DECISIONS

In our modern family life, two of the most crucial decisions are whether to get married, and whether your partner is the right one. Then usually comes the decision on who will handle the money. Another major decision in family life is "shelter"; shall the newly married couple rent, buy, or build. A new development has entered on the Canadian scene since World War II. The family has to decide whether the wife should get a job and supplement the present family income. The increase in married women into the labour force would tend to substantiate that the decision for the woman to work is being made in many Canadian households.

When children come into the scene, new decisions have to be made. Expenses, training, disciplining, and the many other facets of child care cause situations in which major and minor decisions have to be made. These are just a few samples of the many family decisions which are made by husband and wife.

DECISION MAKING STUDY

In order to find out how decisions are made by the families of today, a study was undertaken by the author, of 120 couples. A long questionnnaire was given to the husband and wife of each couple, and they were asked to fill them out separately. Interviews and some tape recordings supplemented the information obtained from the questionnaires.

The characteristics of the couples in the study were that all of them lived in urban areas, had been married only once, were born on this continent, and had attended college (not necessarily graduated). An effort was made to obtain couples of different age ranges, so that we could compare how decision making patterns differ at various stages of married life. This was done by using the concept of the FAMILY LIFE CYCLE.

THE FAMILY LIFE CYCLE

The family life cycle begins with the marriage. The family develops as the husband and wife assume the traditional roles as father and mother with the coming of the first child. As successive children are born, the family enlarges its roles, to bring in the additional children in the family group. Each additional member of the family brings a significant reorganization of family living.

As the children grow older, their parents are also growing older, changing in their needs and desires, their hopes and expectations, as well as their responses to the demands and pressures of growing children. Concurrently, the children are constantly changing in their relationships to their parents, brothers and sisters, and other relatives.

The big, bustling years when the family life runs at a hectic pace eventually gives way to the long, slow-moving years of the "empty nest", when the middle aged parents face the later half of their marriage as a pair, similar to the beginning of the family life cycle.

Each family grows through the years in its own particular way. On the other hand, all families will pass through the stages of the family life cycle. The following table shows the six stages of the family life cycle used in the study.

In each of the stages of the family life cycle, couples were questioned about their decision making pattern, and then the six groups were compared to find the changes at different levels of married life.

What did we find? We will discuss each stage of the family life cycle.

SIX STAGES IN THE FAMILY LIFE CYCLE			
	Stage	Oldest Age of Child	No. of Years Married
I	Beginning families	no children	2
II	Child bearing families	up to 3 years	2-5
III	Families with pre-school children	3-6 years	5-10
IV	Families with school children	6-13 years	10-15
V	Families with teenagers	13-20 years	15-25
VI	Families as launching centres	20-27 years	25 plus

STAGE 1: BEGINNING FAMILIES

It is in this stage where one finds most joint decision making, the highest amount of participation in decision making discussions, the most satisfaction in the areas of decision making used in the study, and the largest amount of consultation in decision making. One can attribute this phenomenon to the fact that the beginning family stage is one in which the men and women are using the first two years of their married life as a period of "finding out about each other". There seems to be an unusual amount of emphasis on "considering the person" and of doing things together. It appears that it is in this stage that the couples share most of their decisions, be they minute and picayune, or large and important. It seems to be important to "agree" with the other spouse, and not to have too many differences.

A 21-year-old newly-wed woman summed up this stage by saying

> ... we seem to be deciding things together all the time, such as what to buy at the supermarket, the kind of drapes to get for the apartment, what friends to invite, and what kind of a car to purchase ... when John comes home from work, we sit down and talk about the day's activities ... I tell him what happened in my teaching

job, and he relates events at his engineering firm ... it's fun to do things like this ... it helps us in our marriage.

In a popular sense this stage can be compared to a boxing bout. At the beginning of a boxing match there is usually the "sparring period", during which the two boxers appear to jab at each other, always very careful not to give away any of their "secret punches". During this sparring they observe each other, and begin to watch their opponent's techniques, and strong and weak points. They move back and forward, trying out various boxing rules and regulations to prepare for the rest of the bout which might last for ten or more rounds.

The emphasis on doing things jointly, such as decision making and other life patterns, is strongly evident in this period, although we have had lately a great surge toward the idea of "togetherness" for the whole family life cycle. One can also assume that it is in this period that the spouses begin to discover the other person's patterns of decision making, patterns of communication, and needs of both psychological and physical nature. There is a lot of catering to the other person. These findings would thus go along with the popular view that the beginning family period is the most "ideal" stage of married life. However, one can look at it in a different light. The transition from bachelorhood and spinsterhood into matrimony brings with it many adjustments and role changes which have to be worked out in mutual discussion, mutual decision making, and a general sharing of views. This "discovery" stage is one in which each spouse begins to learn the pattern of life of the other spouse. In this stage, it is possible to assume that the roles in decision making are solidified and these roles are then kept for the rest of the family life cycle.

STAGE II: CHILD BEARING FAMILIES

Typically, it is during the second year of marriage that the family shifts into this stage. The marriage relationship is subtly and frequently dramatically changed when the first baby arrives, with its own demands. The new roles of father and mother are added to those of husband and wife. Most of the decisions now focus on the new arrival. One of the decisions is the extra financial costs which have to be met and this may result in the husband taking on extra work to supplement his present income. On the other hand, many couples begin to lower their standard of living, and to shift some of the previous expenses to the day by day costs of the baby. Sometimes the couple loses its closeness. At night, mother may be just "too tired" to do things with father, and it is quite possible that their normal sex life diminishes after the birth of the first child. Often the valid excuse is, "I'm just so beat by the time we go to bed, that I just want to snatch some shut-eye, before baby wakes up again."

We found that in our study it appeared that husbands and wives shared child rearing decisions, and also actually shared the baby's care. This defies the traditional pattern of mother being the sole person who looks after the infant, while father brings home the money. A father commented,

I went to pre-natal classes with my wife, and believe it or not, when we brought our baby home, I became an expert in diapering and bathing. At night and on weekends, I help with the baby. It relieves my wife from some of the necessary duties. I must confess I rather enjoy looking after the baby. . . .

There is nothing feminine about a man helping with the baby, and the often heard statement that "I may hurt the baby, I am so rough" is really not applicable to most men.

It is important in this stage not to fall into the pattern of focusing all the attention on the baby and neglecting the husband-wife relationship, because it may be a beginning of distance between the spouses, which widens as the marriage develops.

The wife has to try and pay attention to her husband, and he in turn has to be aware of the strenuous daily routine which the new mother has to follow. The house cannot always be very neat and tidy, and supper may be late. Mother does not "lie down on the job," but has to meet the immediate needs of the helpless infant. As the baby grows a little older, the couple can resume their social life to a limited degree, by allowing a baby sitter to look after the infant, while they attend a party or a play. A 24-year-old mother states:

John and I did not go out for three months after our baby was born. We felt cooped up and blamed our baby for keeping us at home. We were tired of watching T.V., and our friends urged us to go out. Finally it got to the point where we had to go out. I cannot tell you what a difference it made to our relationship. It was like "old times." We are planning to do this regularly now.

A new baby does not mean an end to social life, and it is important to have a change in routine.

STAGE III: FAMILIES WITH PRE-SCHOOL CHILDREN

The children are growing up, and more and more time is spent on child rearing. Decisions have to be made. Should we send Bob to nursery school? Should we have another child? Do we need larger quarters? Should we buy a house? This stage is usually illustrated by the family who has a three-year-old, and is expecting or have just had their second child. Thus they have to watch the growth of the pre-schooler, while looking after an infant with his/her own needs. Responsibilities in the home increase, more money is needed, and space is inadequate. The mother may especially become completely absorbed in keeping the house running and looking after the children.

It seems as if I go from diapers to picking up Joan's toys, which only a three-year-old can throw all around, a young mother said. The baby has colic right now, and at night when he wakes up, our three-year-old also wakes up. My husband comes home from work and expects the house to be clean and neat . . . he does not re- alize that I have a full-time job on my hands right here at home. I have be- come a slave to my children. . . .

Husband and wife may be moving slowly away from each other, and each appears to have found different major interests. He has his work, and mother has the children. A husband ruefully remarked,

My wife has been sloppy. She runs all day after the kids and worries need- lessly. She uses Dr. Spock as her Bible, and every time there is some-

thing wrong with one of our children, she has to find it in his book, and if she does not find it, she immediately bothers our doctor. We used to have so much fun together; all her former charm and "sexiness" seems to have gone. I feel at times like staying late at work, just so that I do not have to come into the house. . . .

Again we find a misunderstanding of each other's roles and functions. There also seems to be a loss of communication. Husband and wife do not talk things out, but let things go, which may result in bringing them emotionally apart. This misunderstanding of each other's role is illustrated by the personal example of when I had to look after our two-month-old son for a day. I was exhausted, and was looking with great anxiety towards the return of my wife, to take over the tir- ing routine which a young infant needs. I feel that I will never again state that "mothers have it easy, all they do is stay home and look after kids."

Co-operation is one of the pillars of this stage. Love of husband and wife is an- other element in keeping husband-wife relationships on an even keel. Love has been defined in so many ways, and each couple has its way of showing love. It en- compasses the wide range from caring about each other, to a normal sexual rela- tionship; from doing things together to celebration of anniversaries; and from recognizing that marriage is not only for children, but for the warm and intimate relationship which can only develop be- tween husband and wife as they grow to- gether in marriage.

STAGE IV: FAMILIES WITH SCHOOL CHILDREN

This stage begins with a feeling of joy and sorrow. A housewife of 35 declares,

It's funny. I waited anxiously for my children to begin school so that I would have more time. Now that they have begun school, I miss them, and am looking for something to keep me occupied. I am planning to take on some part-time work. I used to be a very good secretary. . . .

It is during this stage the husbands are "moving up the ladder" in their jobs, and this requires more of their time for the good of the Company. The slogan "Produce or Perish" is always in the uppermind of eager young men. A husband states, "I have to put in more time at work, so that I will be noticed and promoted. When I get home, it is usually late, and I have work from the office. I know it is a 'rat race,' but what can I do?"

Decisions now centre around discipline problems of the children, T.V. watching time, budgeting for vacations, and frequently a move to another neighbourhood. We found here a beginning of a division of labour in husband-wife decision making. The husband appears to make decisions which involve expenditure of money, such as car purchasing, purchasing of large appliances, and payment of bills. The wife has moved into the area of household decisions almost completely, and rarely consults her husband in this area.

STAGE V: FAMILIES WITH TEENAGERS

This is the stage in which the least satisfaction, the least joint efforts and the least consultation in decision making is found. A close look at this stage of the family cycle will reveal the fact that it is at this time that the men are usually at the height of their working form, they have usually reached a certain plateau in the field of business or in their professional careers, and are busy concentrating a lot of their time and energy on their work. This period is also characterized in our culture by an increase in community activities, and both men and women are active in various community groups. The teenagers at the same time live their own lives and are in and out of the home; they are beginning to make a lot of their own decisions, and are beginning to feel that their parents are "old fashioned" and cannot understand them in their day to day life. It is possible that this stage can be characterized a "busyness" stage in which each member of the family has his or her interests, and the "twains do not meet". The institutions and agencies of the community have taken on much of the former home activities, and are pulling the family members in all directions. One hears often the phrase "there is so little time to do things as a family." A business junior executive comments:

I have to produce in order to get on top . . . social functions are part of my job, and I join communal organizations to meet business contacts. I am rarely home nights. My wife belongs to social agency boards, and works part-time at the Red Cross. Bob, age 14, is at an age when he spends more time with his friends than at home. Jane, age 16, has a steady boyfriend who keeps her occupied. Our home is a place to rest up, before we move to the next activity or meeting. . . .

One must consider also that by this time, the marriage has progressed for about 15-20 years, and the roles have been more or less solidified, and the decision making pattern has been worked out, either verbally or by tacit understanding, that each spouse has the responsibility for certain areas of decision making. A housewife added her comments:

We used to tell each other things, and I remember that at night we would lie in bed and talk into the small hours of the morning. It was a joy to share our experiences, joys and sorrows.

Now we see each other so little, and have so little to say. Something wonderful seems to have gone out of our marriage.

Loss of communication was one of the factors which emerged from the husband-wife relationship during this stage. Decisions were being made on an individual basis, with little consultation. It is important again not to fall apart, but to remember that the husband-wife relationship needs nurturing, care, love and consideration in the same way as care of children and attention to the job in the office.

STAGE VI: THE LAUNCHING PERIOD

An interesting fact about this period of the family life cycle emerged in this study. There appeared a return to some of the "joint" decision making patterns, and the high amount of satisfaction and consultation in decision making items. This was similar to Stage I. It was quite noticeable when one considered that in Stage V, the low point of the cycle emerged.

In our culture, this stage has been characterized by the terms "lonely," "retired" and "new beginning." It is in the launching stage that the spouses find themselves again in a similar position as in the beginning stage. Many men are looking forward to retirement. This may not be a good prospect for many of them, but due to our emphasis on "youth," they are forced to retire. The women have by this time involved themselves quite actively in community affairs and find that suddenly their children, whom they had considered as "babies" for many years, have left and have begun their own families. The shouting of the vibrant teenagers has stopped, the arguments are silenced, and the table is set again for two. A 50-year-old wife reminisces.

I look around me, and I see an empty house. It seems to me it is like the beginning of our marriage 30 years ago, just the two of us. So much has happened since. I wish that we can now take the promised vacation—my children live about 1500 km away, and call once in a while. I keep active in organizational work, but I miss my children. It seems as if a bird flew out of a nest. It is not easy for a mother to see her children leave home. . . .

The spouses have a choice. One is to begin to appreciate each other again, and to "do things" together again. Taking trips and going out much more, there is the possibility that they have more time, and they begin to do things about which they always had been talking, but did not do anything.

In our mobile society, there is the chance that the children live thousands of kilometres away, and thus even as "grandparents," they have little to do. It is possible that it is in this stage that the spouses begin to do many more things together, and there occurs a re-orientation and appreciation of each other.

This stage does not have to be a sad one. Many interests and plans can be carried out as two people, husband and wife. Life can be enjoyed to the fullest, and with our jet planes, any part of the globe can be visited within hours. It is a stage not for "reminiscing" but for effort to solidify the husband-wife relationship and to enjoy each other's company. It is a new beginning, not an old ending.

CONCLUSION

There are some central themes running through the family life cycle in respect to decision making. The first is that it appears as if we have a semi-curvular trend in decision making, which ranges from a great deal of joint decision making in the first two stages of the family cycle, to a low ebb of joint decision making in the families with teenage children. Then appears a renewal of joint consulation and decision making in the launching stage. The second is that husband and wife seem to participate quite actively in child rearing and thus this may be a changing trend from the traditional patterns of child upbringing. The third is that there appeared a division of labour in decision making functions, which supports the popular view that "the wife should tend to the household business" and the husband "should not meddle with the household duties but should look after money matters."

It seemed that as children came on the scene, there was a tendency to reduce the closeness of the husband-wife relationship, and to find that slowly the spouses were drawing apart, and the focus of attention became the children. One gets the feeling that the popular conception of "togetherness" is just a myth which has been promoted by high powered advertising agencies, and which has been great material for satirical cartoons. There is little "togetherness" and much "dispersion" with each member of the family moving in different directions, with different goals, objectives and interests. What we need to do is to stand still and ask where are we running—is it necessary to take part in so many community activities? We hear so little of family gatherings, family picnics, family games. Why not return to some of these family-centered activities?

Dr. Aaron Rutledge, past President of the National Council on Family Relations, has stated that the missing ingredient in present day marriage is "nearness." He has defined it as closeness; the absence of loneliness and of isolation. He points out that "nearness provides emotional-social-spiritual-physical nourishment for the growth, maintenance and smooth functioning of an individual." The family of today seems to have forgotten this important point.

Decision making is a daily activity of husband and wife, and gives a good indication of their relationship in the family cycle. We need to pay more attention to family life and the constant changes in our modern age which affect the family members in their day by day living.

FILMS

David and Hazel: A Story of Communication, NFB, 28 minutes, black/white, 1963.
   The husband makes all the decisions in this family. A major problem arises and tensions develop.

AUDIOTAPES

Available from CBC Learning Systems, Box 500, Station A, Toronto, M5W 1E6.
The Conflicts Between Mothers and Daughters
   Whereas many people, particularly men, think that there's no real conflict between mothers and daughters, the program reveals that there are actually many conflicts. There remain very traditional mothers, but there are others who try to communicate with their daughters vis-à-vis today's social context. Cat. No. 313L: one hour.

QUESTIONS, ACTIVITIES AND PROJECTS

1. *Have the class divide into 6 groups. Each group will deal with one of the 6 life cycles of the family and complete the following:*
   a) *From the chapter, identify the main family tasks of the particular life cycle stage. Beside each task, identify the feelings of both the parents and children that may relate to the task.*
   b) *Research and identify the communication skills that would assist family members in dealing with their feelings during their particular life cycle stage.*
   c) *Identify several family problems that occur during this life cycle stage.*
2. *Choose one family problem that you have identified in (c) above. Use the steps to problem solving which follow to work through a possible solution.*
   (i) *describe and define the problem—using who, what, where, when, why and how questions*
   (ii) *brainstorm possible solutions*
   (iii) *choose a solution*
   (iv) *apply a solution*
   (v) *evaluate the results*
   Share your experiences with the large group.

14
The ABC's of Adolescent Sexuality

Action, especially community action. Talking, slogans, conferences and reports all serve their own purpose but it is time for communities to take positive action insofar as adolescent sexuality is concerned.

Basic Issues underlie the complex topic of adolescent sexuality. We cannot discuss or examine adolescent sexuality in a community without examining these factors. They include the political system, religious beliefs, culture and economy. A thoughtful examination of these basic issues will clarify our view of the sexual politics in our communities.

Control. What type of control should our communities have over sexual behaviour? There exists in the world today a wide range of methods of control. In China there is political, almost total control over the sexuality of adolescents, whereas, in Sweden the attitude is one of laissez-faire.

Double Standard. This double standard makes adolescent women responsible for their actions while adolescent men are not. Instead of the time-worn double standard, we must establish a new standard which should be "equality for all human beings."

Education and in this context, I mean primarily sex education. I do not believe we have really considered many of the practical questions that surround the introduction of sex education into our communities. How should we start? Who should teach sex education? What approaches are best for each individual community? What information should we transmit? to whom?

One of the most important things we have to remember is that each community has different values—different norms. A textbook or training material appropriate for one community may be wholly inappropriate for another.

Father. Let's not leave him out of any discussion that concerns adolescent fertility. We traditionally ignore the father—discussions of his conduct are usually negative and often jocular. I consider adolescent fertility a family affair; babies born out of wedlock are born to two people, a mother and a father. The shadow of this family is the unmarried father. It is time we included him; in a positive, not a punitive way. We must remember he too has feelings and emotions, he too is an adolescent. The experience of fatherhood has, without a doubt, affected him and he may need help.

Grownups or adults. I see grownups as models, not as judges; as examples, not as hypocrites. The old saying, "Do as I say, not as I do" seems to express the situation prevalent in many parts of the world. We should not be surprised that through their actions youngsters reply, "You do not act as you advise, why should I act as you tell me to?" It is time that we, as adults who represent the community, look within ourselves and examine what kind of examples we are setting.

Health. No one would argue the fact that we need good physical and mental health services but sometimes I feel we're so busy building clinics and hospitals that we neglect some of the novel approaches to health care. There is, for example, a whole paramedical approach to working with adolescents that has yet to be explored in many places. There simply are not enough trained doctors in the world to do all the work that is necessary—we can't leave it all up to them. Nor do doctors want to provide some of the health and quasi-medical services which adolescents need; our communities must be ready to provide them via paramedical workers.

Involvement, especially community involvement, with adolescents. Professionals, volunteers, institutions, doctors, teachers, social workers, religious groups, social groups and cultural groups should integrate their work rather than follow a piecemeal approach to health care. Right now, one person is interested in the adolescent's head, another is interested in his/her mouth, diet, etc. There is no one person who sits down and talks with a young man or young woman as a complete person—a whole being.

Justice. Not punitive, but therapeutic justice. Many laws, regulations of social agencies and community policies are punitive and very often they are entirely unenforceable. We need to reexamine them considering both community values and justice for the affected adolescent.

Kindness. It is time for us to begin treating all adolescents with kindness. They are worthwhile human beings who need love. We should stop rejecting them just because their behaviour sometimes clashes with the adult's "ideal." They need understanding, not accusations; they need warmth, not coldness; they need to be included, not isolated from our communities.

Limits. Are there no limits to the acceptable sexual behaviour of adolescents within a community? We have to reintroduce one small word into our communal vocabularies; that word is NO. Sometimes adults appear to want to leave all decisions about sex up to adolescents themselves. The attitude says, "do as you choose." But there are times when adults should say "NO." Most people who have worked with children know that even the most independent adolescent does want some kind of limits set on his/her behaviour. In many places we are moving towards a situation where adolescents do not know what the limits on their behaviour are or if any limits exist at all.

Media. In spite of the fact that there are universal complaints concerning the misuse of television, radio and newspapers there are positive ways we could use the media for adolescent education. Sensitive, well researched, objective programming could be used to educate not only adolescents, but also their parents, about sexuality and fertility.

National Goals. Does our national government support communities who are trying to help adolescents or are we working in a vacuum? For example, a government may announce a sex education policy, but if there is no implementation procedure included with this policy then what is its use?

Openness. We must open our minds to new ideas. We need not blindly accept every new idea, but let's examine them each for their own value. For example, I have found that I, who live in an "industrialized country" can learn a lot from the work being done with adolescents in the so-called "non-industrialized countries." There is much to learn from other countries and from the efforts of other communities in our own country.

Parents. We must get parents involved in our work with adolescents. This is absolutely essential but how should we go about doing this? What's the purpose of getting them involved? We need to help parents for their own sake, as well as for the sake of their adolescent children. Adolescent sexuality and adolescent pregnancy (even the prospect of it) is a major source of anxiety, depression, frustration and general social and psychological maladjustment for parents. Often they need help as much as (or more than) their own teen-age child.

Quality of Life. What is the "quality of life" in our communities? Is there respect for human beings? Do people care for each other? Is the individual adolescent considered and respected as a human being? Is there affection and love?

Research. Certainly no one would deny that research is a vital part of our health care system. There are many areas we should study that deal with adolescent sexuality. Let's look at the different adolescents in our communities. What makes them different? What are their individual and collective beliefs? What do they think about the quality of life in their community? What do they believe the quality of life should be? What are the criteria for their decisions?

We have to remember that research should not be conducted for the sake of research alone. Our goal must be to help communities fulfill their responsibilities to their adolescent citizens.

Services. It is possible to overservice a community. Opening service areas is fairly easy. The problem is often closing them down once there are vested interests opposing any change. As a result, we now have many service units which overlap and duplicate each other. Yes, we do need services, but let's examine the type, our needs and the costs.

Truth. Can we have a true dialogue between adults and adolescents without lies, sham and hypocrisy? What is the "truth" in human sexuality?

Underlying Causes of Pregnancy. This can include boredom, poverty, unemployment, a difficult home life, misinformation about sexuality and the effects of the community's morality on the lives of its adolescents.

Values. Whose values? Should I impose my generation's values on the adolescent? What values do adolescents have? It's all very nice to talk about throwing out old values, but what worries me is that we have to substitute new values. It's too easy to reject this or that basic community value without substituting anything in its place. We cannot live in a valueless society. Yes, adolescents are proposing a few warmed-over old values—what they call new values are really nothing more than old values with a new accent. We now have to consider, at the community level, whether we (or the adolescents themselves, when they become older) would want these "new values" to be a permanent part of our community culture. Sexual values do not exist in a vacuum, they must be consistent with other moral, religious, psychological and social values.

Women and in this case, especially adolescent women. It's time we began to recognize their rights; their sexual rights and their expectations. We must recognize that they have within them the entire spectrum of adult needs, that they want to, and must be encouraged to participate with us as equals.

X-perimental. We need experimental programs. We need innovative programs that do not cost a lot of money but which are imaginative. There are some very beautiful program ideas that should be tried. We could for example, utilize the arts, theatre, literature—the whole creative realm is open to us.

Youth. Do we want to dominate our adolescents? Do we want to work against them, for them or with them? Obviously working with them can be our only fruitful alternative. It is very likely that this is the first time in history where adults and adolescents have had the opportunity to work together as two generations, rather than continuing the intergenerational conflicts of the past. Both generations should seek co-operation, not authoritarianism; dialogue, not monologue; self-help, not external aid; and understanding, not deaf ears and unresponsiveness.

Zip is North American slang suggesting zest, a high morale and readiness. We must become front-line soldiers in our communities in the fight to liberate adolescents and this fight includes their sexual liberation. It takes great energy, fortitude and courage to take this stand. Right now there are a few pioneers who are fighting an almost lone battle on the national level. We need more people and we need this kind of energy and spirit at the community level.

When the words "sex," "adolescence" and "fertility" are mentioned together in local discussion, there should be leaders who will stand up and speak their mind. It is very difficult to stand on a podium and shout aloud to your neighbours, "We need change." Such people are often accused of all kinds of subtle and not-so-subtle motives, nevertheless this is the kind of involvement and community action that we need and we must work towards.

READINGS

Schlesinger, Benjamin, ed. *Human Sexuality in Canada.* Toronto: University of Toronto Press, 1977.
  A collection of 25 articles dealing with selected issues in human sexuality in Canada.
_____. (ed.) *Family Planning in Canada: A Source Book.* Toronto: University of Toronto Press, 1974.
  Thirty-three articles discuss various aspects of family planning in Canada.

QUESTIONS, ACTIVITIES AND PROJECTS

1. Analyze a current song that focuses on adolescent love. What messages does the song project for adolescent sexual behaviour.
2. Although some segments of society feel that a major change in sexual standards has come about in the past 15 years, there are other groups that exert strong pressures against changes in traditional sexual standards. Identify institutions or groups that support the "new morality" and those that support traditional standards. Write a brief rationale for the beliefs of each of these institutions.
3. Discuss the factors that have contributed to the present standards of sexual morality.

15
Singlehood

Rubin Todres

INTRODUCTION

The position of "bachelor" and "spinster" have been with us for as long as the institution of marriage and family, yet little serious attention has been focused upon the characteristics of singlehood, and on how males and females regard their single status.

It is unfortunate that so little analysis of singlehood has been done, since bachelors and spinsters make up approximately 2% of the population in Canada and the United States. For this discussion, bachelors and spinsters are identified as being over the age of 35 and never married. According to 1976 Census data, there were 356 400 spinsters and 375 760 bachelors in Canada[1] and 2 357 000 single males and 2 363 000 single females in the United States.[2]

This study is an attempt to discover more about these groups, by asking such individuals directly about their lifestyles, their family and social relationships, and the experience of being single in a society where couplehood is the norm.

FINDINGS

Demographic Data (115 Singles)

The following table presents a summary of crucial demographic data for the total population of singles. Both females and

SUMMARY OF DEMOGRAPHIC DATA ON SINGLES			
Category		**Single Females**	**Single Males**
AGE		Average = 43	Average = 43.5
EDUCATION	high school or less	30%	28%
	some college	23%	31%
	college degree	48%	34%
OCCUPATION	managerial/professional	58%	no pattern
	office workers	24%	
INCOME	$ 0—$ 6 000	2%	0%
	$ 6 001— 12 000	34%	20%
	$12 001— 18 000	35%	44%
	$18 002 +	22%	36%
	Average Income	$13 000	$19 000
RELIGION	Protestant/Anglican	71%	55%
	Roman Catholic	17%	35%
	Jewish	4%	7%
	Number of Respondents	86	29

males in this study are highly educated, have a higher than average salary and appear to be primarily a middle and upper class white grouping.

Use of Recreational Time

Contrary to public belief that the life of the single is preoccupied with the desire to find a suitable marriage partner, both men and women reported that a majority of their spare time was spent on hobbies (reading, listening to music, etc.), which are solitary activities. Social activities came next, with single males devoting an average of 6 hours a week and single women 9 hours a week to this activity. In addition, less time per week was devoted to participation in clubs or sports.

Family Interaction and Friendship Patterns

Approximately 55% of both men and women reported contacting their parents twice a month or more. Generally they felt that contact with parents was either initiated by them or that both parties shared equally in initiating contact.

It was interesting to note that 24% of the single women described their contact with their parents as infrequent while only 7% of the bachelors reported the same answer. Half of the single women who described their contact with parents as infrequent stated that this was due to the unsatisfactory nature of the relationship with their parents.

In both sub-groups, a great majority (women 94%, men 90%) were not living with their parents at the time of the interview. Single men had left home at an average age of 20.5 years, while the comparable figure for single women was 21 years. Both groups stated that they primarily left home to establish their independence, to attend school or to seek employment. It is perhaps significant to note that 14% of the single females stated they left home to escape an unhappy family situation while only 7% of bachelors left home for that reason. It is possible that single women tend to be more candid about unhappy family relationships than single men. However, it is also possible that single men are more likely than single women to leave their homes as a matter of course, to establish their independence. Both groups reported that approximately one-third of their parents accepted their single status while another one-third of the parents were anxious that they marry.

Approximately one-half of the single men reported that most of their close friends were married, and 17% stated that their friends were equally divided between married and singles. This contrasted with the single women, who suggested that for one-half of them, their primary friends were both married and single, while 37% reported having an equal distribution of men and women friends. Both groups suggested that they had trouble maintaining friendships with married people as they were seen as a threat to the marriage (generally by the friend's spouse), or because their life style was somewhat incompatible with the life style of married people.

Attitudes

The last section of the survey focused on the attitudes of singles toward their single status. Two-thirds of both groups felt that society is geared to the concerns of the married rather than the concerns of singles. Single females felt discriminated against in the areas of travel and taxation: 57% felt that singles are unfairly taxed; 75% felt it was more expensive for single women to travel alone. Single men, agreed that tax laws were unjust and added that they were bothered by the social view that single persons are less stable and responsible than married people.

The respondents were asked to state the advantages and disadvantages of single life. Loneliness was listed by thirty-six women (42%) as the major disadvantage of being single; limited social life and not living in a married state were also mentioned as less frequent disadvantages of single life. Similar findings were reported by the bachelor group. About 75% believed that their singlehood had deprived them of intimacy experienced in marital and family relationship. While many of the bachelors admitted to feelings of loneliness, many suggested that they did not see themselves as differing greatly from married people in this respect.

Freedom was listed by seventy-seven women (90%) as the major advantage of being single; financial security and more free time were also mentioned as advantages of the single life. This view was echoed by the bachelor group.

Attention was focused on the reasons why the respondents were not married and whether they would marry in the future. Forty-four of the women (51%) who gave their reason for being single stated that they had not met the right men. The bachelor group agreed that this was the situation but a number added that they had previously feared the responsibility of marriage and family life.

Eighty women in the study (93%) claimed that they had had the opportunity to marry previously but the major factor which prevented this event was that they were not ready at that time for marriage. This corresponds closely to the male situation, where 93% said that they had the opportunity to marry but were either emotionally unprepared or that the prospective mate had not met their expectations. Finally, a significant majority (83% of the males and 60% of the females) expressed a desire to marry now if a suitable opportunity arose. The main reasons given were the wish for companionship within an intimate relationship and the wish for a family and emotional readiness to make such commitments.

When asked to compare the happiness of single and married men and single and married women, a significantly greater number of the male respondents felt that the married of both sexes are happier. Although the bachelors felt that single men are discriminated against, they perceived single women as suffering an even greater social stigma. However, it would appear from our study that single women feel less discrimination than the bachelors who, unlike the women, felt discriminated against in the areas of employment. They also experienced a fair amount of pressure from their married friends to marry.

Finally, 43% of the women felt that the Women's Liberation Movement changed the way they felt about themselves as single women. They claimed that the movement had provided support and had heightened their awareness as women.

SUMMARY AND CONCLUSIONS

This study is only an initial attempt at understanding the phenomenon of "singlehood." Because the singles volunteered to take part in this study, it is questionable whether the one hundred and fifteen volunteers are necessarily representative of other single men and women in Canada. It is quite possible that others—those who did not feel comfortable enough to discuss their situations—or those who did not hear of the study might have provided entirely different data. However, this study does reveal a great deal about the lifestyles of a particular group of one hundred and fifteen single people whose answers point out some similarities and shared concerns which deserve closer scrutiny.

Contrary to the stereotype of the single

person as isolated, dissatisfied and a victim of circumstance, the singles in this study experience personal fulfillment through varied friendships, careers, economic status and leisure time activities. The single status of the respondents does not seem to prevent them from getting personal satisfaction in areas other than marriage and the family. Some of the characteristics of the men and women are:

1. The fact that a large proportion of the respondents attended college, belonged to the managerial/professional job category and reported a substantially high income. These facts suggest success in their careers and financial stability. These results are consistent with previous research findings indicating high socio-economic status among singles.

2. The singles in the study appeared to be very stable and independent. Stability was indicated by the appearance of very steady residential and social patterns. Not only did most of the singles live alone, challenging the myth that singles live with their families, but both groups reported a mixture of married and single friends, both male and female. In addition, they engaged in an active social and recreational life with these friends.

3. The singles were generally ambivalent toward marriage and toward their single status. While a very high proportion of both groups expressed a willingness to marry at this point in time, should a suitable opportunity arise, most of the respondents cited more positive than negative attributes of singlehood. There were only a few confirmed singles, despite the fact that most of the respondents seemed to have adapted to living alone quite successfully.

4. The study confirmed that our society is oriented towards marriage and couplehood and discriminates against people who are single. Not only were singles hampered in job advancement (more so for bachelors) but they felt that the tax laws discriminated against them financially. In addition, to discrimination, there is some pressure from their married friends and immediate families to get married. While maintaining friendships with married friends was generally considered beneficial, most singles experienced some discomfort in this area.

5. Finally, while the media convey the image of the single as a swinger or a recluse, it appears that this stereotype is very superficial and not necessarily valid. It appears from our study, that there may in fact be three sub-types of singles. The first sub-type is characterized by a single person who has few friends, minimal contact with family, spends most of his (her) time alone and has minimal social interaction. A second sub-type is represented by the single person who wishes to remain unmarried, treasures her (his) independence and yet seems to have a fairly adequate social interaction pattern. Both of these sub-types seem to be the exception rather than the rule. Finally, the largest sub-type is characterized by the single person who has stable and frequent social interaction, treasures his (her) independence yet would marry now if the opportunity arose.

REFERENCES

1. *Marital Status by Age,* 1976 Census.
2. *Statistical Abstract of the U.S., 1977* (98th edition). Washington, D.C.

READINGS

Adams, Margaret, *Single Blessedness.* New York: Penguin Books, 1978.
    A study of the single state.

QUESTIONS, ACTIVITIES AND PROJECTS

1. *Before reading the chapter write down the words that you associate with the terms "spinster" and "bachelor" on small cards or pieces of paper. Collect the cards or paper and develop a list of words written by the class for each term.*

   a) *Compare the images associated with each term.*

   b) *Analyze the societal factors that contributed to stereotyped images of "spinster" and "bachelor."*

2. *Complete one of the following statements: "I think that I would choose to remain single because _____."*

   "I think that I would choose not to remain single because _____."

16
Canada's Working Women

STATISTICS AND TRENDS

The latest statistics and trends related to Canada's working women were released in 1977 and cover the 1975 period. The highlights of this survey were:

—In 1975, there were 3 697 000 women in a total labour force of 10 060 000 persons, thus representing 36.7% of the Canadian labour force.

—The female labour force in 1975 showed a percentage increase of 78.9% compared with the female labour force in 1965; this meant an increase of 1 631 000 women in the labour force in that decade.

—In 1975, there were 8 359 000 women in the population aged 15 years and over. The female labour force in 1975 constituted 44.2% of the female population aged 15 years and over, compared with 31.3% in 1965.

—In 1975, there were 2 204 000 married women in the female labour force, constituting 59.6% of the female labour force.

—In 1975, there were 5 302 000 married women in the total population aged 15 years and over of whom 2 204 000 were in the labour force, representing 41.6% of married women in the population.

—In 1975, 82.0% of all single women in the population aged 25 to 54 were in the labour force; 46.2% of all married women aged 25 to 54 in the population were also in the labour force.

—In 1975, 20.3% of all employed women worked part-time; the comparable percentage for men was 5.1%.

—In 1975, there were 323 000 women employed in medicine and health occupations, representing 75.6% of all persons so employed. There were also 1 228 000 women employed in clerical occupations representing 74.9% of all persons employed in such occupations.

—In 1975, 1.7% of women in the full-time employed labour force were absent from work, because of illness, for the whole of a particular week; the percentage of men in the full-time employed labour force who were absent from work because of illness for the whole of a particular week was 1.7%.

WAGES FOR WORKING WOMEN

We will only present a selected sample of wages for women compared to wages for men in Canada[1] to illustrate the fact that women are still paid less for the same job. However, statistics do show that the gap is narrowing.

—In 1974, the average annual earnings of women employed in sales occupations were $5 638 compared with $12 063 for men. This represents a percentage difference of 114.0%. In clerical occupations women's average annual earnings were $6 253, compared with $9 661 for

[1] Source: *Women in the Labour Force: Facts and Figures. 1976 Edition. Part II Earnings of Women and Men.*

men. The earnings of men exceeded those of women by 54.5%.

—The average annual earnings of men employees in managerial occupations increased by $6 684 from 1969 to 1974 compared with $4 106 for women. For men employees in professional occupations, the average annual earnings increased $4 148 from 1969 to 1974 compared with $3 114 for women.

—The median annual salaries of full professors were $25 250 for women and $27 500 for men. The salaries of men exceeded those of women by 23.0%. In the health professions and occupations the median annual salaries of men exceeded those of women by 5%. (This category excludes doctors and nurses. It includes medical lab technicians, psychiatric attendants, and cooks.) In education, the median salaries of men teachers exceeded those of women by 14.6%.

EMPLOYED MOTHERS

In examining the voluminous literature related to employed mothers the following factors have been shown to increase the probability that a mother will be employed:

—having few rather than many children

—older rather than younger children

—husband's income low rather than high

—mother's education high rather than low

—single-parent mothers more than two-parent homes, since they are the sole earners in a family

Thus we find many Canadian mothers working because they have to. In our economy, the husbands may not be able to earn enough to support their families. For those women whose husbands earn "enough" to support the family the reasons for working include a desire to provide a higher standard of living, to use the wife's earnings for vacations, tuition payments, home repairs, house purchase and other extra essentials for family living. Many women of course would want to work even if they did not need the money. It is their right to feel satisfied in the working world and use their education and training in the same way as men do. This is especially true of university trained or special vocationally trained women in Canada. They want to use their skills and keep up their training in the world of work. Many women do not find great satisfaction in homemaking. It may be a great waste for a woman who wishes to use her skills in outside employment to devote a lifetime to the care and upkeep of a single family.

Work outside the home has several obvious positive attractions. It boosts self-esteem and a sense of self-worth. These qualities may, in turn, beneficially affect children. However, some aspect of employment may in fact make a woman feel less worthy, less competent. Women are often assigned jobs far below their levels of education and skill-training. For example, women with college degrees may be offered only clerical work. The reality is that traditional women's jobs are accorded lower status; earnings are lower than those for men in equivalent jobs; many industries use women as an expendable work force; and men are given preference in hiring where qualified women are available.

Women with young children are often discriminated against because they are thought to be less responsible than men in fulfillment of job requirements, despite good evidence to the contrary.

Studies of decision making and the assumption of responsibility for the family indicate that when mothers are employed, fathers tend to take more responsibility for the day to day management of family affairs.

CHILD CARE AND HOUSEWORK*

When a wife-and-mother spends time away from the home at a paid job, the family must make some decisions about the mechanics of child care and those personal maintenance chores—laundry, food preparation, shopping for minor essentials, house-cleaning, and so on—that are traditionally the principal responsibility of adult women.

There are four different arrangements that families can make when a wife's part-time absence from the home limits the time and energy she has to fulfill the "traditional" domestic responsibilities. It should be noted that while a family may prefer one arrangement, factors such as time, money, ages and number of children, and available facilities may force the family to accept a combination of the four arrangements listed.

1. The wife and mother can herself undertake to carry out both the responsibilities of her paid job and those of domestic needs. For some men and some women, socialized to believe that house-cleaning and child-watching are the primary and sole responsibility of the wife-mother, this is the only thinkable solution.

The principal difficulties in such an arrangement are that (a) it places an enormous burden on the woman, who may feel like a "failure" when she feels tired, or when her housework does not meet some standard of attainment; (b) it leaves the woman very little time or energy for positive personal interactions with other persons in her family, both children and adults; and (c) the woman may struggle with a sense of resentment at the disparity of domestic versus economic responsibility assumed by husband and wife.

*I would like to give credit to Dr. Mary C. Howell of the Harvard Medical School in Boston for her excellent review of literature on employed mothers which appeared in *Pediatrics*, Vol. 52 (August 1973), 252-263.

2. The mother can arrange to hire some person to substitute for herself and carry out her traditional domestic responsibilities in her absence. This person may be a relative (in which case "pay" may be in the form of room and board, other personal assistance, or simply an incurred obligation), or the surrogate may be a formal employee of the family. This person, usually a woman, may live with the family, or may come to the house only when the mother is absent. The mother-substitute arrangement may be considered advantageous because the traditional family function and assumption of responsibility for domestic chores goes undisturbed. It is usually the mother's responsibility to find her substitute, to assess the substitute's acceptability as a replacement for herself and to make special adjustments when the arrangements break down. If the substitute is ill it is usually the unquestioned responsibility of the mother to be absent from her work until a replacement can be found. There is a sense, then, that family function goes on "as usual," especially if the mother substitute can be induced to fulfill her tasks in a style close to that of the mother.

3. The family can agree to "send out" some of the tasks of personal maintenance, by hiring other service agencies to perform fragments of the domestic housekeeping. Thus, laundry, ironing and other clothes-maintenance services may be purchased; cleaning firms may be hired to come to the house on a regular basis; food may be purchased already prepared, or eaten away from home and so on. In a somewhat similar fashion, children may be cared for in day-care centres or in family day-care homes. Although it should be obvious that one does not "send out" a child as one does a shirt, there is analogy in the purchase of child care from an "agency" designated to provide that service.

This arrangement has the advantage of clearly relieving the wife-mother of some of the labour of a double job, and may, depending on attitudes within the family, represent a sharing of responsibility as well. It also enables the family to arrange to have their personal needs cared for without directly exploiting another person, as can be the case in a housekeeper arrangement. The principal disadvantages are that costs are usually very high, and there may be even less guarantee that the services will be performed as the family would like them to be done.

4. Finally, the family can agree to share the responsibility for their joint and individual personal maintenance. The children of employed mothers usually participate more in household chores than do the children of homemaker mothers. Sharing of responsibility by husbands, however, varies (in part) with age of parents. Older couples are more likely to maintain the traditional role patterns. This fourth option is frequently chosen by couples who explicitly question the logic of assigning the income producing role exclusively to the male spouse, and the domestic role exclusively to the female spouse.

Thus, employment may be planned so that one parent can be home at all times when children need care; responsibility for this and personal maintenance chores may be shared or rotated among those members of the family capable of participating; and the family as a group may come to a mutual agreement about the chores essential to their sense of well-being, and the nonessential ones that can be omitted. Families who choose this option often mention as an advantage the satisfaction of not asking other persons to do their "dirty work." Participation of all able family members in caring for themselves and each other offers a sense of community and shared responsibility more commonly found in other societies than in our own. As a new and nontraditional pattern of family life, however, it goes well only

when family members can maintain a willingness to experiment, a tolerance and respect for each other's needs and a sense of humour.

We have scant information about the effects of working in paid employment on a parent's capacity to nurture his or her children. As is so often the case, we cannot readily generalize from the experience of men to the experience of women. It would be important to know whether employment significantly affects "mothering" by altering a woman's self-esteem or her energy resources or by the experience of sharing her child's care with others.

Studies of both employed and non-employed mothers permit a single broad generalization: women who enjoy their work also enjoy the role of parent and mothers who are dissatisfied with their work are more likely to be unhappy, unsure or dissatisfied with parenting. The causes of this generalization are not clear.

If work outside the home enhances a person's sense of competence, achievement and self-worth, this sense is likely to carry over to all areas of their life.

On the other hand, although paid employment may strongly enhance one mother's sense of self-esteem it may reduce that of another. She or her family may see her outside employment as somehow inappropriate; the inequality of employment opportunity for women is well known; she may be unable to provide adequate substitute care for her children. Any parent's ability to positively affect her/his children, give positive direction and provide care may be handicapped by a severely curtailed sense of self-esteem.

There is ample evidence, both from mothers and from professional advisors, that dissatisfaction with shared child-care often comes mainly from a sense of guilt caused by the surrounding society. If, on the other hand, parents feel that provision of affectionate and attentive caretakers for part of the child's day is of positive benefit to the child, their own parenting behaviour may be enhanced.

CONCLUSION

It is a fact of life that in Canada our labour force is nearly half filled by women. More and more women enter our labour force every year. At this time we really know very little about the effects on family life of full-time working mothers. On the other hand we need to support these women who in most cases have to go out and work. New approaches to the child care of working mothers will have to be developed.

READINGS

Bennet, James E. and Loewe, Peter M. *Women in Business*. Toronto: 1975, Maclean-Hunter.
Women's quest for equal opportunity in business.
Canadian Women's Educational Press. *Never Done*. Toronto: 1974.
Three centuries of women's work in Canada.
Canadian Women's Educational Press. *Women Unite*. Toronto: 1972.
An anthology of the Canadian Women's Movement.
Canadian Women's Educational Press. *Women at Work: Ontario 1850-1930*. Toronto: 1974.
Nine essays discuss working women in Ontario during the 1850-1930 period.
The Canadian Review of Sociology and Anthropology, *Women in the Canadian Social Structure*. Sepcial Issue: November 1975.
Cook, Gail C. A. ed. *Opportunity for Choice: A Goal for Women in Canada*. Ottawa: Statistics Canada, 1976.
Curtis, Jean, *Working Mothers*. New York: Doubleday, 1976.
Curtis, Jean, *Working Mothers*. New York: Doubleday, 1976.
Kieran, Sheila. *The Non-Deductible Woman*. Toronto: Macmillan, 1970.
Advice for working wives in Canada.
Kohl, Seens B. *Working Together: Women and Family in Southwestern Saskatchewan*. Toronto: Holt, Rinehart and Winston, 1976.
Nunes, Maxine and White, Deanna. *The Lace Ghetto*. Toronto: New Press, 1972.
A book about women's liberation in Canada.
Shack, Sybil. *The Two Thirds Minority*. Toronto: Faculty of Education, Guidance Centre, 1973.
An examination of women in education in Canada.
Stephenson, Marylee. (ed.) *Women in Canada*. Toronto: General Publishing 1977— revised edition.
Thirteen selections review various aspects dealing with the lives of Canadian women. Contains an excellent 1110 item bibliography.
Women in the Labour Force: Facts and Figures: Ottawa: Labour Canada. 1976 edition. Part II "Earnings of women and men."

American Studies Comparing the Satisfactions of Married Employed Women with those of Full-time Homemakers

Feld, S. "Feelings of Adjustment", in F. I. Nye and L. W. Hoffman, eds., *The Employed Mother in America*. Chicago: Rand McNally. 1965, pp. 331-353.
Howell, Mary C. "Employed Mothers and their Families", *Pediatrics*. Vol. 52, No. 2, August 1973, 252-263 (see pp. 254-255 for marital happiness).
Locke, H. J. and Mackeprang, M. "Marital Adjustment of the Employed Wife", *American Journal of Sociology*. 1949—Vol. 54, p. 536.
Nye, F. I. "Marital Interaction", (In) Nye, F. I. and Hoffman, L. W. eds. *The Employed Mother in America*. Chicago: Rand McNally, 1965, pp. 263-282.

FILMS

Women Want . . . NFB, 28 min., colour, 1975.
A look at the status of women in Canada.
They Called Us: "Les Filles de Roy", NFB, 36 min., colour, 1974.
Quebec women through history.

Working Mothers: NFB, colour, 1974-1975.

A series of 10 films to promote discussion of the issues faced by working women in Canada.

1) *And They Lived Happily Ever After,* 12 min.
   Marriage and motherhood.
2) *Extensions of the Family,* 14 min.
   A "communal" family.
3) *It's Not Enough,* 14 min.
   Why women work.
4) *Like the Trees,* 14 min.
   A Métis woman discusses her life.
5) *Luckily I need little Sleep,* 7 min.
   A mother-nurse discusses her life.
6) *Mothers are People,* 7 min.
   A widow and biologist discusses her life.
7) *Our Dear Sisters,* 14 min.
   A North American Indian woman talks about her life.
8) *They appreciate you more,* 14 min.
   Two parents who work full time in Montreal discuss their family life.
9) *Tiger in a Tight Leash,* 7 min.
   A female university professor talks about her work.
10) *Would I ever like to work,* 9 min.
   A welfare mother discusses her desire to work.

QUESTIONS, ACTIVITIES AND PROJECTS

1. *Divide the class into two groups: (i) those whose mothers worked when they were young and (ii) those whose mothers did not.*
   (a) *Compare ideas on the positive and negative effects of the employed-outside with at-home mothers on the family environment.*
   (b) *List the ways in which a mother employed outside the home copes with her multiple roles.*
   (c) *Compare the responsibilities expected of the members of a family when a mother is employed outside the home with those expected of family members when a mother is a full time homemaker.*
2. *Discuss the considerations to be made in choosing suitable arrangements for children when the mother works outside the home. If you had to choose alternate arrangements for your child, with what situation would you feel most comfortable?*
3. *It has been argued that women are better at parenting than men. Draw up a class list of the arguments in favour of and against this position. Where possible, give reasons for your point of view.*
4. *Interview a full-time working mother to discover her feelings about her work and her family.*

17
Child-Care Services In Canada

The complexities, demands and changing attitudes of contemporary life make it vital that supplementary child-care services be available to all Canadian families. Today many mothers work. Some work because their contribution to the family income is essential. Others want to continue a career. When adequate supplementary child services are available, mothers who wish to can work outside the home, continue their studies or participate in community activities.

Other mothers and fathers, whether widowed, separated or divorced, are trying to raise children alone. For these one-parent families, the need for day-care services is crucial.

Even though many mothers delay going out to work until their children are in school, their day-care problems are not solved. In order to reach their employment on time, parents often have to leave home an hour or more before school doors open. There are no adults at home during the noon hour and many elementary schools do not serve lunch or allow children to remain at school. At the end of the day, these young children are dismissed two hours or more before their parents return home. Responsible adult supervision during these hours is essential.

The increasing popularity of apartment living for city families poses another problem for children today. Small children, who may be ten stories above the street and completely out of sight and earshot, without a suitable place to play or proper supervision from mother, may be confined inside all day in order to be "safe." Concentrated housing frequently lacks facilities for those school-age children who need space and some supervision outside of school hours. Sometimes the family housing unit is too small to make young visitors welcome, even when mother is at home. Often, because of increased family mobility, small children seldom see their aunts, uncles and grandparents, and never come to know their parents' adult friends. Yet the establishment of friendships outside the family circle is an important and necessary part of growing up.

While the need to provide supplementary child-care services may seem a problem peculiar to urban families, it is often even more difficult to establish services in small towns or rural and more isolated areas.

Disadvantaged families have special problems. Although mothers may be at home during the day, they are often unable to provide adequate play activities, constructive toys or sustained interest for their children. There is growing evidence that early learning is valuable to the development of all children. Often a day-care centre or nursery school program can make up for what may be unavailable at home.

Community day-care services also provide health care for children. A medical check-up is required before children are accepted in child-care centres and trained staff often spot health needs that require medical attention, but which might otherwise be neglected until elementary school. Nutritious meals are provided at full day-care centres. Carefully planned snacks are offered during shorter programs. School menus can be made available by the centre staff to help parents plan nourishing meals in the home and set lifetime patterns of good eating habits.

Counselling is also part of a day-care service and provides a professional contact with families. A variety of family problems can receive attention in a way that is easily acceptable to parents. When more serious problems exist in family relationships, referrals can be made to other community services.

Supplementary day-care services can be very valuable for many types of handicapped children. Special programs designed for emotionally disturbed, physically handicapped or mentally retarded youngsters can help them to make the most of their abilities. And since it allows the mothers to establish a more normal household routine, the relief it gives from the constant care which these children require may be a vital factor in stabilizing the entire family.

Most families, at one time or another, need to make use of some form of supplementary child-care service. Readily available day-care services will not mean that parents will neglect their children. Good day-care services supplement what parents do for their children. Supplementary child-care services can assist parents, and at the same time enrich the lives of their children.

TYPES OF AVAILABLE PROGRAMS

What I have described so far is the need for full-time day care as one option for child care in Canada. There are other child-care programs available which range from part-time to full-time care and which meet the special needs of a range of children and the needs of particular parents during the pre-school period. Some of the typical half-day programs are:

Nursery and Kindergarten Schools: The two programs which are most familiar to Canadians are nursery and kindergarten schools. Nursery schools serve children of three and four years old and are usually under some private or voluntary auspices. Kindergarten usually refers to a program for five-year-old children. In many areas, kindergartens are a part of the school system and are publicly supported. Many public schools offer junior kindergarten programs for four-year-olds.

Play School: Play school is a program where mothers volunteer their time under the direction of paid staff to organize activities that emphasize the social development of children from two to five years old.

Montessori Schools: The Montessori Schools are privately run schools which use a prepared environment designed to stimulate the academic and intellectual growth of children. Methods adapted from Montessori Schools, as well as other pre-school programs, are being used by nursery school teachers in day-care centres.

The following are typical full-day programs:

Family Day Care: Family day care is a day-care program involving the selection and supervision by a social worker of private homes which give individual care to children during the day. If the community has day-care centres, these family day-care homes usually serve the children under the age of three and older children who are not able to take advantage of the day-care centre.

Day-Care Centres: A day-care centre is a place that serves, during the day, children up to the school years, through the use of a program prepared by staff especially educated to work with preschool children. The program attempts to insure the child's physical well-being, to deepen emotional growth, to stimulate social skills and to promote the extension of the child's frame of reference through experiences which facilitate his or her conceptual development.

THE STATUS OF DAY CARE IN CANADA

The latest available figures on day care, compiled by the Department of National Health and Welfare, follow.

In 1977, Canada had 1 962 day-care centres, which had 81 651 spaces for pre-school children. This number included 5 534 spaces in family day care. There were 15 237 (18.6%) children under the age of three, 58 626 (71.8%) children ages 3-5 years and 7 788 (9.5%) children age six and over in day care. Thus the majority of children were in the 3-5 year age group. It has been estimated that there were in 1977, 291 000 children under the age of 3 whose mothers were in the labour force, thus 5.23% of these children are receiving day-care services.

It has also been estimated that there were 365 000 children aged 3-5 years whose mothers were working. Of these 16.6% were enrolled in day care.

In 1977, working mothers had 2 108 000 children between the ages of 6-16 years of which .36% were enrolled in day-care services. Many of the other children are "Latch Key Children". This term originated from the observation that many young school-age children of working parents were carrying house keys to gain entrance to their home between the hours that school closed and their parents returned from work. Some day-care services developed to meet the needs of this age group for supervision before classes begin, during the noon hour and after class.

Of course, many of the pre-school children of Canada's working mothers are looked after in their own home by babysitters or relatives. Private arrangements are also made by many parents in the homes of other families.

CHILD CARE IN TORONTO

In 1978, the Social Planning Council of Metropolitan Toronto produced a series of publications dealing with the child-care arrangements of working parents. Table I reproduced from the first report in this series, indicates the estimated numbers of children using various types of care.

Table I

ESTIMATED NUMBERS OF CHILDREN IN METROPOLITAN TORONTO
USING VARIOUS TYPES OF CHILD CARE, BY
AVERAGE WEEKLY HOURS OF USE

Average Weekly Hours of Supervision	Family Member	Friend or Sitter	Full-Time Day Care Centre or School	Nursery/ Kindergarten	Child Cares for Self	Other	Total
1-9	10 241	7 298	570	2 356	471	747	21 683
10-19	7 315	5 671	333	29 693	183	333	43 528
20-29	8 290	5 759	667	1 836	—	239	16 791
30-39	7 803	5 627	2 264	554	—	94	16 342
40-49	18 531	14 683	8 307	139	—	406	42 066
50-168	8 778	4 924	1 750	69	—	141	15 662
							156 072

Source: Social Planning Council of Metropolitan Toronto, *Child Care Patterns in Metropolitan Toronto,* 1977.

The percentage of mothers using different types of child care are listed in Table 2.

Table 2
PERCENTAGE OF MOTHERS USING DIFFERENT TYPES OF CHILD CARE

Type of Care	Percentage of Mothers Using Child Care
Family Member	61.2
Friend or Sitter	44.1
Full-time day care centre or school	13.9
Part-time nursery school or kindergarten	0.6
Other	2.0

The overwhelming predominance of a family member looking after the child appears to be evident.

CONCLUSIONS

We have a long way to go to provide adequate child care for Canada's pre-school and school children whose mothers have to work full-time.

READINGS

Canadian Council on Social Development. *Day Care Report.* Ottawa: 1972. A national study.

Health and Welfare Canada. *Day Care: A Resource for the Contemporary Family.* Ottawa: 1974. Papers and proceedings of a seminar.

————. *Status of Day Care in Canada.* Ottawa, 1978.

————. *Day Care Services: A Bibliography.* Ottawa, 1972.

SOURCE OF MATERIALS ON DAY CARE IN CANADA

National Day Care Information Centre, Social Service Programs Branch, Department of National Health and Welfare, Brooke Claxton Building, Tunney's Pasture, Ottawa, Ontario K1A 1B5.

QUESTIONS, ACTIVITIES AND PROJECTS

1. Assume that you are a parent of a 3-year old child who requires full-time day care.
   (a) List the qualities of a suitable day-care centre. Consider such aspects as: physical environment; food provided; training of personnel; ratio of personel to children; program offered.
   (b) Investigate the availability and cost of a day-care centre in your community which comes close to meeting the requirements you noted in part (a).
   (c) Summarize your findings in report form, and share it with the class.
2. Investigate the reasons why the supply of day-care centres in Canada has not caught up with the demand.
3. The traditional view in Canada has long been that the biological mother is the best person to raise a child. Prepare an oral response to this statement, indicating the extent to which you agree/disagree with the idea.
4. Research and review studies written on the Israeli kibbutz. Report on the effects of communal child-rearing on kibbutz children.

18
Occupation: Canadian Homemaker

In 1975 there were 8 359 000 women in Canada over the age of 15 years, and 3 697 000 (44.2%) were in the labour force. Thus over 4½ million Canadian women may list their occupation as homemaker. Women whose full-time employment is the care of their families and homes comprise one of the largest occupational groups in the economy. Yet they are repeatedly asked, "Do you work or are you a housewife?"

It is obvious that the functions of a homemaker are not generally viewed as an occupation. Little has been done to identify or evaluate household functions. Nor have household functions been subject to the extensive methods studies to which other occupations have been exposed. There is a major obstacle in the way of a study of this kind. While there are certain responsibilities common to virtually all homemakers, the extent of these responsibilities and the tools used vary greatly. Preparing meals for a large family without modern cooking equipment, for example, can be quite a different task from preparing meals for a family of two with all the household appliances available. More than this, the tasks of a homemaker are greatly affected by the ages and numbers of children in the home.

It is apparent that long hours are a characteristic of the occupation of homemaker. The homemaker at home with no children may have shorter working hours than women who work outside the home for pay. On the other hand, the homemaker in the labour force and the homemaker with two or more children are likely to work over 11 hours a day. An 11-hour day on a regular basis would not be permitted in most industries.

THE STATUS OF HOMEMAKERS

Professor Margrit Eichler of the Ontario Institute for Studies in Education has examined the status of homemaker in Canadian society. She points out that the relationship of non-employed homemakers to men is fundamentally different from that of employed women to men. While employed women are ranked on the same criteria as men—occupation, income, education, etc. (thus occupying an independent status)—non-employed homemakers are ranked solely in terms of the men they are attached to, who are, in most cases their husbands. These women, then, derived their status from their husbands. Thus, the wife of a minister or an M.P. may have a higher status than some working woman, although the latter may actually have a higher education.

It is more complicated when one tries to rank non-employed homemakers. Homemakers are found in every stratum of society. They vary as broadly as men in terms of financial means, education, etc. The only factor that unites all homemakers is that they are economically dependent on one individual, usually their husbands.

THE EFFECTS OF TECHNOLOGY ON THE HOMEMAKER'S ROLE

Comparison with much earlier studies suggests that hours spent on housework have not decreased as much as one would expect in a technological age. Has housework been influenced by the same forces of technological change that have transformed and continue to alter the rest of the economy?

Mechanization of the old processes of spinning, weaving, cutting and sewing has transferred the manufacture of clothing from the home to the factory. Commercial laundries have taken over much of the cleaning. Truck-gardening, canning, freezing and pre-cooking have lessened the importance of the home in the production, preservation, and preparation of food.

Mechanization has also entered the home. Electric power, its distribution over long distances and the invention of the small, inexpensive, low-horsepower electric motor have made previously existing inventions practical for the home. A simple mechanical washing machine, for example, was available in 1869, but it took electric power to make it generally useful. Electrical appliances have been developed and their use has become widespread at an ever-growing pace.

Other functions, which had stayed in the home, have been greatly altered. Meal preparation has been changed by the introduction of a wide variety of appliances. New quick-freezing techniques for fresh food, along with improvements in canning and pre-cooking techniques and the addition of chemical fortification of foods, make it possible for the family to eat varied and nutritious meals with much less preparation in the home.

Perhaps the greatest change has been in cleaning, that everlasting and laborious task of the homemaker. Modern heating and air conditioning systems mean less dirt and soot. A variety of new chemical products, from rug shampoos to stain removers, and new materials, including plastics, paints, wallpapers, tiles and treated fabrics take some of the effort out of cleaning.

Technology has also played an important part in the construction of homes, which are now better designed, and are easier to clean and maintain than in the past.

Technology has obviously helped the homemaker in a great many ways. However it may be that technological change has so far only been sufficient to alter the old adage that "women's work is never done" to "women's work is from sun to sun." The disappearance of the extended family of the past, with female relatives who could help out, and the shortage of paid assistance have also served to counteract the impact of technological change on the homemaker's time. Most homemakers today must do all their work themselves.

While technology has had some impact on the time required to care for the child, many child-care functions remain relatively untouched. It has not done a great deal to reduce the personal help and attention required by a child.

Today's homemaker has more to organize than in the past. Since the home is now dependent on outside agencies for many supplies and services, she must keep in touch with them, doing everything from shopping to calling the plumber, the electrician or the television repairman. Organization also involves planning and frequently budgeting. The modern homemaker must decide not only how to organize various tasks, but also what activities should be carried out in the home: whether, for example, the time saved by using pre-cooked food is worth the extra expense. With advances in preventive medicine, she must also allocate time for regularly taking her children to the doctor and dentist. Many wives also act as family chauffeurs.

ESTIMATED VALUE OF UNPAID HOUSEWORK IN CANADA (1971)

If homemakers had been paid for their work, they would have earned between $74-billion and $84-billion last year, according to Statistics Canada.[1]

The agency says in a special study that the value of unpaid household work done in Canada is between 35 and 40% of the gross national product.

If that proportion is applied to last year's GNP of $210-billion, it means the value of work done in the home, mostly by homemakers, was worth between $74-billion and $84-billion, although Statistics Canada gave dollar figures for 1971 only.

However, housework is not currently included in the GNP estimate of the value of production of goods and services in the economy. Only paid housework done by people outside the family unit is counted in the GNP, and only then if it is reported to the tax department.

The estimates for 1971 show that the value of household work was between $32-billion and $38-billion, as compared to the GNP for that year of $95-billion.

"Given about 6.5 million family units (including single-person units) in that year, this comes to approximately $6 000 per family annually," the study says.

It says the value of household work done in Canada is between 35 and 40% as large as the GNP, although it does not give dollar estimates for years other than 1971.

The study notes that housework seems to be a higher percentage of the GNP in Canada than in the United States where it is estimated at between 32 to 36%.

The Statistics Canada study, prepared by Queen's University professor Oli Hawrylyshyn, used three techniques to estimate the value of household work done in Canada.

For 1971, one method of calculation, which evaluates each separate task of household work at its market replacement cost, yielded a value of $38-billion.

A second method estimating the cost of replacing such work by use of a single housekeeper arrived at a $32-billion figure. And a third approach estimating the wages lost because people did household work instead of working at paying jobs pegged the value at $37.5-billion.

About Face a booklet published by the Ontario Status of Women Council in 1977, points out the various Canadian sources which benefit from unpaid housework (pp. 25-26).

1) Our economy is based on mass production. In order for the machines to keep turning out goods profitably, there must be mass consumption. At least a portion of the time that formerly went into producing an item, now goes into selecting it. Housewives who choose, buy, clean, maintain, keep repaired and finally, replace consumer goods, are the backbone of a mass production economy. Without millions of housewives shopping every day, our economy would collapse. Stores, for instance, obviously rely on the premise that one member of the family is free for shopping during regular business ("working") hours.

2) Big employers have the advantage of a cheap and mobile temporary labour force. During the world wars, women proved their capability as employees in all fields. Thirty years later, women are still restricted to certain (usually) service occupations, largely barred from career advancement and paid an average of 40% less than men doing the same work. Part-time and temporary jobs (most suited for homemakers) are even cheaper for employers, since they

pay few or no fringe benefits. Because housework is unpaid, every other "women's" job is paid less; and any woman who doesn't like it can go right back to her kitchen.

3) All levels of government are relieved of the responsibility to provide adequate day care, because the majority of homemakers mind their own children. In our band-aid curative culture, the state's main recognition of child-raising as a public service, occurs when the state takes a mistreated child away from its family.

4) Husbands receive a measure of personal service otherwise unusual in our servantless society. A man who formerly would have needed his wife's goodwill in order to share the vegetables, eggs, chickens and bread she raised, now claims his supper by virtue of having already paid for the commodities. The balance of power within the family has shifted, unevenly. The homemaker is increasingly dependent on her husband (because she produces only services, not goods or income), while the husband is decreasingly dependent on her, because he may view her child care hours as no service at all to him personally.

5) Volunteer work helps many schools, hospitals, churches and charities to meet their budgets. Homemakers are still being pulled into public work through their interest in their children and their communities. Many of our vital public services rely heavily on volunteer workers.

6) Children and homemakers themselves may be better off for having the time to savour early childhood. However, to the extent that this is good for children, it is also good for society. And all the evidence suggests that women might enjoy this satisfaction, if they choose, at a lesser personal cost than at present.

SATISFACTIONS OF A HOMEMAKER

Professor Helena Lopata completed a study of 571 homemakers in the Chicago area. When she asked her subjects to describe a satisfied homemaker, she received the following selected replies.

—One who has a happy family. If there is happiness, there is satisfaction, respect, love and companionship.

—One who is a warm, efficient person, who enjoys all the phases of her work as a homemaker.

—One that keeps her family content and happy by doing the needed things.

—One whose family comes first above everyone else. One who is a good manager and uses good common sense and one who takes an active interest in outside activities.

—One who is satisfied with herself—receives recognition from her husband and children and is looked upon in the community with respect.

—One who caters to the needs of her family and doesn't constantly complain about how much she does, but takes it in her stride as part of the job.

—One who is proud of her family; keeps a clean and comfortable home and makes her house a home.

—One who is very unselfish, but not to the point where she's never considered. She must keep harmony in the family; keep abreast of the times so that she can keep on her level with her husband; and be able to sometimes put herself on her children's level.

In the following table, I have listed some of the satisfactions of a homemaker.

SATISFACTIONS OF A HOMEMAKER

I. **Children**
   having children
   watching children grow

bringing up children
seeing children happy
seeing children healthy
pride in children

II. **Relations**
ability to satisfy and make family happy
response, appreciation, being needed
love

III. **Happy marriage**

IV. **Possessions, home ownership**
pride in homemaking
keeping a clean, neat house

V. **Seeing fruits of one's labour**
getting the job done

CONCLUSIONS

We have to be careful not to assume that every married woman in Canada wants to fulfill herself by full-time employment outside the home. There are personal, social, psychological and emotional satisfactions in being a full-time homemaker. On the other hand, "full-time" does not have to mean 8-12 hours tied to the home. Adult Education courses, part-time work, university degrees, voluntary work, creative activities such as art, pottery, etc. can balance the homemaker role in a meaningful way.

There is nothing shameful about being a homemaker, and one does not have to feel guilty because the neighbour is out working. We cannot assume that all the jobs are satisfying and are superior to homemaking. It is unfair for a small vocal group of so-called "liberationists" to dump a negative image and useless role on the Canadian woman who chooses to fulfill part of her life through "occupation homemaker." We really cannot put a financial value on the varied activities carried out by the homemaker. However, what we can do is to realize the important role that Canadian homemakers play in raising the future generation of Canadians.

Homemaking is a true profession, ancient, honorable and unique. Indeed homemaking is the real oldest profession in the world. It's time that we recognize the positive contributions that our millions of housewives make to Canadian society.

REFERENCES

1. Catalogue 13-566; Oli Hawrylyshyn; *Estimating the Value of Household Work in Canada.* Statistics Canada, Ottawa, June 1978.

READINGS

Eichler, Margrit. "The Industrialization of Housework." Toronto: Ontario Institute for Studies in Education, Grow Paper #3, 1977.
A very good analysis of housework in our society.

Gavron, Hannah. *The Captive Wife.* London: Penguin Books, 1966.
A British study of housebound mothers and their conflicts.

Lopata, Helena Z. *Occupation Housewife.* Toronto: Oxford University Press, 1971.
A sociological study of 1000 American homemakers in the Chicago area.

Ontario Status of Women Council, Toronto, 1977. *About Face: Towards a Positive Image of Housewives.*
An excellent overview of the position of homemakers in Canadian society.

Report of the Royal Commission on *The Status of Women in Canada.* Ottawa: 1970.
This report includes material on Canadian homemakers.

FILMS

This is No Time for Romance, NFB, 28 min., colour, 1966.
A woman reflects on her life and marriage.

A Woman's Place, NFB, 14 min., colour, 1972.
Canadian women discuss woman's place in society.

The Housewife, NFB, 6 min., colour, 1975.
A housewife describes her work.

QUESTIONS, ACTIVITIES AND PROJECTS

1. *Many women today willingly choose the role of a homemaker, particularly during the early child-rearing stages, finding their life to be both rewarding and satisfying. Discuss the positive aspects of being a full-time homemaker.*

2. *Betty Friedan in her book, "The Feminine Mystique" suggests that "housewives have adjusted to their biological role and have become dependent, passive, child-like; they have given up their adult status to live at a lower human level. The work they do is simple, endless, monotonous and unrewarding." Write a reaction to this comment either supporting or opposing her point of view.*

3. *Keep a record, for one week, of the types of jobs done in your home. Indicate (i) who performs each task and (ii) the amount of time spent on each task. Summarize your findings in chart form. From this record draw conclusions focusing on (a) whether tasks are done according to traditional role expectations or according to abilities; (b) whether the household routine is flexible or on a firm schedule; (c) the equality of time spent on tasks by males and females.*

   Comment on how you would like to have household routines handled in your own home in the future.

4. *Prepare a cross generational survey of attitudes within your family to determine attitudes and expectations concerning who does what at home. If possible interview grandparents, parents, older and younger brothers and sisters and any other relatives in your family. Summarize the responses.*

19
Masculinity—Myth or Reality?

INTRODUCTION

In January 1977, the magazine *Psychology Today* published the results of a study of 28 000 readers (men and women) who responded to questions on the topic of masculinity today. Dr. Carol Tavris a social psychologist compiled the results. According to this study the ideal man combines self-confidence, success and the willingness to fight for his family and beliefs with warmth, gentleness and the willingness to lose. The "macho" male who is tough, strong, aggressive and has many sexual conquests is not admired by either sex.

The results of this survey indicate that both men and women are reaching for an ideal which combines so-called masculine and feminine qualities, but they haven't quite caught it. Both sexes support the idea of "men's liberation," which includes efforts to liberate men from their emotional strait jackets. Men want to be warmer and more loving than they feel they are, and women want their men to be more gentle, romantic and expressive.

Masculinity was harder for men to define than for women. Women seemed to know it when they see it, and consider their men more masculine than the men themselves do.

Masculinity today is in fact a set of admirable qualities, appropriate for either sex, rather than a set of merit badges that must be earned and rewon. Most people don't think that men have to prove their manhood any more in daring feats of faucet-fixing or hand-to-hand combat.

In the survey men were asked what were the important traits of an ideal man. They replied in order of importance: able to love, self-confident, stands up for beliefs, intelligent, warm, gentle and successful at work. When women were asked to indicate the important traits of ideal men, they replied in the following order of importance: able to love, warm, gentle, self-confident, intelligent, successful at work and romantic. The fact that both men and women indicated their feelings about an ideal man had a ironic twist. While 86% of the women indicated what an ideal man should be like, only 55% felt that they had an ideal man. Only 42% of the men in the study stated that they felt that they fitted the picture of an ideal man.

STEREOTYPES OF MEN AND WOMEN

I was on a panel dealing with the role of men with Dr. Peter Cole, director of the Family Planning Services Division of the City of Toronto. He developed some ideas about men today, which I would like to share with you.

Table 1 gives you some indication of some personality traits.

In Canada, in many cases you are not considered to be "masculine" unless you possess the traits in Table 1. Similarly women are not considered to be "feminine" if they do not fit into the list.

Table 2, gives some interests of men and women.

Table 1
STEREOTYPED PERSONALITY TRAITS OF MEN AND WOMEN

Men	Women
Competitive	Non-competitive
Aggressive	Passive
Emotionless	Emotional
Independent	Dependent
Analytic/Scientific	Intuitive
Organized	Scatter-brained
Strong	Weak
Uncreative	Creative
Athletic	Non-athletic

Table 2
STEREOTYPED INTERESTS OF MEN AND WOMEN

Men	Women
Sports	Music/Art
Politics	Family
Business	Housework
Gadgets— cars/boats	Fashions

We still seem to have divided male and female interests. You only have to watch the advertising on television to confirm the stereotypes. Even in the work world (Table 3) the male is distinct.

Table 3
JOBS OF MEN AND WOMEN (MAIN CATEGORIES)

Men	Women
Professions	Secretaries
Executives	Salespeople
Managers	Service Jobs
Trades	Factory Workers
Unskilled labour	

We seem to have placed men in certain occupational categories, and so it becomes a "big deal" when a woman becomes a president of a firm, or a member of the board of a bank. On the other hand, if a man takes a job in a nursery school or kindergarten he receives much attention.

The assignment of characteristics based on one's sex is also evident in our relationships with members of the same sex. (Table 4).

Table 4
INTERACTION WITH SAME SEX—MEN AND WOMEN

a. MEN	—no emotional interaction, only superficial relationships —no physical contact, except sports —no risks in confidence —compete with each other over work, women —major interaction is intellectual
b. WOMEN	—can be more open, emotional —develop closer relationships with each other —more confidence in relationships —still wary of each other concerning men, competitive

We have a real double standard in our relationships. The male is supposed to show coolness, while the female exhibits warmth. This double standard is also evident in our interaction with the opposite sex. (Table 5).

The double standard clearly turns up here. The pressure for sexual conquest rather than friendship is an all pervasive factor in men. Strength, knowing it all, cool, authoritarianism are all valued. Men do not cry, sigh, "let down their hair", reveal inner feelings or lean on women for emotional support. They are not gentle and warm.

A MANIFESTO FOR MEN'S LIBERATION

There are men who are trying to free

Table 5
EXPECTATIONS IN INTERACTION WITH OPPOSITE SEX

a. MEN
—aggressive, bustling
—initiate interaction and continue to make first move
—must always appear as the authority, know everything
—pillars of strength, problem solvers, pep-talkers

b. WOMEN
—cannot expect to have friendships without sex
—must be passive, react to male initiative
—generally dress, behave to attract men

---

themselves from sexual stereotypes. One such group, the "Berkeley Men's Center" in California issued a manifesto in 1973. I have chosen a few of their statements to illustrate how some men seek their liberation.

1. We, as men, want to take back our full humanity. We no longer want to strain and compete to live up to an impossible oppressive masculine image— strong, silent, cool, handsome, unemotional, successful, master of women, leader of men, wealthy, brilliant, athletic and "heavy". We no longer want to feel the need to perform sexually, socially, or in any way to live up to an imposed male role, from a traditional American society or a "counterculture."

2. We want to relate to both women and men in more human ways—with warmth, sensitivity, emotion and honesty. We want to share our feelings with one another, to break down the walls and grow closer. We want to be equal with women and end destructive competitive relationships between men. We don't want to engage in ego battles with anyone.

3. We are oppressed by conditioning which makes us only half-human. This conditioning serves to create a mutual dependence of male (abstract, aggressive, strong, unemotional) and female (nurturing, passive, weak, emotional) roles. We are oppressed by this dependence on women for support, nurturing, love and warm feelings. We want to love, nurture and support ourselves and other men, as well as women. We want to affirm our strengths as men and at the same time encourage the creation of new space for men in areas such as childcare, cooking, sewing and other "feminine" aspects of life.

4. We believe that this half-humanization will only change when our competitive, male-dominated, individualistic society becomes cooperative, based on sharing of resources and skills. We are oppressed by working in alienating jobs, as "breadwinners." We want to use our creative energy to serve our common needs and not to make profits for our employers.

5. We believe that Human Liberation does not stem from individual or social needs alone but that these needs are part of the same process. We feel that all liberation movements are equally important; there is no hierarchy of oppression. Every group must speak its own language, assume its own form, take its own action; and when each of these groups learns to express itself in harmony with the rest, this will create the basis for an all embracing social change.

6. As we put our ideas into practice, we will work to form a more concrete analysis of our oppression as men, and clarify what needs to be done in a socially and personally political way to

free ourselves. We want men to share their lives and experiences with each other in order to understand who we are, how we got this way and what we must do to be free.

MALE ROLES IN THE FUTURE

Because of social change men, both young and old, are beginning to realize that the psychological baggage they have been carrying is far too heavy. They need a rest for the old values, with their incessant demands for stiff deportment, are tiring. Taboos, restrictions and constrictions are disappearing, but "masculinist" rulings die hard. At present Canadian males are experiencing guilts as they abandon old roles. The roles, after all, were once sanctified and revered.

Where do men go now? They stand at new crossroads. Many are unable as yet to see the damage wrought as they strain themselves to be domineering and competitive. All men who are determined to be self-regulating and self-dependent must help to bring about changes without resorting to old "masculinist" methods of one-upmanship. They must be confident enough to say "no" when the society around them insists that they should live by outdated ideas. The choice facing them requires courage. It is a choice between integrity and appearance. The man who chooses integrity is not afraid that others will run roughshod over him. He has confidence in his life and himself.

How will we define masculinity and male roles in Canada in the year 2000? We really do not know at this time what will be rejected and accepted. What we do know is that male liberation may bring with it a feeling of being one's self, without always proving to everyone how "tough" and "macho" one is.

As we examine the forces that have put us into the "male" mold, we may decide to change, to adapt or to retain some of the qualities which move us nearer to "personhood." I believe definitely that there are differences between men and women. I am not a champion for "unisex". What we have to decide is what qualities are necessary to reach the stage of "ideal manhood."

THE EFFECT OF A CHANGING MALE ROLE ON THE FAMILY

The family, of course, is the most critical factor in the development of the individual. The increase in the number of mothers working outside the home has created a strong impetus for a shift from separate male and female roles to less differentiation.

As women participate more in the larger world outside the domestic sphere, men, of necessity in many cases, will take on a greater share of responsibility for homemaking and child care. As a result, both will expand their sensibilities and capacities by adding those previously ruled out by the traditional sex roles. Children will have as models parents who are not restricted to sex stereotypes.

Equally important, the relationship of such parents will not be the conventional one of the father being catered to and serviced by the mother, all in the name of his role as economic provider. As women move into positions of status equal to that of their men, a shift takes place in the balance of power—the hierarchical structure of the relationship breaks down. The model from which children draw their earliest and most powerful expectations that men will and should dominate women is replaced by a more balanced egalitarian structure.

If work and child care are fully shared by the father and mother, the children will be more or less equally attached to them. Each parental relationship will have its nurturing and its performance-oriented sides. Rivalry for affection and attention will be diminished since the child's dependence will be more evenly divided. And each parent will provide a model of both aspects of human behaviour from which the young boy, because of the insignificance of sex roles, will be free to choose what best suits his individual temperament and needs. Any general tendency to identify with and imitate the father as opposed to the mother will be slight, limited to those few areas—having to do primarily with sexual orientation—in which gender is still a differentiating factor, and will be the result of the boy's gradual elaboration of these differences rather than pressure from parents suddenly anxious that he be "a man." A change in masculinity may mean that fathers will not be the president of the company but will move to become members of the board of directors of the institution called "the family."

READINGS

Fasteau, Marc Feigen. *The Male Machine.* New York: Dell Publishing, 1975.
An examination of masculinity in North American society.

Nichols, Jack. *Men's Liberation.* New York: Penguin Books, 1975.
A pioneering book discussing masculinity.

Peck, Joseph H. and Sawyer, Jack eds. *Men and Masculinity.* New York: Spectrum Books, 1974.
A collection of readings dealing with roles of men in our society.

Stoll, Clarice Stasz. *Female and Male: Socialization, Social Roles, and Social Structure.* Dubuque, Iowa: Wm. C. Brown Co., 1978, 2nd edition.
A review of gender identity.

QUESTIONS, ACTIVITIES AND PROJECTS

1. *Before reading this chapter list the words that you associate with "masculinity."*
   a) *Compare your list with that of a student of the opposite sex. What differences do you perceive?*
   b) *After reading the chapter compare your list with the one in Table 1.*

2. *Assign two class members to role play the following situations. The rest of the class should record feelings on masculine and feminine roles that come out of the discussion.*
   Mother and Dad have a four-year-old son, James, and a six-year-old daughter, Jennifer.
   a) *James wishes to play dolls just as his sister does.*
   b) *Grandma wishes to teach the two children to crochet.*
   c) *James loves to be the same as his sister and wishes to have pink wallpaper in his room too.*
   d) *Father jokingly comments that "Men should be the boss in the family."*

3. *Take a poll of your class. Ask each student to list their*
   1) *favourite subject*
   2) *favourite recreational activities*
   3) *greatest ambition*
   4) *what they want to be at age 40*
   What similarities and differences do you find in the responses of males and

females? Can you generalize about male and female roles from the results of your poll?

4. *Collect advertisements from Canadian newspapers and magazines which use the masculine image to "sell" products. List the "male" characteristics you find in these advertisements. Display the ads on a bulletin board.*

20
Grandparents: Giving Roots to Canadian Families

For too long, we have ignored the important contributions which grandparents can make to our Canadian families.

Alex Haley, the author of *Roots* (a book which told the story of his family over generations) stated in an interview: "I tell young people to go to the oldest members of their family to get as much oral history as possible. Many grandparents carry three or four generations of history in their heads but don't talk about it because they have been ignored. And when the young person starts doing this, the old are warmed to the cockles of their souls and will tell a grandchild everything they can muster."

WHAT IS A "GOOD" GRANDMOTHER?

In examining various studies related to grandparenting we found the following qualities listed to describe a "good" grandmother: she is a person who loves and enjoys granchildren, sets a good example, helps grandchildren when needed or asked, does not interfere with parents and can use discipline with grandchildren if needed. Grandchildren feel that a good grandmother is one who loves and enjoys grandchildren, visits with them, shows an interest in them, helps grandchildren when needed, is loving, gentle, understanding, industrious, smart, a friend, talkative and funny. The least important quali-

ties are that she should be childish, dependent, a mediator, a companion and a teacher.

TYPES OF GRANDPARENTS

Grandparents could be categorized in the following groups: the *formal style* grandparents are those who do what grandparents are supposed to do; the *fun seekers* are usually younger grandparents who play with the grandchildren; *the surrogate parents* are the grandparents who take care of the children while the parents work; the *reservoir of family wisdom* are those grandparents who are authoritarian figures who dispense special skills; and the *distant figures* are grandparents who are benevolent but remote.

GRANDPARENTHOOD: A CANADIAN STUDY

In 1978, with a group of 17 graduate students at the Faculty of Social Work, and Professor Win Herington, we completed a study of 137 grandparents of whom 99 were grandmothers and 38 were grandfathers. We interviewed all of them in their homes.

SATISFACTIONS OF GRANDPARENTING

Their satisfaction in grandparenting can be found in the following table.

Table I SATISFACTIONS OF GRANDPARENTING	**Table 2:** DISSATISFACTIONS OF GRANDPARENTING
—helping grandchildren —listening to grandchildren —seeing grandchildren —talking to grandchildren —watching grandchildren grow up —providing an example or model to grandchildren —passing on family traditions —giving affection/love —getting affection/love —being a confidant to grandchildren —entertaining grandchildren —helping to raise grandchildren —getting respect from grandchildren —taking pride in grandchildren —teaching and guiding grandchildren —giving extra time to grandchildren —being a steadying influence on grandchildren —providing continuity over the generations —being needed by grandchildren —being a moral/spiritual advisor to grandchildren —giving time out to parents of grandchildren —buying presents or giving financial help	—not having enough time with grandchildren —being "used" as a grandparent —their own children holding back the grandparent's enthusiasm —looking and feeling like a grandparent —not having more grandchildren —the grandchildren living far away —not being appreciated —remembering grandchild is not their own child —being asked not to say anything about the way children handle grandchildren —their children expecting them to be available for "babysitting" —grandchildren not being raised in religious faith of grandparents —jealousy and rivalry among grandchildren for grandparents' attention —apartment living restricting what grandchildren can do with grandparent —being unable to share knowledge and experience with grandchildren —conflicts with parents of grandchildren —grandchildren not calling or visiting frequently —not seeing grandchildren brought up like grandparent would like them brought up —the mobility of grandchildren —grandchildren who do not understand/respect grandparents enough —loss of tranquillity in house when grandchildren visit

Here are some statements from our grandparents related to how they see their relationships with their grandchildren and their role as grandparents today:

"To listen to them and to give them advice when they need it."

"To be there—to be with them and to add to the happiness of the grandchildren."

"You can give them a feeling of safety and security."

"To pass on family background and history."

"To provide an example to others of how to live with dignity."

"To offer the special kind of love that grandparents give grandchildren that is different from parental love."

"To be a friend to the grandchildren and make them feel that they are important to you."

"Being someone who loves their grandchildren unconditionally."

"I love them and cherish them. It is a wonderful feeling. I take pride in their accomplishments. We are friends."

"My son and daughter-in-law are better parents than I was. It's satisfying to see that. My son has learned from my mistakes and my good points and has become a better parent . . . You can enjoy the grandchildren without the worry you have as a parent."

A GRANDMOTHER SPEAKS

The following is an account of an interview with Mrs. Y., a great-grandmother, seventy-six years of age. She is a very active and healthy woman, currently employed for fourteen hours per week in a small library.

The interview is recorded as accurately as possible, and no attempt has been made to organize or re-order the structure of the conversation.

"I am close to my grandchildren, they come to me with all their troubles, they say I keep the family together, they wouldn't hurt my feelings for a million dollars. I have a girlfriend, and her grandchildren won't even stay overnight with her, yet while he was in university my grandson stayed overnight from Monday to Thursday. Now it is a tradition for them all to come over for a big dinner at certain times of the year, like Christmas when I have twenty-six of them over.

"My husband died when the kids were young, forty-six years ago, so that my kids, and there were eight of them at the time, became very attached to me. Now the kids have me involved. Last Sunday I didn't want to go on a hike and said that I wasn't feeling well. So they went without me and came back early. It was the worst thing I could have said! They worry too much!

"My great-grandchildren are always phoning me. They're five and seven now. Last year I went on a ten day holiday with my son and his children. We went to Florida and we are planning to do the same thing this year. Tonight I'm having John (the son who went to Florida) over for his birthday dinner, along with his wife and three kids.

"All my kids have married well and they are all really good to me. My grandchildren go away and bring me things. Their mothers sometimes ask, 'What did you bring for me?' and they just say, 'Well I thought Mamie (my affectionate family nickname) would like this.'

"One time my grandson Leo was staying overnight at my apartment. I belong to a bridge club so I didn't come in until 1 a.m. The house was all lit up when I got home and Leo was perched on the end of the bed, 'I thought you were dead, does your family know that you keep these late hours?' I just told him, 'Now you know how your parents feel when you're out late!'

"During the school year, my grandson often brings friends over from school during the lunch hour, for a while some of my grandchildren even studied at my house.

"I never really got along with my grandmother. My mother was a convert and my grandmother was a real Irish Catholic. I can remember walking past my grandmother's house and my mother saying, 'Stay away from grandmother, you're always getting into trouble and she's telling your father.'

"I don't fight with the kids, and I am careful not to interfere. My granddaughter is getting married next April and I've met her financée. I'd never tell them that I thought his hair was too long.

"It's a parent's responsibility to look after discipline. My girlfriend is always telling her children how to do things. It's not any business of a grandparent to interfere, but I wouldn't tell her that.

"My niece called to tell me that she was pregnant for the ninth time. She couldn't tell anyone else as all her relatives complain, but I had eight kids, so she called me.

"Nearly every weekend someone invites me out to their house. I don't like to say no, but sometimes I'd like to stay home. I have another wedding cake to make for Susan. I really like to do that.

"Once when my son was away in Europe, Bob was at home by himself. I went over to pick him up on the way to meet his parents at the airport. The house was a mess, the lawn wasn't cut and the dishes were piled up. It was crazy to do that, because Bob's father is a real crab. I told him to get things cleaned up and together we straightened up the house. His father still thought it was dirty, but we just winked at each other. I could have yelled at Bob for letting it get like that, but I didn't.

"I'm happy. My grandchildren bring over guests for Christmas dinner. I'm glad they do that.

"The trouble with me is that I'm all alone. If my husband was living we would do things. So I have time to make things for the kids when I might be with my husband or he might tell me not to do it. I often make special treats for the kids. If you're making something, it's just as easy to make what they like."

CONCLUSIONS

Grandparents should be included in the lives of our families. Their contribution can enhance family life to a great extent. They can also supply roots to our families.

READINGS

Goude, Ruth. *A Book for Grandmothers.* New York: Macmillan, 1976.
A discussion of grandmothers.

Shedd, Charles W. *Then God Created Grandparents.* New York: Doubleday.
A grandfather discusses grandparenting.

FILMS

Antonio, NFB, 28 min., black/white 1966
An Italian widower living with his memories.
Great Grandmother, NFB, 28 min., colour 1975
An appreciation of women who settled the prairies. An historical documentary.
Growing Old, NFB, 15 min., colour 1972
This film raises many questions about growing old in our society.
Nell and Fred, NFB, 28 min., black/white 1971
Two elderly citizens consider the pros and cons of entering an old people's home.
Where Mrs. Whalley lives, NFB, 28 min., black/white 1966
An examination of an aging grandmother who lives with her family.

AUDIOTAPES

Available from CBC Learning Systems, Box 500, Station A, Toronto, Ontario. M5W 1E6

Fathers
A young man who has just become a father realizes that all his criticisms and suggestions to his own father were simply theories. Now, faced with reality, he is able to better see his father's viewpoint. Cat. No. 315L: one hour

What Shall We Do With Mom and Dad? (2 audiotapes)
Dealing with the problems of being old in an increasingly youth-oriented society, the programs include interviews with different people in various situations: the old living with their offspring; those in homes for old people; those wanting to preserve their independence and so living alone on their pensions; ethnic groups in which three generations live under the same roof. Cat. Nos. 300L and 301L: each one hour

QUESTIONS, ACTIVITIES AND PROJECTS

1. *Describe the role that your grandparent(s) played in your life when you were*
   (a) *5 years old*
   (b) *10 years old*
   (c) *15 years old*
   (d) *today*
   Write a brief description of the role you would like your parents to play in the lives of your children.

2. *Interview grandparents about their satisfactions and dissatisfactions with their roles. Compare the results of your interviews with those listed in the tables in this chapter.*

3. *Research the ways that two of the following societies accommodate the needs of their elderly and compare their methods to those commonly found in Canada:*
   (a) *Germany* (b) *India* (c) *Portugal* (d) *China* (e) *Italy* (f) *an island in the West Indies*

4. *Anthropologist Dr. Margaret Mead has said that "Grandparents have now become the living repositories of change, living evidence that human beings can adjust, can take in the enormous changes which separate the pre-1945 generation from those who were reared after the war." She goes on to suggest that "we have to get the older people back close to growing children if we are to restore a sense of community, a knowledge of the past and a sense of the future to today's children."* (The Education Digest, *March 1975).*
   (a) *List the contributions that grandparents can make in helping their grandchildren adjust to rapid societal changes.*
   (b) *Investigate the programs in your community which utilize the knowledge and experiences of grandparents. (One example might be grandparents working in day-care centres).*

V

THE CANADIAN FAMILY OF THE FUTURE

21
The Canadian Family: A Backward Glance and a Look Ahead

It is clear that the family in a mass society, of which Canada is a dramatic example, has been transformed from an extended family to a nuclear family. It has changed, too, from a three-generation or four-generation family to a two-generation family.

The family has lost many of its functions or has experienced a reduction of them. In our past, when we lived in small, often isolated communities, the family functioned as a production unit, a consumption unit, a religious unit, an educational unit, a socialization unit, an affectional unit and a protective unit. In Canada today, the family is certainly no longer a production unit, and it is increasingly not a consumption unit. Usually it does not function as a religious unit or as an educational unit. The family is increasingly less important as a unit of socialization. It has less and less impact on the child, as specialized institutions emerge that strongly affect him/her. Moreover, the family in most cases is not a strong affectional unit. It must compete with many other sources of affection. And is it a protective unit? What about the impact of our social services, including medical insurance?

The Canadian pattern of marriage has also changed. It is still described as monogamy, but it is no longer the monogamous marriage of the past. Rather, it is becoming a form of serial monogamy; an increasing proportion of men and women have had several marriages.

A profound alteration in the nature of the family life cycle has occurred. This change has been caused by a combination of demographic and social trends. Some of the phenomena that account for this change are a slight decrease in the number of marriages; the tremendous increase in the proportion of the population that is married; the increasing age of the partners at the time of marriage; the increasing age at which childbearing begins; the increased concentration of childbearing in the years before the woman reaches thirty-five years of age; and the almost universal employment of family planning methods. As a result of all these changes, the age of the parents when the last child leaves home for marriage has been lowered; the number of years in which parents are freed from childbearing and childrearing activities has tremendously increased; and the age at which the death of one spouse is experienced has risen markedly.

The role of women has changed. The woman in Canada is being transformed from "a female" into "a person." The transformation is still not complete. In a small community the woman's role was circumscribed and centred chiefly in her female attributes as wife and mother. In a mass society she may engage in an ever wider spectrum of activities, many of them previously open only to men. Her changing role, including her wider participation in social, economic and political activities, has had tremendous impact on the family.

The relationship between husbands and

wives is increasingly egalitarian. The family structure is less patriarchal.

A LOOK INTO THE FUTURE

Predicting the future is a precarious undertaking. But since many are making prophecies, I am joining them.

It seems certain that the family will lose its utilitarian functions—survival, protection, economic security, education, production of goods and services, recreation. These are now taken over by the community.

It is suggested that parenthood will become a specialized function, with children being raised by professional "upbringers," at the expense of the state. So far this idea has not become reality.

The new function of the family will be to provide emotional security to people living in a vast, impersonal society. People will find love, acceptance, identity and a sense of worth in the family. These are very deep needs of men, women and children today, and will continue to be. No other institutions that can serve this function on a dependable and lasting basis, are in sight.

Concern for the environment, plus a variety of personal motives have made planned parenthood common. The availability of various birth control measures have made it easier. Women in the future will not see themselves primarily as child-bearers and nurturers. Men will perceive themselves not primarily as providers of financial support, but as partners in a relationship which may or may not produce a child. Both can feel freer to share in money-earning, work activities, home activities and leisure-time activities.

The single child or childless marriage will become the popular family size of the future. This may mean that more and more couples will consider adopting hard-to-place children with handicaps or mixed parentage. Several couples may plan to share a house in order to share the pleasure and responsibility of child care. The desire to have a child will not be conditioned away, but rather young married people will deliberately plan for their children. To insure that pregnancies will be planned, sex education, including information on birth control and devices, will become a part of the regular school curriculum.

There will be more child-care centres, more day-care groups in charge of "retired" grandparent managers and sharing of child care in one large household which will allow the young parent to have other activities. Parents can "spell" each other in employment or continue education, rather than one person giving up outside activities when a child is born.

There will be far fewer children than there are today and, therefore, each will be more individually valued. It should be clear, under those circumstances, that children are wards of society in general and not merely the property of their biological parents. Children, few in number and therefore not to be wasted, must be "used" wisely, as would be true of any resource that was at once crucially important and in short supply.

The nuclear family will not only persist into the twenty-first century, but it will be stronger than ever. We live in a time of rising psychological as well as economic expectations. The family as an institution will not be abolished, because people expect more of it and are more apt to express and act on their dissatisfactions. I do not agree with people who say that marriage will be replaced by the new "alternative life styles." I do believe that other forms—group marriages, single parent households, communes—will probably become more prevalent as our society becomes more tolerant of individual choice and differences. But ultimately, for biological reasons, and more immediately for psychological reasons, the pairing husband and wife relationship and the exclusive parent-child relationship will endure.

I was on a panel dealing with the family in May 1977* with Dr. Michael Novak a professor of philosophy at Harvard University. I remember that when he was asked, "Why is the family important?" he replied: "The answer I want to make to 'Why the family?' is this—unless we have children, there isn't any future. It's very simple. And unless we have children who are brought up in an environment with a certain quality, the promise of our future is much diminished. And, therefore, we have to pay special attention to those members of society, even if it is not all members of society, who do take up the task of the future, who do nurture children. We have an absolutely profound interest in what is done by such citizens. More so than in what is done by other citizens who choose not to have families."

My own feeling is that the family will endure. Alternate family life styles will not take over the majority of the Canadian

population. I strongly believe that as we move to the year 2000, Canadian families will survive with greater strengths and inner fortitudes. Long live our Canadian families in all their forms!

AUDIOTAPES

Available from CBC Learning Systems, Box 500, Station A, Toronto, Ontario, M5W 1E6

The Family
Traditional attitudes to the family are changing, but "There never has been a successful civilization in which the family was not the basic unit," according to Dr. Wilder Penfield, eminent Canadian neurosurgeon and the first president of the Vanier Institute of the Family. Cat. No. 126L: one hour

Images of Childhood
Dr. Norman Bell, sociologist, chairs a discussion among historians and sociologists in which we are able to see some different attitudes towards child-rearing and the role of the child in the family and society as well as some commonly shared attitudes and experiences. Cat. No. 782L: one hour

* *Think About the Family. A Seminar on the Family in Today's Society.* Toronto: Provincial Secretariat for Social Development, 1977.

QUESTIONS, ACTIVITIES AND PROJECTS

1. *Set up a series of class debates on the pros and cons of alternatives to traditional marriage such as: communal living, trial marriages, group marriages, marriages with detailed contracts.*
2. *Anthropologist Dr. Margaret Mead has proposed that marriage be contracted in two steps, although the second step needn't ever be taken.*
   The first step would be an "individual marriage." The couple would be committed for as long as they wished, but could not have children. The next step toward a "parental marriage" could only take place when both partners showed their ability to raise and support children. Couples entering this second stage of marriage would need a special license and ceremony. (a) What are the practical difficulties of putting this proposal into practice? (b) If the difficulties could be overcome, do you think that this proposal would be a valid one? Explain your answer in a short essay.
3. *Study the format of the marriage contract in the Appendix (page 191). Ana-*

lyze it in terms of how well it would meet your needs. If you would like to change it, specify how. Draw up your own version of a marriage contract.

4. *Make your own predictions for family life in Canada in the year 2000. Produce a chart of your predictions, titled* Families: Canada, Year 2000.

APPENDIX

Table 1

POPULATION BY MARITAL STATUS AND SEX, FOR CANADA AND PROVINCES, 1971 AND 1976

(Based on 100% data—Basé sur les données à 100%)

Census year and sex	Total	Single (never married)			Married			Widowed	Divorced
		Total	Under 15 years of age	15 years of age and over	Total	Married	Separated		
CANADA									
1971 T.	21 568 310	10 671 570	6 380 900	4 290 670	9 777 605	9 406 240	371 365	944 025	175 115
M.	10 795 370	5 641 130	3 263 480	2 377 645	4 888 760	4 726 700	162 060	191 130	74 360
F.	10 772 945	5 030 445	3 117 415	1 913 030	4 888 840	4 679 535	209 305	752 895	100 760
1976 T.	22 992 600	10 672 600	5 896 180	4 776 420	10 973 905	10 593 155	380 750	1 043 565	302 535
M.	11 449 525	5 666 590	3 020 010	2 646 580	5 474 235	5 310 925	163 310	189 665	119 035
F.	11 543 080	5 006 005	2 876 165	2 129 840	5 499 670	5 282 230	217 440	853 900	183 505
Newfoundland									
1971 T.	522 105	295 615	194 585	101 030	207 655	204 255	3 400	18 100	740
M.	266 105	156 975	99 350	57 625	104 300	102 910	1 390	4 540	290
F.	256 000	138 640	95 235	43 410	103 355	101 345	2 010	13 560	445
1976 T.	557 725	296 945	187 765	109 180	238 670	234 505	4 165	20 040	2 070
M.	283 385	158 695	96 205	62 495	119 445	117 595	1 850	4 395	850
F.	274 340	138 250	91 560	46 685	119 225	116 910	2 315	15 645	1 220
Prince Edward Island									
1971 T.	111 640	59 245	35 405	23 840	46 055	44 745	1 310	5 890	450
M.	56 225	31 670	18 065	13 600	23 055	22 435	620	1 295	210
F.	55 415	27 575	17 340	10 240	23 000	22 310	690	4 595	240
1976 T.	118 230	58 910	33 225	25 685	52 310	50 745	1 565	6 240	770
M.	59 325	31 680	17 195	14 485	26 120	25 430	695	1 185	335
F.	58 900	27 230	16 030	11 195	26 190	25 320	875	5 050	430
Nova Scotia									
1971 T.	788 960	399 630	240 765	158 860	344 795	332 100	12 695	39 425	5 110
M.	396 465	213 210	123 390	89 825	172 620	167 065	5 550	8 375	2 260
F.	392 495	186 415	117 375	69 040	172 175	165 030	7 140	31 055	2 850
1976 T.	828 570	396 455	223 735	172 815	380 395	368 035	12 360	42 170	9 460
M.	414 150	212 225	114 770	97 455	190 030	184 525	5 505	7 925	3 970
F.	414 420	184 320	108 965	75 360	190 365	183 510	6 855	34 240	5 490
New Brunswick									
1971 T.	634 555	333 755	203 100	130 650	269 345	260 610	8 735	28 290	3 165
M.	319 425	176 975	104 310	72 665	134 985	131 115	3 870	6 005	1 450
F.	315 135	156 780	98 795	57 985	134 360	129 495	4 860	22 280	1 715
1976 T.	677 250	331 585	193 095	138 485	309 345	299 430	9 915	30 750	5 570
M.	339 335	176 650	98 985	77 665	154 405	150 105	4 300	5 895	2 385
F.	337 915	154 930	94 115	60 820	154 940	149 325	5 615	24 855	3 185
Québec									
1971 T.	6 027 760	3 175 620	1 785 535	1 390 085	2 593 550	2 494 995	98 560	233 545	25 050
M.	2 994 550	1 640 290	912 545	727 745	1 294 500	1 252 805	41 700	49 050	10 705
F.	3 033 215	1 535 335	872 990	662 345	1 299 045	1 242 185	56 860	184 495	14 345

1976	T.	6 234 445	3 001 555	1 550 335	1 451 220	2 906 970	2 823 190	83 785	259 950	65 970
	M.	3 084 645	1 562 700	794 585	768 115	1 447 990	1 414 125	33 865	49 290	24 670
	F.	3 149 800	1 438 860	755 750	683 105	1 458 980	1 409 060	49 920	210 660	41 300
Ontario 1971	T.	7 703 110	3 628 925	2 208 490	1 420 435	3 645 855	3 501 745	144 115	358 235	70 095
	M.	3 840 910	1 923 130	1 131 090	792 040	1 821 215	1 758 205	63 020	68 340	28 215
	F.	3 862 200	1 705 790	1 077 400	628 395	1 824 640	1 743 545	81 095	289 890	41 875
1976	T.	8 264 465	3 706 100	2 073 785	1 632 320	4 052 515	3 891 810	160 700	395 495	110 360
	M.	4 096 865	1 967 260	1 062 980	904 280	2 019 495	1 950 905	68 590	68 285	41 825
	F.	4 167 600	1 738 840	1 010 805	728 035	2 033 020	1 940 905	92 110	327 210	68 535
Manitoba 1971	T.	988 245	478 960	286 795	192 165	452 005	435 590	16 415	49 215	8 070
	M.	494 610	255 585	146 180	109 400	225 770	218 620	7 145	9 855	3 410
	F.	493 635	223 375	140 610	82 760	226 240	216 965	9 270	39 365	4 660
1976	T.	1 021 505	471 150	265 105	206 045	484 815	467 595	17 215	52 615	12 930
	M.	508 010	251 495	135 645	115 850	242 005	234 495	7 510	9 390	5 125
	F.	513 495	219 660	129 460	90 195	242 810	233 105	9 705	43 225	7 805
Saskatchewan 1971	T.	926 245	457 435	280 435	177 005	417 700	405 170	12 530	45 570	5 535
	M.	470 725	249 160	143 150	106 010	209 250	203 890	5 365	9 720	2 600
	F.	455 520	208 280	137 280	70 995	208 450	201 280	7 165	35 855	2 935
1976	T.	921 325	429 780	248 015	181 765	435 865	424 305	11 565	47 445	8 230
	M.	464 770	234 350	126 460	107 895	218 155	212 910	5 245	8 680	3 580
	F.	456 550	195 430	121 555	73 870	217 710	211 390	6 320	38 765	4 650
Alberta 1971	T.	1 627 875	807 815	514 505	293 310	737 485	712 785	24 705	61 285	21 285
	M.	827 785	436 110	263 100	173 010	369 505	358 550	10 955	12 970	9 200
	F.	800 085	371 705	251 405	120 300	367 985	354 235	13 750	48 310	12 085
1976	T.	1 838 035	869 265	503 130	366 135	865 470	839 700	25 765	69 410	33 895
	M.	932 370	472 705	257 445	215 260	433 000	421 500	11 500	12 695	13 970
	F.	905 670	396 560	245 685	150 880	432 470	418 205	14 265	56 715	19 925
British Columbia 1971	T.	2 184 620	1 003 435	609 975	393 460	1 042 525	994 475	48 050	103 475	35 190
	M.	1 100 375	540 950	311 305	229 650	523 045	501 075	21 970	20 620	15 760
	F.	1 084 245	462 485	298 670	163 810	519 475	493 395	26 080	82 855	19 430
1976	T.	2 466 610	1 074 300	595 125	479 170	1 221 530	1 168 865	52 665	118 230	52 550
	M.	1 232 510	578 690	303 965	274 725	610 405	586 735	23 675	21 510	21 905
	F.	1 234 095	495 610	291 165	204 445	611 125	582 130	28 995	96 715	30 645
Yukon 1971	T.	18 390	9 745	6 370	3 380	8 080	7 620	460	335	230
	M.	9 920	5 515	3 295	2 215	4 150	3 875	270	125	135
	F.	8 470	4 235	3 070	1 165	3 930	3 740	190	205	95
1976	T.	21 835	11 245	6 425	4 820	9 815	9 330	480	405	375
	M.	11 705	6 400	3 350	3 050	4 975	4 705	270	120	205
	F.	10 135	4 845	3 075	1 770	4 835	4 625	210	285	170
Northwest Territories 1971	T.	34 805	21 395	14 940	6 455	12 555	12 155	400	655	200
	M.	18 280	11 565	7 695	3 870	6 360	6 155	210	235	120
	F.	16 525	9 830	7 250	2 585	6 195	6 005	190	425	80
1976	T.	42 610	25 215	16 435	8 780	16 205	15 640	560	825	370
	M.	22 450	13 735	8 430	5 305	8 210	7 905	305	290	215
	F.	20 160	11 475	8 005	3 475	7 995	7 735	255	535	155

Source: 1976 Census of Canada: *Population: Demographic Characteristics: Marital Status.* Cat. #92-824-Bulletin 2, 5, March 1978.

Table 2
MARITAL STATUS OF POPULATION 15 YEARS AND OVER BY AGE GROUP
AND SEX—CANADA—1976

	Men	Women	Total	%
Single	2 646 580	2 129 840	4 776 420	28
Married	5 310 925	5 282 230	10 593 155	62
Separated	163 310	217 440	380 750	22
Widowed	189 665	853 900	1 043 565	6
Divorced	119 035	183 505	302 540	2
Total	8 429 515	8 666 915	17 096 430	100

Source: Calculated from 1976 *Census of Canada, Marital Status.*
Cat. #92-824, March 1978.

Table 3
FAMILIES IN CANADA

No. of families: 5 727 895
    Intact families: 90.24% of all families
No. of lone-parent families: 559 330—9.76% of all families
    No. of male lone-parents: 94 990—17% of all lone-parents
    No. of female lone-parents: 464 345—83% of all lone-parents

Increase and decrease in families since 1971 census
All families: +13.4%
All lone-parent families: +17%
All male lone-parents: −5.4%
All female lone-parents: +23.1%
All husband-wife families: +13.0%

Source: 1976 census of Canada. *Families by Family Structure and Family Type.* Catalogue #93-822 Bulletin 4.3,
May, 1978.

Table 4
ESTIMATED NUMBER OF FAMILIES BY NUMBER OF CHILDREN 24 YEARS
AND UNDER AT HOME—CANADA—1975

Total Number of Families: 5 564 000

Number of Children	Number of Families	Percentage
0	1 808 000	32
1	1 218 000	22
2	1 253 000	22.7
3	697 000	12.7
4	323 000	5.9
5	149 000	2.7
6+	116 000	2.0
Total	5 564 000	100.0

Source: Calculated from Table 2—Estimates of Families in Canada—1975—Cat. #91-204—Annual,
Ottawa: August 1977, pp. 6-7.

Table 5

NUMBER OF LIVE-BORN CHILDREN IN ORDER OF LIVE BIRTHS, BY AGE OF MOTHER, 1974[1]

Order of birth of child	Age of mother									All ages	% of total
	Under 15	15-19	20-24	25-29	30-34	35-39	40-44	45 and over	Age not stated		
1st child	309	31 715	61 262	42 035	9 617	1 878	356	15	246	147 433	44.0
2nd	3	5 963	38 345	47 825	16 219	3 073	398	15	18	111 859	33.4
3rd	—	566	9 272	20 194	11 845	3 011	462	26	6	45 382	13.5
4th	—	58	1 943	6 128	5 723	2 211	482	21	4	16 570	5.0
5th	—	3	454	1 842	2 329	1 424	409	21	2	6 484	1.9
6th	—	—	96	719	1 078	891	306	25	—	3 115	0.9
7th	—	—	20	302	586	584	227	26	1	1 746	0.5
8th	—	—	5	119	352	350	180	20	1	1 027	0.3
9th	—	—	3	38	187	260	125	11	—	624	0.2
10th	—	—	1	17	126	166	111	12	—	273	0.1
11th	—	—	1	4	49	120	92	7	—	176	0.1
12th	—	—	—	—	16	88	68	4	—	101	—
13th	—	—	—	2	8	38	50	3	—	61	—
14th	—	—	—	—	5	17	30	8	1	35	—
15th	—	—	—	—	—	17	13	5	—	18	—
16th	—	—	—	—	—	2	13	3	—	8	—
17th	—	—	—	—	—	—	5	3	--	3	—
18th	—	—	—	—	—	—	3	—	—	2	—
19th	—	—	—	—	—	1	—	1	—	1	—
20th and over	—	—	—	—	—	1	—	—	—		—
Not stated	—	9	7	13	2	1	3	—	23	58	—
Total	312	38 314	111 409	119 238	48 142	14 133	3 333	226	302	335 409	100.0
% of total	0.1	11.4	33.2	35.5	14.4	4.2	1.0	0.1	0.1	100.0	—

[1] Excludes Newfoundland.

Source: Canada Year Book 1976-1977. pp. 199-200.

Table 6
THE FEMALE LABOUR FORCE AND PARTICIPATION RATES, BY AGE GROUP, CANADA, 1965, 1970 and 1975

Age group—Groupes d'âges	Female labour force			Participation rate		
	1965	1970	1975	1965	1970	1975
	'000	'000	'000	%	%	%
14-19* years	318	369	529	30.2	30.4	47.4
20-24 years	357	526	697	52.6	58.5	66.9
25-34 years	368	532	919	31.1	39.0	52.9
35-44 years	425	506	645	34.1	40.2	51.5
45-54 years	372	464	564	37.0	40.6	46.1
55-64 years	191	251	293	27.0	29.8	30.8
65 years and over	45	43	50	6.0	5.0	4.8
All ages	2 076	2 690	3 697	31.3	35.5	44.2

* In 1975 this age group was changed to 15-19 years of age.

Source: Women in the Labour Force,
Facts and Figures. Part 1
Labour Force Survey, Ottawa
Labour Canada, 1977, p. 21

Table 7
FEMALE POPULATION AND FEMALE LABOUR FORCE, BY MARITAL STATUS, AND PARTICIPATION RATES OF WOMEN IN THE LABOUR FORCE, CANADA, 1965, 1970 and 1975

Marital status	Female population		Female labour force		Participation rate of women in the labour force
	Number	Percentage of the total population [a]	Number	Percentage of the total labour force [b]	
	'000	%	'000	%	%
			1965		
Single	1 658	12.6	807	11.3	48.7
Married	4 255	32.4	1 073	15.0	25.2
Other [c]	709	5.4	196	2.7	27.6
Total	6 623	50.4	2 076	29.1	31.3
			1970		
Single	1 948	13.0	925	11.0	47.5
Married	4 763	31.7	1 525	18.2	32.0
Other	863	5.7	240	2.9	27.8
Total	7 575	50.4	2 690	32.1	35.5
			1975		
Single	1 937	11.8	1 146	11.4	59.2
Married	5 302	32.2	2 204	21.9	41.6
Other	1 120	6.8	347	3.4	31.0
Total	8 359	50.8	3 697	36.7	44.2

[a] The total population figures used here were (in thousands): 1965: 13 128; 1970: 15 016; 1975: 16 470.
[b] The total labour force figures used here were (in thousands): 1965: 7 141; 1970: 8 374; 1975: 10 060.
[c] Widowed, divorced or separated.

Source: Women in the Labour Force: Facts and Figures, Part 1
　　　　Labour Force Survey, Ottawa
　　　　Labour Canada, 1977, p. 33

Table 8

AGES OF CHILDREN REGISTERED IN DAY CARE IN 1973, 1974, 1975, 1976 and 1977

Ages	1973		1974		1975		1976		1977	
	No.	%	No.	%	No.	%	No.	%	No.	%
Under 3	3 626	13.19	11 351	20.57	10 859	15.52	11 829	14.16	15 237	18.66
3-5	22 074	80.35	38 952	70.59	53 730	76.80	63 501	76.03	58 626	71.80
6 and over	1 773	6.45	4 878	8.83	5 363	7.66	8 190	9.81	7 788	9.54
	99.99		99.99		99.98		100.00		100.00	

Source: Status of Day Care in Canada: 1977 Ottawa: Health and Welfare Canada, 1978, p. 9

Table 9

DIVORCES: CANADA 1975

Divorces: 50 611 (1974: 45 019; 1973: 36 704; 1972: 32 389; 1971: 29 685)

Rank Order of Divorces per Province:

1.	Ontario	17 485
2.	Quebec	14 093
3.	British Columbia	7 543
4.	Alberta	5 475
5.	Manitoba	1 984
6.	Nova Scotia	1 597
7.	Saskatchewan	1 131
8.	New Brunswick	758
9.	Newfoundland	380
10.	P.E.I.	75
11.	N.W.T.	56
12.	Yukon	43
	TOTAL	50 611

Table 10

DIVORCE BY AGE OF HUSBAND AND WIFE AT TIME OF THEIR MARRIAGE: 1975

Age	Husbands	Percent	Wives	Percent
under 20 yrs.	6 758	13.4	21 839	43.2
20-24 years	26 979	53.3	19 792	39.1
25-29 years	9 608	19.0	4 305	8.5
30-34 years	3 076	6.1	1 417	2.8
35-39 years	1 329	2.6	729	1.4
40-44 years	662	1.3	423	0.8
45-49 years	400	0.8	260	0.5
50+	518	1.0	341	0.7
not stated	1 281	2.5	1 505	3.0
TOTAL	50 611	100.0	50 611	100.0

Note: This table gives us the age of husbands and wives *at the time they married.*

Table 11
DIVORCE BY AGE OF HUSBAND AND WIFE AT TIME OF DIVORCE—1975:

	Husbands	Percent	Wives	Percent
under 20 yrs.	44	0.1	294	0.6
20-24 years	2 685	5.3	6 301	12.4
25-29 years	10 442	20.6	12 352	24.4
30-34 years	9 980	19.7	9 293	18.4
35-39 years	7 470	14.8	6 434	12.7
40-44 years	6 083	12.0	5 102	10.1
45-49 years	4 884	9.7	4 037	8.0
50+	7 798	15.4	5 334	10.5
not stated	1 225	2.4	1 464	2.9
TOTAL	50 611	100.0	50 611	100.0

Average age at divorce: 1975—husbands   35.4 years
                                    wives   38.3 years
  —the average age has been declining steadily since 1969.

Median duration of marriage: 11.4 years (1974—11.7 years; 1972—12.1 yrs.)
  —the median duration of marriage prior to divorce is declining steadily.

Table 12
MAJOR GROUNDS FOR DIVORCE IN RANK ORDER: 1976

Percent of Divorces

1) Separation for not less than 3 years	33.
2) Adultery	30.
3) Mental Cruelty	16.5
4) Physical Cruelty	13.9
5) Desertion not less than 5 years	3.0

Table 13
AVERAGE AGES AT MARRIAGE—CANADA 1975

	Men	Women
1. At first marriage	24.9	22.5
2. All marriages	27.6	25.0
3. Divorced and married for second time	38.3	34.9
4. Widowed and married for second time	58.8	53.1

Table 14
AVERAGE INCOME OF FAMILIES IN CURRENT AND CONSTANT DOLLARS BY REGION, SELECTED YEARS, 1951-74

Region	1951	1961	1967	1971	1973	1974
Current dollars						
Atlantic provinces	2 515	4 156	5 767	7 936	9 965	11 647
Quebec	3 523	5 294	7 404	9 919	12 024	13 742
Ontario	3 903	5 773	8 438	11 483	13 912	16 144
Prairie provinces	3 261	4 836	6 908	9 309	11 760	14 755
British Columbia	3 669	5 491	7 829	11 212	13 942	15 620
Canada	3 535	5 317	7 602	10 368	12 716	14 833
Constant (1971) dollars						
Atlantic provinces	3 810	5 544	6 667	7 936	8 839	9 318
Quebec	5 337	7 062	8 559	9 919	10 665	10 994
Ontario	5 913	7 701	9 754	11 483	12 340	12 915
Prairie provinces	4 940	6 451	7 986	9 309	10 431	11 804
British Columbia	5 559	7 325	9 050	11 212	12 367	12 496
Canada	5 356	7 093	8 788	10 368	11 279	11 866

Table 15
AVERAGE INCOME OF FAMILIES IN EACH REGION AS A PERCENTAGE OF THE AVERAGE FOR CANADA, SELECTED YEARS 1965-74

Region	1965	1967	1969	1972	1973	1974
Atlantic provinces	79.3	75.9	76.0	80.9	78.4	78.5
Quebec	95.8	97.4	96.9	95.9	94.6	92.6
Ontario	109.9	111.0	110.8	110.0	109.4	108.8
Prairie provinces	93.0	90.9	91.0	92.7	92.5	99.5
British Columbia	104.6	103.0	103.3	101.3	109.6	105.3
Canada	100.0	100.0	100.0	100.0	100.0	100.0

Table 16
PERCENTAGE DISTRIBUTION OF FAMILIES IN CONSTANT (1971) DOLLARS, SHOWING AVERAGE AND MEDIAN INCOMES, SELECTED YEARS, 1965-74

Income group in constant (1971) dollars	1965	1967	1969	1971	1973	1974
Under $3 000	12.1	9.9	9.6	9.0	6.5	5.6
$ 3 000-$ 4 999	14.9	13.5	13.0	11.5	10.3	9.7
5 000- 6 999	19.5	17.6	14.6	12.2	10.8	10.2
7 000- 9 999	26.4	26.9	25.2	22.0	20.8	18.5
10 000- 11 999	10.9	12.0	13.0	14.0	13.4	14.3
12 000- 14 999	8.6	10.2	11.5	14.2	15.5	17.0
15 000- 19 999	4.6	6.4	8.1	10.9	14.0	14.9
20 000 and over	2.7	3.5	4.9	6.2	8.6	9.8
Total	100.0	100.0	100.0	100.0	100.0	100.0
Average income	$ 8 127	8 788	9 490	10 368	11 279	11 866
Median income	$ 7 320	7 906	8 465	9 347	10 217	10 827

Median income refers to the middle or central value when incomes are ranged in order of magnitude. Meidan income is lower than average income in these tables since it is not as affected by a few abnormally large values in the distribution.

THE VANIER INSTITUTE OF THE FAMILY

What is the Vanier Institute of the Family (VIF)? What does it stand for? What does it do?

The Institute, which came into existence in 1964, has declared that it has the following foundations for its existence:

The Vanier Institute of the Family has chosen as its purpose to focus attention on the importance and significance of family life, and to further the well-being of all Canadian families.

The Institute's approach is one of open and full exploration of our society. The purpose is to acquire a deeper understanding of the factors and forces behind the new, developing shape of our society.

Out of its searching probes has come an appreciation of the variety of family life in Canada. The multi-faceted Canadian mosaic includes extended families in many rural regions, communes of different kinds, urban families where both parents work and tribal mixes among many of our native peoples. Some of these many forms are new and experimental, others are old, with long traditions.

The VIF considers the family as a unique institution for the development of human potential. Within the family self-realization, caring, love, support and equal respect for oneself and others, as shown in mutual and increasing personal responsibility, can develop.

With today's breakdown in the nuclear family we find that many people are going back to the older forms and wider networks of familial support. The Institute sees hope in the current strengthening of bonds in the search for new ways of community.

The programs of the Vanier Institute of the Family reflect a continuing concern for our whole way of life. Few other organizations have been willing to undertake close examination of the many issues that affect family life, community and the nation.

Learning for Family Living

In the area of family life education VIF is exploring with a number of North American experts the premise that our most important learning is taking place in the home among family and close friends. The Institute's Task Force on the Conceptual Framework on Learning is pursuing this topic as well as establishing the necessary conceptual frameworks to help us all to apply this understanding in our lives. A comprehensive bibliography on learning has been prepared.

The first of a series of community consultations was held in Saint John, N.B. and another is being planned in Sault Ste. Marie. These consultations provide deeper understandings of family life and human relations.

The Family and the Law

The Institute's Task Force on the Family and the Law continues to probe our understanding of the law and to examine the basic assumptions underlying it and to explore the impact it has on our primary relationships. The Institute has held dialogue meetings with representatives of the federal and provincial law reform commissions in Canada. VIF has responded to the Law Reform Commission of Canada's Working Paper No. 1, *The Family Court,* and will continue to react to these commissions when law reform recommendations affect family living.

Work and Income

The Institute's concerns about the impact of our various social systems on familial life has extended itself into the area of work and income distribution. A Task Force on Work and Income has been initiated to probe issues in this field.

Immigration

The Institute is responding to the Federal Government's Special Joint Committee on Immigration Policy Green Paper, because of the serious effects such a proposed policy will have on the family life of immigrants.

The Arts

The VIF has developed a tape program, "Music as a Social Indicator." These tapes have been used as teaching aids in universities and hospitals. They seek to help us understand our society and are an experiment in using the arts as a valid sphere of social indicators. The CBC has arranged with the Institute for two national network broadcasts using the material.

As an initial approach to communications policy VIF recently considered the CRTC's new FM radio regulations. Its concerns have been expressed in an article in the Institute's publication, "Transition," and further exploration in the broad field of communications will continue. The Institute has given support to Vancouver's new co-op FM radio station for an experimental series of family life programs. It was involved in the work of the Ontario Royal Commission on Violence in the media.

Lifestyle Research

VIF has given support to research projects and workshops that will encourage the research community to explore the varying forms of familial relationships. Two workshops were held in British Columbia to explore alternative familial lifestyles. A seminar brought together the Institute's Research Task Force on Frameworks on Contemporary Familial Lifestyles. Bibliographies on contemporary lifestyles and alternative lifestyles are available.

Publications

A complete list of papers, documents, submissions and reports as well as membership and subscription to *Transition*, the newsletter of the institute can be obtained by writing to:

Vanier Institute of the Family
151 Slater Street
Ottawa, Ontario.
K1P 5H3

THE FAMILY LAW REFORM ACT, ONTARIO 1978*

*From a pamphlet published by the Ministry of the Attorney-General for Ontario.***

The old law assigned ownership of matrimonial property to the spouse who paid for it. This meant, in many traditional marriages, that the husband owned everything and the wife owned nothing, because she had no income from which to buy property. The contributions of a spouse in homemaking and child care were not recognized. Also, contributions toward family vacations and consumable items were not recognized. Public response has favoured sharing matrimonial property between husband and wife, including where one spouse's contributions are non-financial.

- The new law adopts the "family assets" approach to matrimonial property. This means a house, a car, household goods, a boat—whatever the family uses together for shelter or transportation or for household, educational, recreational, so-

*The new laws apply to all Ontario residents, including persons who were married outside Ontario or were married before the legislation came into force, except those who have a marriage contract or separation agreement.

**Copies of this material and a booklet with a more detailed explanation of the new law, including a copy of the Family Law Reform Act, 1978, are available from:
COMMUNICATIONS OFFICE
MINISTRY OF THE ATTORNEY
  GENERAL
18TH FLOOR
18 KING STREET EAST
TORONTO
M5C 1C5
Or
PUBLICATIONS CENTRE
5TH FLOOR
880 BAY STREET
TORONTO
M7A 1N8

cial or aesthetic purposes—will be shared equally as assets that belong to both spouses if the marriage breaks down.

- The court can change those equal proportions in favour of the husband or the wife, or order the couple to share other assets, such as business assets, if necessary to avoid unfairness in an individual case.
- This system applies only if the couple do not have a marriage contract which spells out exactly what each of them can retain if their marriage comes to an end.
- The family assets system applies only as long as both husband and wife are living, and only when their marriage breaks down. During their marriage, the spouses are free to deal with their own property as they wish, except the matrimonial home.

Support

- Under the new legislation, a judge, having considered a couple's ages, health and financial resources, can order either one to support the other, and in what amount. The question of support is answered by whether it is needed—not by where the fault lies for the adultery, cruelty or desertion that may have preceded the marriage breakdown. Basically, the principle of the new support legislation is that as long as one of the spouses can show need and the other spouse can pay, support must be provided.
- A husband or wife can buy the necessities of life against the credit of the other, although both are legally bound to pay the debt. That right ends if the spouses separate or if one of them notifies creditors that he or she will no longer be responsible for the other's debts.
- Either spouse of a common law relationship can claim support after they have lived together for at least five years, or if there has been some continuity to their living together and they have a child.

- Parents are responsible for supporting their children up to age 18, unless the child is 16 or over and withdraws from the parents' control. If a child marries before 18, the parents are automatically relieved of the support obligation.
- Support is available for children born outside marriage, as well as for those born to legally married couples, and for children taken in by a person and raised as members of the family.
- If a creditor sues a minor to recover money owing for necessities, the minor's parents can also be liable, if they are responsible for that minor's support.
- Natural parents who have cared for and supported a child and those who have treated a child as one of their own family can claim support from a child over 18, if the parent is in need and the child can afford to support the parent.
- Where a person is supported by a public agency, the agency can claim support on that person's behalf from his or her spouse.
- A spouse who fails to make court-ordered support payments can have part of his or her wages deducted by an employer under a court order to do so, to satisfy the support order.
- Where a person from whom support is claimed cannot be found, a court can order disclosure to a court official from government or private records of the address, and only the address, of the person for the purposes of obtaining or enforcing a court order for support.

Matrimonial Home

The new legislation abolishes dower, the ancient common law right which entitled a wife to a life interest in one-third of her husband's real estate after he died. Dower is replaced by laws that protect the rights of both spouses in the matrimonial home.

- Either spouse can seek a court order for possession of the matrimonial home and contents, regardless of which of the spouses is the legal owner, or whether it is a rented home or not. But before a court makes such an order, it must be satisfied that financial support alone would be inadequate.
- Neither spouse can sell the matrimonial home without the other spouse's consent in writing. This protects the family by ensuring its members shelter. Where a spouse's consent cannot be obtained because he or she is unreasonably withholding it, is mentally incompetent or cannot be located, the court has power to order a sale without consent.

Domestic Contracts

- A couple can define in a marriage contract what their property rights, support obligations and child-rearing responsibilities will be during marriage, on the death of one of them or if they separate or divorce. A court may, however, alter a contract if it was drawn up fraudulently or under duress or undue influence, if its provisions are not in the best interests of a child, or if its provisions regarding support are unconscionable.
- A man and a woman who are living together but not married to each other can sign a cohabitation agreement, which is like a marriage contract.
- A marriage contract or cohabitation agreement cannot limit a spouse's right to live in the matrimonial home or to control the sale of it. It also cannot grant rights regarding the custody of children; those can only be spelled out in a separation agreement.
- Domestic contracts must be in writing and signed in the presence of at least one witness.

The Children's Law Reform Act

- The new Children's Law Reform Act abolishes the status of illegitimacy. All children now have the same legal rights, whether or not they were born within marriage.

- It is now possible to obtain a court declaration that a person is the child of another particular person, if such a declaration is necessary to settle a dispute.

The Marriage Act

- The new Marriage Act requires persons 16 or 17 years old to obtain both parents' consent to marry. Marriage under 16 is not permitted.
- Non-religious marriage ceremonies can be performed by judges and designated justices of the peace.

The Succession Law Reform Act

- The new Succession Law Reform Act governs the rights of surviving spouses and other family members on the death of a family member.
- If a person dies without a will, the surviving spouse receives the first $75,000 of the estate plus half of any remainder, if there is one child, or one third of the remainder if there are two or more children. If there are no children, the surviving spouse receives the entire estate.
- If the deceased left a will, the surviving family members receive what the will says is to go to them. However, if this is inadequate, they can apply to a court for a greater share of the estate. This right is available to the spouse, parents, children, brothers and sisters of the deceased if the deceased was supporting them or was under a legal obligation to support them.

A SAMPLE MARRIAGE CONTRACT

The following sample of a marriage contract was drawn up by a lawyer in Ontario. Because the Civil Code of Quebec is derived from the Napoleonic Code, a marriage contract in that province would contain several different clauses from one which might be used in the other 9 provinces, whose legal systems are derived from English Common Law. As Family Law varies from province to province, you should contact the Attorney-General's office in the province where you live for up-to-date information on marriage contracts.

Note that there are three items in the Ontario Family Law Reform Act, 1978 (see pages 188-190) which persons cannot contract out of. These involve custody of children, access to children, and a spouse's rights to part of the matrimonial property.

THIS MARRIAGE CONTRACT

made _____
                                (month)

19__
 (year)

BETWEEN:

_____   (Name of Husband
                            or Husband to be)

-and-

_____   (Name of Wife
                            or Wife to be)

WITNESSES:

The parties were married to each other (or are to shortly marry) at _____(name of City, Town of Village), in the Province of _____ on the _____ day of _____, 19__. Throughout this contract they are called respectively the "husband" and "wife", even if they are not married.

As a result of their marriage (or in contemplation of their marriage) the parties have agreed to enter into this contract during marriage (or before their marriage, to exist during such marriage) as to their respective rights and obligations, such rights and obligations to continue during cohabitation, or upon separation or dissolution of such marriage, as to ownership of property, support obligations, the upbringing of their children and all other matters in the settlement of their affairs, and the parties further agree that this contract sets out their mutual understanding as to the financial obligations and rights between them.

THEREFORE, the husband and wife agree as follows:

1. USE OF WIFE'S NAME DURING MARRIAGE:
   (1) The wife shall be at liberty to use her maiden name as she wishes (or, the wife shall be at liberty to use her maiden name in hyphenated form with that of the husband during marriage)

2. CHILDREN, THEIR NAMES, AND UPBRINGING:
   (a) The husband and wife agree that they shall have two children at such time as the wife has been employed for a period of __years;
   (b) In the event, for any medical reason, or any other reason, the husband and wife do not have children, they shall adopt two children, subject to the provisions of the agreement, as in paragraph 2(a) above.
   Or
   The husband and wife agree that they shall not have children.

(c) The husband and wife agree that their children shall be brought up in the _____ religion;

(d) The husband and wife agree that the wife will not be employed for a period of time until each of their children are __ years of age;

(e) The children's education will be to the best of their academic abilities, however, no decisions shall be made affecting the children's education without joint agreement between the husband and the wife and if such joint agreement cannot be reached, the husband and wife will submit such issue to mediation by mediator appointed pursuant to the provisions of this agreement;

3. HUSBAND AND WIFE'S PLACE OF RESIDENCE:

The husband and wife agree that they shall live in the City of _____ in the Province of _____ and in the event that either the husband or wife's employment requires that they live in a City, Town or Village, other than in the City of _____ in the Province of _____, the husband and wife will jointly agree to such relocation in order to further their respective careers.

4. HOUSEHOLD DUTIES AND UPBRINGING OF CHILDREN:

The husband and wife agree to equally share household duties and child rearing and when the wife is not employed, or if the wife no longer seeks employment, the husband shall divide with the wife such duties and responsibilities.

5. FINANCES:

(a) In the event that both the husband and the wife are employed, they shall deposit to a joint account their respective incomes and pay all expenses and after payment of such expenses each of the husband and wife shall divide equally the net surplus, if any.

6. MARRIAGE CONTRACT RENDERS INOPERATIVE THE PROVISIONS OF THE FAMILY LAW REFORM ACT, 1978:

The husband and wife agree that this marriage contract is entered into between them and notwithstanding the force and effect of the Family Law Reform Act, 1978 (Statutes of Ontario, 1978, c. 2) the terms and conditions herein and hereinafter expressed and the husband and wife expressly agree that no claim for support, division of family assets or any other entitlement shall be made by either of them pursuant to the provisions of the Family Law Reform Act.

7. SEPARATION OR DISSOLUTION OF THE MARRIAGE:

In the event that the husband and wife separate, they agree as follows:

(a) They shall obtain counselling with a view to marriage reconciliation, or to conciliation as to separation or ultimate divorce;

(b) In the event of separation being inevitable after appropriate counselling, they shall split their family assets as defined from time to time under the Family Law Reform Act, 1978.

(c) In the event that the children are no longer dependent upon either the husband or wife and living permanently elsewhere other than with the husband and wife, the husband and wife agree that any matrimonial home shall be listed for sale and the net equity split equally between them;

(d) In the event of separation or dissolution of the marriage, and in the event that the children are still dependent upon the husband or wife, and that the husband or wife have custody of the children, the non-custodial spouse shall pay to the custodial spouse, 30 per cent of his or her gross income as maintenance for the children.

(e) In the event that the parties separate or the marriage is dissolved and the wife is unemployed, the husband shall support the wife in an amount equal to a further 20 per cent of his income or a period of __ months following the separation;

8. MEDIATION:

In the event that the parties disagree in respect of any of the terms of this agreement, save and except those terms setting out their financial obligations the one to the other, they do now agree to the appointment of _____ as mediator to resolve any disputes between them and to conciliate such disputes.

9. The parties to this marriage contract each acknowledge that each:
   (a) has had independent legal advice;
   (b) understands their respective rights and obligations under this agreement; and
   (c) is signing this Marriage Contract voluntarily.

IN WITNESS WHEREOF the husband and wife have signed this Marriage Contract on the date stated in this Marriage Contract.

SIGNED, SEALED
AND DELIVERED
in the presence of:

_____ (Husband)

_____

_____ (Wife)

SOURCES OF INFORMATION AND MATERIAL RELATED TO CANADIAN FAMILY LIFE

Advisory Council on the Status of Women, Box 1541, Ottawa, Ontario, K1P 5R5

Canada Law Reform Commission, 130 Albert St., Ottawa, Ont. K1A O1G

Canadian Council on Social Development, Box 3505, Station C, Ottawa, Ont. K1Y 4G1

Community Contacts for the Widowed, 460 Jarvis St., Toronto, Ont., M4Y 2H5

Faculty of Education, University of Toronto, Guidance Centre, 1000 Yonge St. Toronto, Ont. M4W 2K8

National Council of Welfare, Brooke Claxton Bldg., Ottawa, Ont. K1A 0KA

Ontario Institute for Studies in Education, 252 Bloor St. W., Toronto, Ont., K5S 1V6

Ontario Status of Women Council, 801 Bay St., 3rd Floor, Toronto, Ont., M5S 1Z1

Vanier Institute of the Family, 151 Slater, Ottawa, Ont. K1P 5H3